THE HISTORY OF RELIGIONS

ESSAYS IN DIVINITY

VOLUME I

JERALD C. BRAUER, GENERAL EDITOR

The History of Religions

Essays on the Problem of Understanding

BY JOACHIM WACH, MIRCEA ELIADE
JOSEPH M. KITAGAWA, CHARLES H. LONG, KEES W. BOLLE
THOMAS J. J. ALTIZER, PHILIP H. ASHBY
CHARLES S. J. WHITE, CHARLES J. ADAMS, H. BYRON EARHART
JEROME H. LONG, PAUL TILLICH

Edited by JOSEPH M. KITAGAWA
with the collaboration of
Mircea Eliade and Charles H. Long

THE UNIVERSITY OF CHICAGO PRESS

CHICAGO AND LONDON

In Memory of

JOACHIM WACH (†1955)

and

PAUL TILLICH (†1965)

THE UNIVERSITY OF CHICAGO PRESS
CHICAGO AND LONDON
The University of Toronto Press, Toronto 5, Canada

Library of Congress Catalog Card Number: 67–20574

Printed in the United States of America

General Editor's Preface

The present volume is the first in a series of eight books which will be published under the general title "Essays in Divinity." This does not appear, at first glance, as a particularly auspicious moment for such a formidable enterprise. At the very moment the so-called radical theologians announce that "God is dead," an eight-volume series investigating various dimensions of the study of religion or of theology begins publication. Is this not an ill-timed venture?

On the contrary, in America the discipline of theology was never in a healthier state. To be sure, there are no giants such as Tillich or Niebuhr on the scene, but there are many new and exciting factors in the picture. The very presence of the "God is dead" movement is evidence of a new vitality among the younger theologians. In no sense does such a movement herald the end of systematic theology or the impossibility of using God-language. It is but one attempt to focus on the serious task of reconstructing Christian theology, and it is not the only attempt.

One fact alone is sufficient to mark this new age — the dominance of dialogue in all aspects of divinity. Basic conversation between Roman Catholicism, Protestantism, and Judaism is just beginning, and its full effect on theological construction is only in its preliminary stages. Before the discipline of systematic theology had passed beyond even the preliminary phase of dialogue, Paul Tillich's last lecture pointed to the future of this discipline in relation to the world's religions. Dialogue is not to be taken as the "in" movement in religion today; it is to be understood as providing a new base that will profoundly affect not only the systematic study of doctrines and beliefs but every dimension of religious studies.

Another mark of the vitality of religious studies today is its dialogic relationship to other disciplines. Studies in divinity have never been carried on in complete isolation from other areas of human knowledge, but some epochs have exhibited a greater interrelationship than others. The contemporary scene is marked by the increasing tempo of creative interchange and mutual stimulation between divinity and other disciplines. Several new theological disciplines have emerged recently and documented this fact. The interplay between theology and literature, between theology and the psychological sciences, and between theology and other social sciences bids fair to reshape the traditional study of religion, and this is rapidly becoming central in major theological faculties.

The emergence and increasing role of the History of Religions is a case in point. Until recently it has been a stepchild in the field of religious subjects. Today it is beginning to come to the front as one of the most provocative and fruitful ways to study religion. It is developing a methodology that will soon prove influential in all dimensions of theological study. It might not win the day, but it will have a profound influence. History of Religions appears to be the way that most state universities are willing to take in order to introduce the serious and disciplined study of religion into strictly humanistic curriculums.

These are but a few of the factors that demonstrate the present vitality of the study of religion today. It makes both possible and necessary a series of books such as this. The occasion for the publication of "Essays in Divinity" is supplied by the one hundredth anniversary of the Divinity School of The University of Chicago and by the University's seventy-fifth anniversary. Such occasions call for special plans.

The editor of this series proposed to celebrate the event by holding seven conferences to be attended only by graduates and present faculty of the Divinity School. Out of the conferences a set of eight volumes would emerge that would at once mark the progress in the various dimensions of theological study and point to the ongoing tradition of scholarship in the Divinity School. Of course, something is lost by not inviting the best scholars from throughout the world to contribute to the volumes. On the other hand, something is gained by inviting only those men who have been educated or are now teaching at a single theological center of America long noted for its scholarship and its education of theological professors.

This limitation will enable an observer to determine the extent to which a series of generations has shaped—and has been shaped by—a particular institution. It will be possible to note the variations of approach and concern that mark respective generations of that institution. Furthermore, it will help to assess the particular genius, if any, that a given institution possesses. It will demonstrate to what extent its graduates and professors are in the midst of contemporary theological scholarship. It is to be hoped that the series will provide both a bench mark for today's scholarly discussions and research in religion and a record from which future generations can assess the contributions of an institution at the turn of its first century.

No one of the volumes pretends to be definitive in its area; however, it is hoped that each will make a worthy contribution to its area of specialization and that the entire series will provide an over-all assessment of religious scholarship at the present moment. The intent is to have each volume deal with a particular issue that is of special significance for scholarly research today. Thus, one will not be confronted by a disconnected series of essays but by a group of writings each of which deals with a general problem from the point of view of the author's own problem. One will not find articles on the new prominence of dialogue or on the deeper concern of religion for culture today. Rather, these will be reflected in the essays themselves as they seek to develop their particular problems.

It is appropriate that the first volume to appear should be that on the History of Religions. Known previously as Comparative Religions, the History of Religions has always been an important subject in the curriculum of The University of Chicago. Although the Department of Comparative Religions was for many years a part of the Graduate School of Arts and Literature (later Humanities), it always worked closely with the Divinity School. Not only George Stephen Goodspeed, who from 1892 until his retirement held the chair of Comparative Religions and Ancient History, and Albert Eustace Haydon, who held the chair of Comparative Religions between 1910 and 1945, but many scholars in the Oriental Institute and other departments of the University co-operated in the teaching and in research on various aspects of History of Religions.

In addition, the Haskell Lectureship, established in 1895 by the generous gift of Mrs. Caroline Haskell, has brought a host of eminent scholars in this field to the campus from all over the world. Among them are John Henry Barrows of Oberlin, Karl Budde of Marburg, Duncan B. Macdonald of Hartford, J. J. M. DeGroot of Berlin, Morris Jastrow, Jr., of Pennsylvania, Franz Cumont of Brussels, A. V. William Jackson of Columbia, Maurice Bloomfield of Johns Hopkins, Carl Bezold of Heidelberg, Christian Snouck Hurgronie of Leiden, Masaharu Anesaki, Daniel C. Holtom, Hideo Kishimoto, and Ichiro Hori of Tokyo, George Foot Moore of Harvard, Frederick Jones Bliss of Beirut, Kenneth Saunders of Bombay, Sarvepalli Radhakrishnan and K. Natarajan of India, Mordecai Kaplan of New York, Wing-tsit Chan of Dartmouth, Hamilton A. R. Gibb of Oxford, Louis Massignon of Paris, Friedrich Heiler of Marburg, and Mircea Eliade, then of Paris. Thanks also to the Barrows Lectureship, another gift of Mrs. Haskell, a number of the scholars of The University of Chicago, including among them Charles Gilkey, Joachim Wach, Bernard Eugene Meland, and R. Pierce Beaver, visited India and other Asian countries for lecturing and exchange of ideas.

In 1946 Joachim Wach was called to head the newly organized History of Religions field, which offered a Ph.D. program through what was then called the Federated Theological Faculty. In 1951 Joseph M. Kitagawa joined the faculty. The untimely death of Joachim Wach in 1955 was followed by the appointment in 1956 of Mircea Eliade, who assumed the chairmanship of the field in 1957. In 1957, Charles H. Long joined the faculty. In addition, the field of History of Religions invited a number of visiting professors from abroad, such as U Pe Maung Tin of Burma, Shoson Miyamoto of Tokyo, Friedrich Heiler of Marburg, and Jacque Duschene-Guilleman of Liége. Currently, the Field consists of Mircea Eliade (chairman), Gösta Ahlström, Robert M. Grant, Joseph M. Kitagawa, and Charles H. Long, and its teaching and research is augmented by the work of numerous scholars from various departments of the University.

The theme of this volume is the problem of understanding or hermeneutics as seen from the perspective of the History of Religions. This is one of the major problems confronting the study of religion today. It involves the development of a methodology adequate to interpret and understand the data of religion, and it also embraces the attempt to correlate religious rites, beliefs, and actions with contemporary culture. It looks both to the past and to the present, but it tends to see the present from a perspective supplied by an analysis of the religious forms and vitalities of the past.

In one sense, the volume represents an attempt at self-understanding on the part of History of Religions as a particular discipline. Perhaps its title ought to have been *History of Religions: Essays on the Problem of SELF-Understanding*. Professors Kitagawa, C. Long, and Bolle deal directly with this problem, and all of the other essays touch on it in one way or another. Professor Altizer's analysis of the "Death of God" theology in the context of insights provided by other religions proves most enlightening both for his own point of view and for the entire movement itself. Professors Ashby, White, Adams, Earhart, and J. Long each deal with a particular religion or a particular problem within a religion as seen from the perspective of the discipline of the History of Religions. Thus, they demonstrate that the History of Religions is a distinct discipline, yet a discipline which, by its own nature, is interdependent with such other disciplines as Buddhology, anthropology, and Islamics.

The articles by Professor Eliade and the late Professor Paul Tillich both deal with the contemporary significance of History of Religions and its contribution to the problem of understanding. Eliade, in his typically brilliant fashion, sheds light on a number of the key movements in contemporary life by viewing them from the perspective of man's religious history. It is a model exemplification of History of Religions' contribution to understanding the contemporary cultural setting. Tillich's article, which was delivered at the opening of the one hundredth anniversary conference, proved to be the last words he uttered. After three years of a joint seminar with Eliade, he addressed himself to the task of Christian self-understanding when undertaken in dialogue with other religions and particularly with the discipline of History of Religions. He foresaw the future of Christian theology as developing in this new context. Only history will prove him right or wrong; meanwhile, he pointed to a fresh, new direction.

It was thought appropriate to include a special introductory article by the late Professor Joachim Wach, who founded the modern tradition of the History of Religions at The University of Chicago. Prior to his coming to the Divinity School in 1946, the comparative study of religions had been the approach in the search for certain common elements in all religions. As Wach's article makes clear, the discipline of the History of Religions is completely different in both method and interest. This article, "The Meaning and Task of the History of Religions (*Religionswissenschaft*)," originally appeared in German in *Zeitschrift für Missionskunde und Religionswissenschaft* (Vol. L, No. 5).

This volume was edited by Professor Joseph M. Kitagawa, with special assistance from Professor Charles S. J. White, of the University of Pennsylvania, and Mr. Alan L. Miller, a graduate student in History of Religions in the Divinity School.

JERALD C. BRAUER, *General Editor*

CONTENTS

Introduction: The Meaning and Task of the History of Religions (Religionswissenschaft)

JOACHIM WACH

On special occasions . . . a discipline has the right and the duty to look about and to examine the correctness of its path, to ask about the well-being of its method, and to ascertain what shall be the purpose of its task. What is the meaning of *Religionswissenschaft*? There is an old traditional discipline already concerned with religion, namely, theology. Why need there be a *Religionswissenschaft* at its side? When this discipline took shape during the nineteenth century in a very fascinating process of development, there were many – and they still may be found now and then – who thought that *Religionswissenschaft* was called to supplant theology. Recent *Religionswissenschaft*, insofar as it need be taken seriously, has definitely departed from this error. At this point it is widely separated from the work of a meritorious scholar such as Ernst Troeltsch. Theology has its own task in identifying its own confessional norms, and none may take this task from it. Theology is concerned with understanding and confirming its own faith. Foreign religions, to a certain and not inconsequential degree, belong to its realm of study; namely, as they exhibit close or distant relationships in their respective histories or in their concerns. But this can never be the reason for ascribing to theology the immense task of studying and describing the foreign religions in their manifold fulness. At the same time, the development of religious studies tells us that the proposition "he who knows one religion knows all" is false. Thus, theology has every reason to show and to cul-

This article was first published in *Zeitschrift für Missionskunde und Religionswissenschaft*, L (1935), No. 5. It has been translated by Karl W. Luckert with the help of Alan L. Miller.

tivate a lively interest in the results of studying other religions. It nevertheless leaves the study itself to the discipline which has come into existence especially for this purpose. Quantitatively and qualitatively *Religionswissenschaft* thus has a field of study distinct from that of theology: not our own religion but the foreign religions in all their manifoldness are its subject matter. It does not ask the question "what must I believe?" but "what is there that is believed?" According to this definition, it may now seem that the question raised by *Religionswissenschaft* is a superfluous, idle, even harmful curiosity—for the satisfaction of which we can waste neither time, nor energy, nor motivation today—especially at this juncture when we ought to concentrate on what is absolutely necessary. It is good that difficult times now and then compel people to recognize the superfluous for what it is and to throw it overboard and then to limit themselves to what is essential. For us this means that if *Religionswissenschaft* is only an aesthetically interesting or purely academic matter, then, indeed, it has no right to exist today.

The religions of exotic or primitive peoples have often, as has their art, been regarded as curiosities. This is an insufficient, as well as an improper, motive for occupying oneself with them. But even the pure, academic study of foreign religions, which ethically can be fully justified inasmuch as it rests on a broad desire for truth, must today be prepared to defend its right to exist. It cannot be denied that many a recent attempt in *Religionswissenschaft* is more or less exposed to the threefold criticism of lifelessness, intellectualism, and historicism. This accusation is often brought against the scientific disciplines in our own time. But it is an empirical, not a basic, shortcoming. *Religionswissenschaft* can as little do without learned research as can any other discipline. Nevertheless, this purely learned pursuit stands in the servitude of a higher purpose. Where research in religions, as a consequence of individual inability or from a basically false attitude, appears in the guise of a herbarium—a collection of and for linguists, ethnologists, and historiographers of religions—and where it appears as an occupation with theoretical and abstract formations of thought which dissolve values in unlikely comparisons, there it misses the purpose of *Religionswissenschaft.*

Religionswissenschaft, as we think of it, is alive; moreover, it is positive and practical. It is a living concern to the extent that it remains aware that the religion with which it deals is the deepest and the noblest in the realm of spiritual and intellectual existence, although, to be sure, it is difficult to see into the dark depth of that inwardness. *Religionswissenschaft* is alive, further, in that it recognizes the dynamic nature of religion, in that it knows that its goal will never be reached, and in that it can never sufficiently express that which it hopes to express. For the study of religious expressions, this means a never-ending task. *Religionswissenschaft* is also positive. A rather justified suspicion to the contrary has repeatedly been expressed—and not on the part of insignificant people. This suspicion has been nourished by the sounding from within our own realm of negative, overly critical, destructive, and nihilistic opinions. These tendencies could not help but produce justified defensive reactions since the enemies of religion disguised themselves as scholars.

However, *Religionswissenschaft* in its true intention does not dissolve values but seeks for values. The sense for the numinous is not extinguished by it, but on the contrary, is awakened, strengthened, shaped, and enriched by it. And as research in religions discloses religious feeling, desire, and action, it helps to reveal more fully the depth and breadth to which religiosity may radiate. A history of religions (*Religionsgeschichte*) which is inwardly connected with the history of cultures can accomplish much in this respect. When we have at last stated that *Religionswissenschaft* has a practical aspect, we must however protect this assertion against a possible misunderstanding. The practical benefit which justifiably is to some degree also demanded of all scientific disciplines must not be seen and sought too directly—which happens now as ever and which is supported by the spokesmen of contemporary need. How far-reaching in its often broad and indirect effects has been what appeared at first to be a very abstract philosophical investigation! The practical aspect must not be understood too narrowly. *Religionswissenschaft* cannot and must not serve the current moment in this bad sense.

What than is the practical significance of *Religionswissenschaft*? It broadens and deepens the *sensus numinis*, the religious feeling and understanding; it prepares one for a deeper conception of one's own faith; it allows a new and comprehensive experience of what religion is and means. This is as true of the religious experience as such as it is of the doctrinal and dogmatic aspect of religion, of its practice in the cult, and of the organization of the congregation. The effectiveness of the religious genius, the power and the formation of the religious community, the shaping of culture by religion — all these are experienced in new and manifold ways which do not paralyze but rather strengthen and fortify religious impulses.

Let us here remember the comparative approach; it has been much too overworked in the past, and too great expectations have been held concerning it. Now, in turn, it is easily underestimated. To observe the multiplicity of religious life and of religious expression, to discover similarities and relationships, need not, as some fear, have a sobering or paralyzing effect on one's own religiosity. On the contrary, it could become a support and an aid in the battle against the godless and estranged powers; it ought to lead to the examination and preservation of one's own religious faith. The value and significance of this may be recognized more clearly through that which is related but not identical. As Christians we have no reason at all to shy away from comparison — at any rate, not insofar as the idea and the impulse of our religion is concerned, although more, perhaps, in regard to practice. But there, precisely, the results of *Religionswissenschaft* could have very enlivening and encouraging effects. Precisely because the young person of our time has often very little living knowledge of the final and decisive religious experiences, the detour through examples and analogies from other religions may serve many a purpose.

Personally, I have many times seen young and open-minded students, in the study of the great subjects of *Religionswissenschaft*, attain, to their own surprise, a new understanding of the essentials of their own faith. The study of our various creeds—not as the dry enumeration of various doctrinal opinions, but as actual introductions into the piety of particular Christian movements—may accomplish something new. For example, in understanding the meaning of the cultic expressions of Catholicism, we may effect a richer and more forceful unfolding of our own religious life. As an instance from the general history of religions, the understanding of the immense role which the ethical aspect plays in the life of Buddhists will in theory and in practice lead increasingly to a more intensive unfolding of the motives contained in the imperative of the Christian ethic. *Out of life and for life*—even though it is to be understood in the above-described sense—is the motto of every scientific discipline and consequently also of *Religionswissenschaft.*

It is of course especially clear that the discipline concerned with religion must be inwardly alive (more, perhaps than the disciplines concerned with economics, law, language, and art), that it can proceed finally only with the austerity and sacred depth appropriate to its great subject matter, with an ever renewing openness, with enthusiasm and thoroughness. It is an exaggeration, but nevertheless understandable, when some people in principle and because of the depth and delicacy of religious matters question the possibility of a *Religionswissenschaft* or of "understanding" religion. Perhaps there is here a greater justification than there is for those who seek to interpret the documents of religious life no differently from documents of a business nature or than there is for those who cast judgment from the ivory tower of a modern intellectual enlightenment upon the customs and beliefs of the primitives. In any case, *Religionswissenschaft* would choose to assert rather less than too much. Happily, at least among us, it has freed itself from the pathos of optimistic positivism.

However much the work of *Religionswissenschaft*, as research, will always be careful about particulars—for here the meditation on the insignificant, of which Jakob Grimm spoke, cannot be thorough enough—the goal of *Religionswissenschaft* remains to understand and to present as living totalities the religions studied. After they have been disclosed and studied, its desire will always be to place the individual beliefs and ideas, the customs and communal modes, into that context in which alone they live; to connect them and to show them together with the spirit of the entire religion, with the basic intention that animates them, and with the creative religious intuition at their source.

Schleiermacher has said that every religion represents one aspect of the divine and develops a certain attitude toward it, an attitude which unfolds within the major spheres of religious expression, in doctrine, and in community. It is the task of *Religionswissenschaft* to show how strong, how weak, how enduring, the spirit (*Geist*) of a religion is, or how, in ever new beginnings it manifests itself externally. In this the hermeneutic circularity need not frighten us. This spirit must be understood by means of its dogmatic, cultic, and sociological expressions so that it may then be presupposed in the interpretation of these same manifestations. Religious language in the broader sense of "expression" (*Ausdruck*) is always a code which points beyond itself. This is the truth of the hermeneutic of depth-exegesis, which we encounter in all great religious complexes and which—however arbitrary and unprovable its interpretation of the particulars may seem—has an eternal right over against all rationalism in the understanding of religious expressions.

In a religious doctrine, or in a cultic act, there is always more intended than can be recognized (because expressions in word, pitch, and gesture always limit that which is to be expressed). And then again in excess of what is intended, there is also something in an expression of the religious totality which is represented by it and hinted at by it. The demand to do justice always to all these relationships is put on the student of religions. It is exactly the decisive trend, the central motivation of a given religiosity, which is often very difficult to grasp, to trace, and to describe. And still, this apparently theoretical and abstract undertaking is of special practical significance. It is significant for missions; they are just as much entitled to make use of the work of *Religionswissenschaft* as the latter will always thankfully accept for study—and this does not exclude criticism—the results of missionary reports about other religions. For the sake of contact (*Anknüpfung*), it will be very important to recognize the primary motivating forces of the religiosity which one confronts. These forces are definitely not always expressed in the ideas and beliefs of the primary official doctrine. It is important to identify them, to determine where and to what extent a religion is alive and has power to live. It is important to determine where the negative and sensitive spots are that require considerate care and to determine where positive values appear, the admiration of which is required for contact and communication to occur.

From what has been discussed, it should be clear that the central concern of *Religionswissenschaft* must be the understanding of other religions. Before we speak about this understanding proper, we shall venture yet a few words toward the further clarification of what has been said. Today, especially, the study of religions which are not our own is obliged to defend its ambitions. First, it has to defend itself against the theological objection that "he who knows one religion knows them all." Then, further, it must defend itself not only with respect to external opportunity (Can one afford to occupy oneself beyond the present concerns of our nation and our hemisphere with the religions of distant lands and times?) but also against skepticism that knowledge is possible about that which transcends one's own vital and spiritual life, feeling, thought, and will. To the point respecting opportunity, we may add that *Religionswissenschaft* in its presentations and in its research has to distinguish between what is important and what is less important, what is interesting and what is peripheral, what is necessary to know and what is worthy of knowing. But this is essentially a didactic matter.

It is understandable that today in lectures and in courses it is primarily the religions which appeal to the wider public that must be discussed: those which stand prior historically to our Christianity — as for example, the Germanic religion as the early faith of our people — or, in another way, the high religions with which our own struggles today at so many places. In this, *Religionswissenschaft* will have to claim the totality of religious phenomena as the task of its research — to study them and to understand them — but it will also have to claim penetration into most distant realms. A discussion of the final reasons for this would lead us deeply into the systematic problems of philosophy of religion, on the one hand, and into the methodology of the intellectual disciplines, on the other. Therefore, in the present context we must omit such a discussion. But since again and again in the course of time the possibility of understanding other religions has been doubted, *Religionswissenschaft* has a fundamental interest in this question.

The student of religions must be clear about the difficulties to which critics have rightly pointed. We refer here to the difficulties contained in the very naïve assumption that religious phenomena, if only sufficient mterials were available, could readily be understood through the scientific approach. This assumption still plays a great role among the various types of positivism, as well as in that study of religions which is determined by it. Of course, a radical skepticism as a consequence of either religious indifference or of agnosticism or as a result of historical skepticism (where the history of religions, as all history, is a *fable convenue*) must be rejected just as must be any naïve optimism concerning phenomenological imagery.

The difficulties in our understanding are of various types. *First*, they are quantitative in nature: for example, the often considerable distance in time and space, especially serious with respect to the "dead," the exotic, and the primitive religions. With the consequent lack of information, with the discontinuities and transformations among the traditions or source materials, may one still hope at all to attain a more or less true picture of the religions from the distant past and from distant realms? One need only think for instance of the religions of Egypt, Babylonia, China, and Mexico. *Second*, there are the qualitative difficulties that hinder our understanding: the uniqueness of foreign inwardness, which is likewise inherent in its expressions. Spengler, to name only one widely known thinker, has recently pointed especially to the uniqueness of ancient thought, feeling, and perceptivity. Who is there who has not felt the unfathomable depths that inhabit the religious representations of the Far East or the demonic so typical of African religions?

However, not only *Religionswissenschaft* is burdened with both of these types of difficulties; rather, all intellectual disciplines concerned with cultures, especially the historical disciplines, share them. In long and toilsome work they have sought to develop methods and criteria which would allow to some degree the mastery of these difficulties. If one looks to the results of these labors, one will have to admit how astonishingly and how extensively they have been crowned with success. We actually have a body of knowledge about the religions of peoples long since past as well as of distant places. This knowledge can withstand the most exacting tests and controls; it completes, broadens, and extends itself continuously, and it constitutes more than a subjective picture of particulars. Moreover, we are even able to test against the certain results of research the false pictures which are based on insufficient and onesided information; here the error of poor subjectivity appears to be eliminated to a very great extent. Nevertheless, nobody will therefore underestimate the difficulties that have been mentioned.

We continuously have reasons to examine within an ever-extending problematic the possibilities, the chances, and the limits in understanding other religions. How difficult it is even to obtain a clear picture of the religiosity of a person near to us—still within the realm of common faith and familiarity! How difficult it is to comprehend the piety of our predecessors of perhaps only a few decades, of the faiths of neighboring lands, of the faith of Islamic peoples who still have certain religious influences in common with Europe, and finally of the people of India and China.

With this we actually have arrived at the *third* major difficulty with which the understanding of other religions must struggle. This difficulty is unique in that it concerns the nature of the religious. It will certainly be less difficult to obtain a picture of the legal customs and of the linguistic and artistic expressions of a people than of their religion. The last is above everything else kept in high esteem. It may even be fearfully hidden from foreign eyes and guarded as an arcanum. And even when it is possible to look into it, it is really not easy to grasp its meaning. A simple example will point this out: a Roman Catholic mass, in which so much is interrelated and unfamiliar, even foreign, to the Protestant who attends. If it is a church service according to the Greek, the Coptic, or the Armenian rite, the strangeness is immediately greater. This foreignness grows again as we encounter no longer a Christian but, for example, a Jewish, or an Islamic, or even a Buddhist worship service. How difficult for consequent understanding are the religious root-conceptions and root-customs of taboo, totem, nagual, and others. How different the baroque mythology of Japanese Shinto, the orgiastic cults of certain Indian Shiva sects, the fanaticism of the Islamic Shi'ah, appear to us. Here our discussion closes in on a great and serious problem: the secret of plurality among religious experiences. We can only lead up to this problem, for its consideration is a concern for philosophy of religion and for theology. Here we shall deal only with the question whether and how it is possible for *Religionswissenschaft* to understand other religions. We have already seen that many practical proofs of its possibility are available. Hermeneutically, on what does this possibility rest?

We have spoken above of what is generally representative of spiritual, and therefore also of religious, expressions. The expression then becomes transparent; it allows something to shine through of the specific and perhaps unique spirit (*Geist*) of a certain religious context. Thus it is that views into the depths (*Tiefenblicke*) become possible. Not always and not to everybody do they open themselves. But it is amazing how much a small and peripheral aspect, taken from the conceptions and customs of a faith, can disclose to a gifted and trained mind. Actual intuition (*Divination*) here, as always, is the exception. Synthesis (*Kombination*) stands in the foreground of all intellectual endeavors, as it does in *Religionswissenschaft.* If then, perhaps, in a happy and fruitful interplay of both avenues to knowledge, some decisive characteristics of a foreign religiosity have emerged for the researcher, he may then dare to grasp and describe its basic intention. In this it is a great help for the human understanding that in the structure of spiritual expressions (of such great and deep experiences as are the productively religious ones) there is inherent an amazing continuity (*Folgerichtigkeit*). Nor is this continuity absent in the structures of the historical religious systems.

It is not very difficult for one who has really comprehended the central intuition of Islam, its experience of the deity, as this is expressed in the original revelation to the prophet Muhammed, to discover it again in the doctrine, theology, cosmology, anthropology, soteriology, and cult. In spite of all other influences, this central intuition develops within the framework of these expressions. The experience of suffering within a world of change, fundamental for Buddhism, is displayed with such a continuity in its doctrine, is presented in its symbols, and is shaped within its ethic, so that the understanding of this may, like a great key, unlock an otherwise strange-appearing world of expressions.

Such considerations certainly ought not minimize the difficulties; they ought not delude us about the levels and degress of understanding, about the differences involved among its various risks. But by considering and by honoring differences, an old truth must not be forgotten. As Goethe and Wilhelm have formulated it, in every man there dwell all the forms of humanity. Novalis asked at one time: How can a man have an understanding of something of which he does not have the seed within himself? This insight in no way implies the lack or the weakness of him who does the understanding; rather, it implies the conviction that in all of us is contained more than becomes manifest in the co-operation of circumstances and fate.

Only very recently Eduard Spranger in his illustrative investigation of the primary levels of reality-consciousness (*Abhandlungen der Akademie der Wissenschaften* [Berlin], 1934) has proven that in all of us there are latently present certain more primeval structures of consciousness. What is called "mind" has the ability to activate these and to understand, so to speak, the atavistic and distant expressions of our soul, the expressions which are alien to our present consciousness. Novalis again says: We stand in relationship with all parts of the universe, with the future and with the past. What relationship we shall primarily develop and what relationship for us shall become primarily effective and important depend only on the direction and duration of our attentiveness. This means that in principle there could resound in each of us something of the ecstatic, the spectral, the unusual—something of that which to us, the children of another age, of another race, and of other customs, appears strange among the religious expressions of distant lands. Where this natural disposition is developed through training, there also the prerequisite for an actual understanding of foreign religiosity exists.

This can be illustrated through the example of myth. In myth, religious experience is expressed in unique categories. As recent ethnological and psychological research has shown, our logical norms are not necessarily valid for these categories. Thus the myths of primitive peoples with their identifications, their theriomorphisms, and so on, at first seem abstruse to the uninformed, contemporary reader or listener. And still, it does not seem impossible to sense something of the intended reality of the myth. Such immersions into archaic modes of consciousness are generally more easily attained by young people. Such modes of consciousness are almost self-evident and present for them. I am reminded of our youth associations and their experience, their symbolism and their customs; in them the world of primitive man (*Natur-*

mensch) is not only imitated externally but actually felt in participation, and it becomes clear that their experience of it is not a purely intellectual affair.

In the human understanding, as the excellent hermeneutics of Wilhelm Dilthey has shown, the totality of mind and soul (*Totalität des Gemüts*) is effective. Concretely stated, the religious content of myth cannot be found alone in a careful and thorough, though necessary, analysis of its ideological elements and motives; rather, the entire personality of him who studies and understands is spoken to. If he wishes to understand the attitude from which the mythological faith and custom have issued, he must respond. An inner aliveness and broadness is necessary if we actually wish to understand other religions. In this connection it should be stated explicitly that the one-sided advancement of a particular point of view is bad for the understanding. As justified and fruitful as may be the co-operative approaches of psychology, sociology, and typology, pure psychological, pure sociological, and pure typological answers do not help us to understand foreign religiosity. Unfortunately, our discipline is rich in one-sided attempts that have been based on false, narrow, and oblique conceptions of the nature of religion.

It appears to be a truism to say that hermeneutics demands that he who wishes to understand other religions must have a sense (*Organ*) for religion and in addition the most extensive knowledge and training possible. Many still think that one of these two prerequisites is sufficient. While all sorts of dilettantes (a famous example is the interpretation of Laotse's *Tao te King*) err in one of these directions, often philologists, ethnologists, and other specialists go amiss in the other. The first demand is stated by some in a still more strict and narrow sense. Well aware of the above-mentioned difficulties in understanding other religions, they think that one must actually belong to a community of believers if one wishes to grasp its actual concern. This is a significant assertion, and it must be seriously examined. If it proves to be fully correct, the ground on which *Religionswissenschaft* builds will have been withdrawn. Here, too, a glance at the results of a century rich in religious studies of the most varied kinds will reveal in fact that even those who have not studied another religion as a member of that particular religious community may be successful. The same can likewise hardly be denied of knowledge concerning the entire realm of expressions, that is, of the doctrine, cult, and constitution of the religious community concerned.

But the matter gets more difficult when we are dealing with the inner experience, the understanding and intention to which such expressions bear witness. There can be no question that growing up within a tradition, belonging to the community of faith, can be a favorable precondition. However, the effect of habit, the absence of distance, and so on, may certainly also be negative influences. Standing within a tradition is nevertheless important. It could perhaps be an advantage in certain situations for the convert over the outsider. It could enable him to grasp the conscious ambition of the community which he joins. But one would want to ask, with respect to understanding Buddhism, for example, whether he who through conversion has been accepted into the community actually has a greater insight than the outsider, perhaps a Westerner, who for a long time has immersed himself in Buddhist studies. We may admit without reservation that standing in a tradition is something that is difficult to replace and that—provided the other prerequisites which we have found necessary are also present—the chances for understanding the actual intention of a religious community are increased. But in practical confrontation with the multiplicity of phenomena, with which the student of religions must deal, such a participation will not be possible. Thus, the demand that one belong to the religious community which one wishes to understand cannot be made a prerequisite—not to speak of the new errors which could arise under these circumstances. The problem of knowledge and faith, of faith and understanding, cannot be discussed here. Only this much must be summarized: being rooted in a personal faith—a faith which may well blind one to other things but which, in contrast to the opinion of many, need not do so—does not necessarily mean a disadvantage for him who seeks to understand. The demand of a *tabula rasa* has long been recognized as utopian; and even though such objectivity might be desirable, it is actually impossible. Schleiermacher has seen that we must learn from our personal religious life in order to encounter the foreign. We need not a blank sheet but an impregnated one, one that will preserve the pictures projected onto it.

Is it at this point that *tout comprendre c'est tout pardonner*? In other words—and in connection with the above—is not the result of *Religionswissenschaft*, then, a hopeless relativism? Is it of such a nature that in its own best interests the Christian mission should be warned against a closer touch with *Religionswissenschaft*? I hope that with the foregoing I have succeeded in showing that contemporary *Religionswissenschaft* no longer pays obeisance to the historicist fallacy which in its time has fettered the so-called *Religionsgeschichtliche Schule*, namely, that norms may be attained from history itself. If history of religions were supposed to tell us what we ought to believe, we would wait for such information for a long time. No, since it no longer thinks about giving such advice and since it has recognized that its field of study is sufficiently large as it is and that it has many concrete tasks that can ambitiously be attacked, we would be doing it a grave injustice to have this sort of suspicion. Certainly, it seeks to understand foreign religiosity. We have also seen that its motivation for this is ethically beyond reproach. How does it stand now with respect to forgiveness? Does the study of *Religionswissenschaft* weaken the sense of value, the courage and the ability to decide?

The ability to decide "what must I believe?" lies—and this we have repeatedly emphasized here—outside the sphere of a scientific discipline. We no longer are good enough rationalists and positivists to believe that an intellectual discipline can replace religion, not even that it necessarily limits it. In practice, it is, however, still the case, as we can see among those peoples who have not yet emerged from their susceptibility to the scientific faith, that an Eastern student graduated from a Western university returns to his home region and deems himself toweringly exalted above the "superstition" which "still" prevails there. As we have said, with us this is no longer the case. It is not a good sign for a faith if it allows itself to be shaken by an intellectual discipline. True decision for a faith, I would like to say, is not only not impaired but is aided and deepended by *Religionswissenschaft*. But what about the sense of value? Nietzsche, who must be understood not only as a dogmatist but also as a critic, has said in his famous discussion of the advantages and disadvantages of historiography, in behalf of the life of the concrete force (*plastische Kraft*), that it would be impaired if the great museum of human history—and thus also that of history of religions—were spread out without choice and distinctions before the people of today. The nineteenth century, to which Nietzsche held up the mirror, was stuck deeply in historicism; its anarchy of values was destined to have its full effects only at the beginning of the twentieth century.

We now have again found the right and the courage to evalute. *Religionswissenschaft* will seek to grasp with understanding all that foreign religions produce of faith, cult, custom, and community. It will seek to grasp the actual meaning, the religious intention, out of which spring all these; otherwise, and this it knows well, it will have only empty shells to tinker with. *Religionswissenschaft* does not abstain from using scales and standards; on the contrary, it makes much use of them. It seeks to overcome all superficial presuppositions, all the binding tendencies; it attempts to see the phenomena of other religious life; it tries to understand and honor this life in its actuality. For once, the student of religions looks at a particular religion immanently, from within. He asks himself what a conception or a characteristic looks like, how it integrates within the totality of the religion concerned. He asks further—and here the reference to value in his study becomes quite clear—about the amount of religious productivity and vitality which speaks from within the specific phenomenon. If, for example, we consider the faith in a god (*Gottesglauben*) of a certain African tribe, we must determine the degree of perfection to which this belief in a god is expressed by this particular community; then we must honor the level of theistic experience which appears attained therein. This certainly is no easy task. Good sense, manners, and experience are needed in order to appraise correctly, to appraise, beyond all naïve absolutizing of one's own personal beliefs and feelings, the religious quality among the particular phenomena of religious life. This is so precisely because standards which are taken from elsewhere, from the realm of aesthetic and ethical evaluation, very easily creep into the place of the only decisive religious point of view. It is understandable that from a didactic point of view, the more history of religions increases the amount of data and the more data it pushes into our horizon, the more the separation of the important from the unimportant, the great from the small, will have to be worked out.

An introduction to *Religionswissenschaft* should not consist of a non-selective enumeration of encyclopedic facts — as is said to be the case occasionally in academic presentations. Rather, it should be concerned with describing the great and classic figures in the history of religions, and of these, again — for each of these great inspirations, too, represents something typical — there should be pointed out the typical and the significant, the personal and the characteristic. The world religions have a claim to a special and thorough consideration. To this introduction also belongs the study of the history of a particular religion — perhaps the history of a significant one from among the more advanced as well as one from among the primitive cultures; then, further, the structure of that religion (its central point of doctrine, the major aspects of the cult, the hinge-point of the organization) and the major phases in its development must be identified clearly enough to make a comparison possible. For this, the role of the leading religious personalities, as well as the transformation of the official religion by popular piety, must also be presented. In all this the decisive thing is to make visible that in which true religiosity is present — a religiosity which may further be cultivated to determine secondary formations, for example, where petrification and degeneration have set in. An exemplary model for training oneself to grasp the significant from the fulness of the materials of *Religionswissenschaft* is still Rudolf Otto's *Das Heilige*. This study, besides being important for the phenomenology of religion, also has great methodological significance.

We have spoken of scales and of choice. It becomes readily clear that here again there is an important starting point with practical consequences. The missionary will find it valuable to have worked out for himself scales of the type hinted at here. From his point of view, he will know well the religion of the nation or tribe with whom he primarily deals. But he gladly and in addition would also like to acquire the greater background against which he can still more deeply understand this religion. In this context we cannot talk in detail about the various relationships between *Religionswissenschaft* and the study of missions. To cultivate and to deepen this knowledge, has already been the special task of this periodical. The more the insight spreads and deepens — as has happened especially in recent times — the more in all Christian missions one motive must stand decisively in the foreground: that behind the religious motive all other motives must retreat to the background, and that the people whom we missionize ought to be led to a religiosity appropriate to themselves and to their uniqueness. So the thorough study of their uniqueness becomes an increasingly important task; to this, too, *Religionswissenschaft* can contribute its share.

> I invite you to observe every faith which human beings have ever confessed, every religion which you have designated by a certain name or label and which perhaps has long since degenerated into a codex of empty customs, into a system of abstract concepts and theories; and when you investigate it at its source and through its more original constituents, you will discover that all this dead slag at one time was a red-hot pouring of the inner fire, the fire which is contained to a greater or

lesser degree in all religions; you will discover in their true nature that, as I have presented it, each of these unique formations has been the one which the eternal and never-ceasing Religion had necessarily to assume among finite and limited characteristics.[1]

[1] Friedrich Schleiermacher, *Über die Religion. Reden an die Gebildeten unter ihren Verächtern* (3d ed.; Berlin: G. Reimer, 1821), pp. 364–65.

1

Cultural Fashions and the History of Religions

MIRCEA ELIADE

The question that I should like to discuss in this paper is the following: What does a historian of religions have to say about his contemporary *milieu*? In what sense can he contribute to the understanding of its literary or philosophical movements, its recent and significant artistic orientations? Or even more, what has he to say, as a historian of religions, in regard to such manifestations of the *Zeitgeist* as its philosophical and literary vogues, its so-called cultural fashions? It seems to me that, at least in some instances, his special training should enable him to decipher meanings and intentions less manifest to others. I am not referring to those cases in which the religious context or implications of a work are more or less evident, as, for example, Chagall's paintings with their enormous "eye of God," the angels, the severed heads and bodies flying upside down—and his omnipresent ass, that messianic animal *par excellence*. Or Ionesco's recent play, *Le roi se meurt*, which cannot be fully understood if one does not know the *Tibetan Book of the Dead* and the *Upanishads*. (And I can testify to the fact that Ionesco *did* read these texts—but the important thing for us to determine is what he accepted and what he ignored or rejected. Thus it is not a question of searching for *sources* but a more exciting endeavor: to examine the renewal of Ionesco's imaginary creative universe through his encounter with exotic and traditional religious universes.)

There are instances when only a historian of religions can discover some secret significance of a cultural creation, whether ancient or contemporary. For example, only a historian of religions is likely to perceive that there is a surprising structural analogy between James Joyce's *Ulysses* and certain Australian myths of the totemic-hero type. And just as the endless wanderings and fortuitous meetings of the Australian cultural heroes seem monotonous to those who are familiar with Polynesian, Indo-European, or North American mythologies, so the wanderings of Leopold Bloom in *Ulysses* appear monotonous to an admirer of Balzac or Tolstoi. But the historian of religions knows that the tedious wanderings and performances of mythical ancestors reveal to the Australian a magnificent history in which he is existentially involved—and the same thing can be said of the apparently tedious and banal journey of Leopold Bloom in his native city. Again, only the historian of religions is likely to catch the very striking similarities between the Australian and Platonic theories of reincarnation and *anamnesis.* For Plato, learning is recollecting. Physical objects help the soul withdraw into itself and, through a sort of "going-back," rediscover and repossess the original knowledge that it possessed in its extraterrestrial condition. Now the Australian novice discovers, through his initiation, that he has already been here, in a mythical time; he was here in the form of a mythical ancestor. Through initiation he again learns to do those things which he did at the beginning, when he appeared for the first time in the form of a mythical being.

It would be useless to accumulate more examples. I will only add that the historian of religions is able to contribute to the understanding of writers as different as Jules Verne and Gerard de Nerval, Novalis and Garcia Lorca.[1] It is surprising that so few historians of religion have ever tried to interpret a literary work from their own perspective. (For the moment I can recall only Maryla Falk's book on Novalis and Stig Wikander's studies of French writers from Jules Michelet

[1] Cf., for example, Léon Cellier, "Le Roman initiatique en France au temps du romantisme," *Cahiers Internationaux de Symbolisme,* No. 4 (1964), pp. 22–44; Jean Richer, *Nerval: Expérience et création* (Paris, 1963); Maryla Falk, *I "Misteri" di Novalis* (Naples, 1939); Erika Lorenz, *Der metaphorische Kosmos der modernen spanischen Lyrik, 1936–1956* (Hamburg, 1961).

to Mallarmé. Duchesne-Guillemin's important monographs on Mallarmé and Valéry could have been written by any excellent literary critic, without any contact with the History of Religions.) On the contrary, as is well known, it is the literary critics, especially in the United States, who have often not hesitated to use the findings of the History of Religions in their hermeneutical work. One need only call to mind the frequent application of the "myth and ritual" theory or the "initiation pattern" in the interpretation of modern fiction and poetry.[2]

My purpose here is more modest. I will try to see whether a historian of religions can decipher some hidden meanings in our so-called cultural fashions, taking as examples three recent vogues, all of which originated in Paris but are already spreading throughout western Europe and even the United States. Now, as we all know well, for a particular theory or philosophy to become popular, to be *à la mode, en vogue*, implies neither that it is a remarkable creation nor that it is devoid of all value. One of the fascinating aspects of the "cultural fashion" is that it does not matter whether the facts in question and their interpretation are true or not. No amount of criticism can destroy a vogue. There is something "religious" about this imperviousness to criticism, even if only in a narrow-minded, sectarian way. But even beyond this general aspect, some cultural fashions are extremely significant for the historian of religions. Their popularity, especially among the intelligentsia, reveals something of Western man's dissatisfactions, drives, and nostalgias.

To give only one example: Fifty years ago, Freud thought that he had found the origin of social organization, moral restrictions, and religion in a primordial murder, namely, the first patricide. He told the story in his book *Totem and Taboo.* In the beginning, the father kept all the women for himself and would drive his sons off as they became old enough to evoke his jealousy. One day, the expelled sons killed their

[2] I discussed some of these interpretations in my article "L'Initiation et le monde modern," *Initiation*, ed. C. J. Bleeker (Leiden, 1965), pp. 1–14; see esp. pp. 11 ff.

father, ate him, and appropriated his females. "The totemic banquet," writes Freud, "perhaps the first feast mankind ever celebrated, was the repetition, the festival of remembrance, of this noteworthy criminal deed."[3] Consequently, Freud holds that God is nothing other than the sublimated physical father; hence in the totemic sacrifice it is God himself who is killed and sacrificed. "This slaying of the father-god is mankind's original sin. This blood-guilt is atoned for by the bloody death of Christ."[4]

In vain the ethnologists of his time, from W. H. Rivers and F. Boas, to A. L. Kroeber, B. Malinowski, and W. Schmidt, demonstrated the absurdity of such a primordial "totemic banquet."[5] In vain they pointed out that totemism is not found at the beginnings of religion, that it is not universal — that not all peoples have passed through a "totemic stage" — that Frazer had already proved that of the many hundred totemic tribes only *four* knew a rite approximating the ceremonial killing and eating of the "totem-god" (a rite assumed by Freud to be an invariable feature of totemism), and furthermore, that this rite has nothing to do with the origin of sacrifice, since totemism does not occur at all in the oldest cultures. In vain Wilhelm Schmidt pointed out that the pretotemic peoples knew nothing of cannibalism, that patricide among them would be a "sheer impossibility, psychologically, sociologically, and ethically," and that "the form of the pretotemic family, and therefore of the earliest human family we can hope to know anything about through ethnology, is neither general promiscuity nor group-marriage, neither of which, according to the verdict of the leading anthropologists, ever existed at all."[6] Freud was not in the least troubled by such objections, and this wild "gothic novel," *Totem and*

[3] Sigmund Freud, *Totem und Tabu* (Zurich, 1913), p. 110. Cf. A. L. Kroeber, "Totem and Taboo: An Ethnological Psychoanalysis," *American Anthropologist*, XXII (1920), 48–55.

[4] Wilhelm Schmidt, *The Origin and Growth of Religion*, trans. H. J. Rose (New York, 1931), p. 112.

[5] Cf. Mircea Eliade, "The History of Religions in Retrospect: 1912–1962," *Journal of Bible and Religion*, XXXI, No. 2 (April, 1963), 98–109, esp. 101 ff.

[6] Schmidt, *op. cit.*, pp. 112–15.

Taboo, has since become one of the minor gospels of three generations of the Western intelligentsia.

Of course the genius of Freud and the merits of psychoanalysis ought not to be judged by the horror stories presented as objective historical fact in *Totem and Taboo*. But it is highly significant that such frantic hypotheses could be acclaimed as sound scientific theory in spite of all the criticism marshaled by the major anthropologists of the century. Because psychoanalysis won the battle against the older psychologies, and for many other reasons, it became a cultural fashion, and after 1920 the Freudian ideology was taken for granted in its entirety. A fascinating book could be written about the significance of the incredible success of this *roman noir frénétique, Totem and Taboo*. Using the very tools and method of modern psychoanalysis, we can lay open some tragic secrets of the modern Western intellectual: for example, his profound dissatisfaction with the worn-out forms of historical Christianity and his desire to violently rid himself of his forefathers' faith, accompanied by a strange sense of guilt, as if he himself had killed a God in whom he could not believe but whose absence he could not bear. For this reason I have said that a cultural fashion is immensely significant, no matter what its objective value may be; the success of certain ideas or ideologies reveals to us the spiritual and existential situation of all those for whom these ideas or ideologies constitute a kind of soteriology.

Of course there are fashions in other sciences, even in the discipline of History of Religions, though evidently they are less glamorous than the vogue enjoyed by *Totem and Taboo*. That our fathers and grandfathers were fascinated by *The Golden Bough* is a comprehensible, and rather honorable fact. What is less comprehensible, and can be explained only as a fashion, is the fact that between 1900 and 1920 almost all the historians of religions were searching for Mother Goddesses, Corn-Mothers, and Vegetation Demons—and of course they found them everywhere, in all the religions and folklores of the world. This search for the Mother—Mother Earth, Tree-Mother, Corn-Mother, and so on—and also for other demonic beings related to vegetation and agriculture is also significant for the understanding of the unconscious nostalgias of the Western intellectual at the beginning of the century.

Let me remind you of another example of the power and prestige of fashions in History of Religions. This time there is neither god nor goddess involved, neither Corn-Mother nor Vegetation Spirit but an animal – specifically, a camel. I am referring to the famous sacrifice of a camel described by a certain Nilus who lived in the second part of the fourth century. While he lived as a monk in the monastery of Mount Sinai, the Bedouin Arabs raided the monastery. Nilus had the opportunity to observe at first hand the life and beliefs of the Bedouins, and he recorded many such observations in his treatise *The Slaying of the Monks on Mount Sinai.* Particularly dramatic is his description of the sacrifice of a camel, "offered," he says, "to the Morning Star." Bound upon a rude altar of stones piled together, the camel is cut into pieces and devoured raw by the worshippers. Devoured with such haste, Nilus adds, "that in the short interval between the rise of the day star, which marked the hour for the service to begin, and the disappearance of its rays before the rising sun, the entire camel, body and bones, skin, blood and entrails, is wholly devoured."[7] J. Wellhausen was the first to relate this sacrifice in his *Reste arabischen Heidenthumes* (1887). But it was William Robertson Smith who established, so to speak, the unique scientific prestige of Nilus' camel. He refers to this sacrifice innumerable times in his *Lectures on the Religion of the Semites* (1889), considering it "the oldest known form of Arabian sacrifice,"[8] and he speaks of the "direct evidence of Nilus as to the habits of the Arabs of the Sinatic destert."[9] From then on, all the followers of Robert Smith's theory of sacrifice – S. Reinach, A. Wendel, A. S. Cook, S. H. Hooke – abundantly and untiringly referred to Nilus' account. It is

[7] Summarized by W. Robertson Smith, *Lectures on the Religion of the Semites* (rev. ed.; London, 1899), p. 338.

[8] *Ibid.*, p. 338.

[9] *Ibid.*, p. 281.

still more curious that even those scholars who did not accept Robertson Smith's theory could not—or dared not—discuss the general problem of sacrifice without duly relating Nilus' story.[10] In fact, no one seemed to doubt the authenticity of Nilus' testimony, even though a great number of scholars rejected Robertson Smith's interpretation. Thus by the beginning of this century Nilus' camel had become so exasperatingly omnipresent in the writings of historians of religions, Old Testament scholars, sociologists, and ethnologists, that G. Foucard declared, in his book *Histoire des religions et méthode comparative*, "it seems that no author has any longer the right to treat of History of Religions if he does not speak respectfully of this anecdote. For it is indeed an anecdote . . . , a detail related as an 'aside'; and on a unique fact, so slender, one cannot really build up a religious theory valid for all humanity."[11] With great intellectual courage, G. Foucard summed up his methodological position: "Concerning Nilus' camel, I persist in the belief that it does not deserve to carry on its back the weight of the origins of a part of the History of Religions."[12]

G. Foucard was right. Meticulous textual and historical analysis has proved that Nilus was not the author of the treatise *The Slaying of the Monks on Mount Sinai*, that this is a pseudonymous work written probably in the fourth or fifth century, and, what is more important, that the text is full of literary clichés borrowed from the Greek novels; for example, the description of the killing and devouring of the camel—"hacking off pieces of the quivering flesh and devouring the entire animal, body and bones"—has no ethnological value but reveals only a knowledge of the rhetorical-pathetic genre of the Hellenistic novels. Nonetheless, although these facts

[10] Cf. the bibliography in Joseph Henninger, "Ist der sogennante Nilus-Bericht eine brauchbare religionsgeschichtliche Quelle?" *Anthropos*, L (1955), 81–148, esp. pp. 86 ff.

[11] G. Foucard, *Histoire des religions et méthode comparative* (2d ed.; Paris, 1912), pp. 132 ff.

[12] *Ibid.*, pp. lxv ff.; "Et pour le chameau de saint Nil, je persisterai à croire qu'il ne mérite pas de porter sur son dos le poids des origines d'une partie de l'histoire des religions."

were already known after the First World War, thanks especially to Karl Heussi's painstaking analysis,[13] Nilus' camel still haunts many recent scientific works.[14] And no wonder. This short and colorful description of the presumably original form of sacrifice and the beginnings of religious communion was tailor-made to gratify all tastes and inclinations. Nothing could be more flattering for that great number of Western intellectuals who were convinced that prehistoric and primitive man was very nearly a beast of prey and, consequently, that the origin of religion should reflect a troglodytic psychology and behavior. Furthermore, the communal devouring of a camel could not but substantiate the claim of the sociologists that religion is merely a social fact, if not just the hypostatic projection of the society itself. Even those scholars who called themselves Christians were somehow happy with Nilus' account. They would readily point out the immense distance that separates the total consumption of a camel—bones and skin included—from the highly spiritualized, if not merely symbolic, Christian sacraments. The splendid superiority of monotheism and especially of Christianity over against all preceding pagan creeds and faiths could not be more convincingly evident. And, of course, all these scholars, Christians as well as agnostics or atheists, were supremely proud and happy at being what they were: civilized Westerners and champions of infinite progress.

I do not doubt that the analysis of the three recent cultural fashions to which I referred at the beginning of this lecture will prove as revealing for us, although they are not directly related to History of Religions. Of course they are not to be considered equally significant. One at least may very soon become obsolete. For our purposes, it does not matter. What matters is the fact that during the last four or five years Paris has been dominated—one might almost say conquered—by a magazine called *Planète* and by two authors, Teilhard de

[13] See especially *Das Nilusproblem* (Leipzig, 1921). The bibliography of Heussi's work on Nilus is presented and discussed by Henninger, *op. cit.*, pp. 89 ff.

[14] Cf. the bibliography *ibid.*, pp. 86 ff.

Chardin and Claude Lévi-Strauss. I hasten to add that I do not intend to discuss here the theories of Teilhard and Lévi-Strauss. What interests me is their amazing popularity, and I will refer to their ideas only insofar as they may explain the reasons for that popularity.

For obvious reasons, I shall begin with the magazine *Planète.* As a matter of fact, I am not the first to have pondered the cultural meaning of its unheard-of popularity. Some time ago the well-known and extremely serious Parisian paper *Le Monde* devoted two long articles to this very problem, the unexpected and incredible success of *Planète.* Indeed, some eighty thousand subscribers and one hundred thousand buyers of a rather expensive magazine constitute a unique phenomenon in France—and a problem for the sociology of culture. Its editors are Louis Pawels, a writer and a former disciple of Gurjdeef, and Jacques Bergier, a very popular scientific journalist. In 1961 they published a voluminous book, *Le Matin des Sorciers,* which rapidly became a best seller. In fact, *Planète* was launched with the royalties earned by *Le Matin des Sorciers.* The book has also been translated into English, but it has not made a comparative impact on the Anglo-American public. It is a curious mélange of popular science, occultism, astrology, science fiction, and spiritual techniques. But it is more than that. It tacitly pretends to reveal innumerable vital secrets—of our universe, of the Second World War, of lost civilizations, of Hitler's obsession with astrology, and so on. Both authors are well read and, as I have already said, Jacques Bergier has a scientific background. Consequently, the reader is convinced that he is being given *facts*—or at least responsible hypotheses—that, in any case, he is not being misled. *Planète* is constructed on the same premises and follows the same pattern: there are articles on the probability of inhabited planets, new forms of psychological warfare, the perspectives of *l'amour moderne,* Lovecraft and American science fiction, the "real" keys to the understanding of Teilhard de Chardin, the mysteries of the animal world, and so on.

Now in order to understand the unexpected success of both

the book and the magazine one should recall the French cultural milieu of five or six years ago. As is well known, existentialism became extremely popular immediately after the liberation. J. P. Sartre, Camus, and Simone de Beauvoir were the guides and models inspiring the new generation. Sartre in particular enjoyed a popularity equalled by no other French writer since the days of Voltaire and Diderot, Victor Hugo, or Zola during the Dreyfus affair. Marxism itself had not become a real attraction for the young intellectuals before Sartre proclaimed his own communist sympathy. Very little was left of the French Catholic renaissance of the early 1920's. Jacques Maritain and the Neo-Thomists had already gone out of fashion at the beginning of the Second World War. The only living movements inside Catholicism, besides the Christian existentialism of Gabriel Marcel, were those which produced at that time the rather modest group of *Études Carmelitaines* (stressing the importance of mystical experience and encouraging the study of the psychology of religion and of symbolism) and the *Sources Chrétiennes*, with their re-evaluation of Greek patrology and their insistence on liturgical renewal. But of course these Catholic movements had neither the glamour of Sartre's existentialism nor the charisma of communism. The cultural milieu, from philosophy and political ideology to literature, art, cinema, and journalism, was dominated by a few ideas and a number of clichés: the absurdity of human existence, estrangement, commitment, situation, historical moment, and so on. It is true that Sartre spoke constantly of freedom; but in the end *that* freedom was meaningless. In the late fifties, the Algerian war prompted a profound malaise among the intellectuals. Whether existentialists, Marxists, or liberal Catholics, they had to make personal decisions. For many years the French intellectual was forced to live almost exclusively in his "historical moment," as Sartre had taught that any responsible individual should do.

In this gloomy, tedious, and somehow provincial atmosphere — for it seemed that only Paris, or rather Saint Germain-des-Près, and now Algeria really counted in the world —

the appearance of *Planète* had the effect of a bombshell. The general orientation, the problems discussed, the language—all were different. There was no longer the excessive preoccupation with one's own existential "situation" and historical "commitment" but a grandiose overture toward a wonderful world: the future organization of the planet, the unlimited possibilities of man, the mysterious universe into which we are ready to penetrate, and so on. It was not the scientific approach as such that stirred this collective enthusiasm but the charismatic impact of "the latest scientific developments" and the proclamation of their imminent triumphs. Of course, as I have said already, science was supplemented with hermeticism, science fiction, and political and cultural news. But what was new and exhilarating for the French reader was the optimistic and holistic outlook which coupled science with esoterism and presented a living, fascinating and mysterious cosmos in which human life again became meaningful and promised an endless perfectibility. Man was no longer condemned to a rather dreary *condition humaine* but was called both to conquer his physical universe and also to unravel the other, enigmatic, universes revealed by the occultists and gnostics. But in contrast to all previous gnostic and esoteric schools and movements, *Planète* did not disregard the social and political problems of the contemporary world. In sum, it propagated a *saving* science, scientific information which was at the same time soteriological. Man was no longer estranged and useless in an absurd world, into which he had come by accident and to no purpose.

I must stop here with my rapid analysis of the reasons for *Planète's* success, for I realize that many of the things which I have said in connection with this magazine can be applied almost identically to the vogue of Teilhard de Chardin. It should be unnecessary to add that I am not speaking of the scientific and philosophic merits of Teilhard, which are unquestionable, but of the tremendous success of his books, all of which, as is well known, were published posthumously. And it is a strange paradox that the only Roman Catholic thinker who has gained a responsible and massive audience was prevented by his ecclesiastical authorities from publishing those very books which today are bestsellers both in the old and in the new world. What is even more important, at least one hundred volumes and many thousands of articles have been published all over the world, in less than ten years, discussing — in most cases sympathetically — Teilhard de Chardin's ideas. If we take into consideration the fact that not even the most popular philosopher of this generation, J. P. Sartre, attained such a massive response after twenty-five years of activity, we must acknowledge the *cultural* significance of Teilhard's success. We have no books at all, and only a very few articles, about the ideas of Louis Pawels and G. Bergier (both articles in *Le Monde* are concerned with the popularity of their magazine *Planète*), but the majority of books and articles written about Teilhard discuss his philosophy and his religious conceptions.

Most probably the readers of *Planète* and of Teilhard de Chardin are not the same, but they have many things in common. To begin with, all of them are tired of existentialism and Marxism, tired of continual talk about history, the historical condition, the historical moment, commitment, and so on. The readers of both Teilhard and *Planète* are not so much interested in history as they are in *nature* and in *life*. Teilhard himself considers history to be only a modest segment in a glorious cosmic process which started with the appearance of life and which will continue for billions and billions of years, until the last of the galaxies hears the proclamation of Christ as Logos. The ideology of *Planète* and the philosophy of Teilhard de Chardin are fundamentally optimistic. As a matter of fact, Teilhard is the first philosopher since Bergson who has dared to express faith and confidence both in life and in man. And when critics attempt to prove that Teilhard's basic conceptions are not a legitimate part of the Christian tradition, they usually point to his optimism, his belief in a meaningful and infinite evolution, and his ignoring of original sin and evil in general.

On the other hand, the agnostic scientists who read Teilhard admit that for the first time they have understood what it can mean to be a religious man, to believe in God and even in Jesus Christ and in the sacraments. It is a fact that Teilhard has been the first Christian author to present his faith in terms accessible and meaningful to the agnostic scientist and to the religiously illiterate in general. For the first time in this century the agnostic and atheistic masses of scientifically educated Europeans know what a Christian is speaking about. This is not because Teilhard is a scientist. Before him there were many great scientists who did not conceal their Christian faith. What is new in Teilhard, and explains his popularity at least in part, is the fact that he has grounded his Christian faith in a scientific study and understanding of nature and of life. He speaks of the "spiritual power of matter" and confesses an "overwhelming sympathy for all that stirs within the dark mass of matter." This *love* of Teilhard's for the cosmic substance and the cosmic life seems to impress scientists greatly. He candidly admits that he has always been a "pantheist" by temperament and "less a child of heaven than a son of earth." Even the most refined and abstruse scientific tools — the electronic computer, for example — are exalted by Teilhard because he considers them to be auxiliaries and promoters of life.

But one cannot speak simply of the "vitalism" of Teilhard, for he is a religious man and life for him is *sacred*; moreover, the cosmic matter as such is susceptible of being sanctified in its totality. At least this seems to be the meaning of that beautiful text entitled "The Mass on the Top of the World." When Teilhard speaks of the penetration of the galaxies by the cosmic Logos, even the most fantastic exaltation of the bodhisattvas seems modest and unimaginative by comparison — because for Teilhard the galaxies in which Christ will be preached millions of years hence are *real*, are living matter. They are not illusory and not even ephemeral. In an article in the magazine *Psychè* Teilhard once confessed that he simply could not believe in a catastrophic end of the world — not now, and not after billions of years — he could not even believe in the second law of thermodynamics. For him the universe was real, alive, meaningful, creative, sacred —

and if not eternal in the philosophical sense, at least of infinite duration.

We can now understand the reason for Teilhard's immense popularity: he is not only setting up a bridge between science and Christianity; he is not only presenting an optimistic view of cosmic and human evolution and insisting particularly on the exceptional value of the human mode of being in the universe; *he is also revealing the ultimate sacrality of nature and of life.* Modern man is not only estranged from himself; he is also estranged from nature. And of course one cannot go back to a "cosmic religion" already out of fashion in the time of the prophets and later persecuted and suppressed by the Christians. One cannot even go back to a romantic or bucolic approach to nature. But the nostalgia for a lost mystical solidarity with nature still haunts Western man. And Teilhard has laid open for him an unhoped-for perspective, where nature is charged with religious values even while retaining its complete "objective" reality.

I will not say too much about the third recent vogue, that of Claude Lévi-Strauss—first, because it is of more modest proportions and, second, because it is interrelated with a broader interest in structural linguistics and structuralism in general. Whatever one may think of Lévi-Strauss' conclusions, one cannot but recognize the merits of his work. I personally consider him to be important primarily for the following reasons: (1) Although an anthropologist by training and profession, he is fundamentally a philosopher and he is not afraid of ideas, theories, and theoretical language; therefore, he forces anthropologists to *think*, and even to think hard. For the empirically-minded Anglo-American anthropologist, this is a real calamity, but the historian of religions cannot help but rejoice in the highly theoretical level on which Lévi-Strauss chooses to discuss his so-called primitive material. (2) Even if one does not accept the structuralist approach *in toto*, Lévi-Strauss' criticism of anthropological historicism is very timely. Too much time and energy have been expended by anthropologists in trying to reconstruct the *history* of primitive cultures and very little on *understanding their meaning.* (3) Finally, Lévi-Strauss is an excellent writer; his *Tristes tropiques* is a great book, in my opinion his most important work. Furthermore, Lévi-Strauss is what I might call a "modern encyclopedist," in the sense that he is familiar with a great number of *modern* discoveries, creations, and techniques—for example, cybernetics and communication theory, Marxism, linguistics, abstract art and Bela Bartok, dodecaphonic music and the "new wave" of the French novel, and so on.

Now it is quite probable that some of these achievements have contributed to the popularity of Lévi-Strauss. His interest in so many modern ways of thinking, his Marxian sympathies, his sensitive understanding of Ionesco or Robbe-Grillet—these are not negligible qualities in the eyes of the younger generation of intellectuals. But in my opinion the reasons for Lévi-Strauss' popularity are primarily to be found in his anti-existentialism and his neopositivism, in his indifference to history and his exaltation of material "things"—of matter. For him, "la science est déjà faite dans les choses": science is already effected in things, in material objects. Logic is already prefigured in nature. That is to say, man can be understood without taking *consciousness* into consideration. *La Pensée Sauvage* presents to us a thinking without thinkers and a logic without logicians.[15] This is both a neopositivism and a neonominalism, but at the same time it is something more. It is a reabsorption of man into nature—not, evidently, dionysiac or romantic nature or even the blind, passionate, erotic drive of Freud, but the nature which is grasped by nuclear physics and cybernetics, a nature reduced to its fundamental structures, which are the same both in the cosmic substance and in the human mind. Now, as I have already said, I cannot discuss Lévi-Strauss' theories here. But I would

[15] For a critical appraisal of the neopositivism of Lévi-Strauss, see Georges Gusdorf, "Situation de Maurice Leenhardt ou l'ethnologie française de Lévy-Bruhl à Lévi-Strauss," *Le Monde Non Chrétien*, LXXI–LXXII (July–December, 1964), 139–92. See also Paul Ricoeur, "Symbolique et Temporalité," *Ermeneutica e Tradizione*, ed. Enrico Castelli (Rome, 1963), pp. 5–31; Gaston Fessard, S.J., "Symbole, Surnaturel, Dialogue," *Demitizzione e Morale*, ed. Enrico Castelli (Padua, 1965), pp. 105–54.

like to remind the reader of one of the most distinctive characteristics of the French "new-wave" novelists, particularly Robbe-Grillet: the importance of "things," of material objects — ultimately, the primacy of space and of nature — and the indifference to history and to historical time. Both in Lévi-Strauss, for whom "la science est déjà faite dans les choses," and in Robbe-Grillet, we witness a new epiphany of "les choses," the elevation of physical nature to the rank of the one, all-embracing, reality.

Thus all three recent vogues seem to have something in common: their drastic reaction against existentialism, their indifference to history, their exaltation of physical nature. Of course, there is a great distance between the rather naïve scientific enthusiasm of *Planète* and Teilhard's mystical love for matter and life and his confidence in the scientific and technological miracles of the future, and there is an even greater distance between Teilhard's and Lévi-Strauss' conceptions of man. But what we might call their "worlds of image" are somehow similar: in all three instances we are confronted with a kind of *mythology of matter*, whether of an imaginative, exuberant type (*Planète*, Teilhard de Chardin) or a structuralist, algebraic type (Lévi-Strauss).

If my analysis is correct, then the anti-existentialism and the antihistoricism which is patent in these fashions and their exaltation of physical nature are not without interest for the historian of religions. The fact that hundreds of thousands of European intellectuals are enthusiastically reading *Planète* and the works of Teilhard de Chardin has another meaning for the historian of religions than it might have for a sociologist of culture. It would be too simple for us to say that the terror of history is again becoming unbearable and that those European intellectuals who can neither take refuge in nihilism nor find solace in Marxism are looking hopefully toward a new — because approached scientifically — and charismatic cosmos. We certainly cannot reduce the meaning of these vogues to the old and well-known tension between "cosmos and history." The cosmos presented in *Planète* and in the works of Teilhard de Chardin is itself a product of history, for it is the cosmos as understood by science and in the process of being conquered and changed by technology. But what is specific and new is the almost religious interest in the structures and values of this natural world, of this cosmic substance so brilliantly explored by science and transformed by technology. The antihistoricism which we have identified in all three fashions is not a rejection of history as such; it is rather a protest against the pessimism and nihilism of some recent historicists. We even suspect a nostalgia for what might be called a macrohistory, a planetary and later a cosmic history. But whatever may be said about this nostalgia for a more comprehensive understanding of history, one thing remains certain: the enthusiasts for *Planète,* for Teilhard de Chardin, and for Lévi-Strauss do not feel the Sartrian *nausée* when they are confronted with natural objects. They do not feel themselves to be *de trop* in this world; in brief, they do not experience their own situation in the cosmos as an existentialist does.

Like all fashions, these new vogues will also fade out and finally disappear. But their real significance will not be invalidated: the popularity of *Planète,* of Teilhard de Chardin, and of Claude Lévi-Strauss reveals to us something of the unconscious or semiconscious desires and nostalgias of contemporary Western man. If we taken into consideration the fact that somehow similar intentions can be deciphered in modern art, the significance of these recent vogues for the historian of religions becomes even more startling. Indeed, one cannot fail to recognize in the works of a great number of contemporary artists a consuming interest in matter as such. I will not speak of Brancusi, because his love for matter is well known. Brancusi's attitude toward stone is comparable to the solicitude, fear, and veneration of a neolithic man when faced with certain stones that constitute hierophanies for him—that is to say, they also reveal a sacred and ultimate reality. But in the history of modern art, from cubism to *tachisme,* we have been witnessing a continuing effort on the part of the artist to free himself from the "surface" of things and to penetrate into matter in order to lay bare its ultimate structures. I have already discussed elsewhere the religious significance of the contemporary artist's effort to abolish form and volume, to descend as it were into the interior of substance while disclosing its secret or larval modalities.[16] This fascination for the elementary modes of matter betrays a desire to deliver oneself from the weight of dead forms, a nostalgia to immerse oneself in an auroral world.

If our analysis is correct, there is a decided convergence between the artist's attitude toward matter and the nostalgias of Western man, as they can be deciphered in the three recent vogues which we have discussed. It is a well-known fact that, through their creations, artists often anticipate what is to come — sometimes one or two generations later — in other sectors of social and cultural life.

[16] See "The Sacred and the Modern Artist," *Criterion* (Spring, 1965), pp. 22–24. The article was originally published as "Sur la permanence du sacré dans l'art contemporain," *XX Siècle*, No. 24 (December, 1964), pp. 3–10.

2

Primitive, Classical, and Modern Religions: A Perspective on Understanding the History of Religions

JOSEPH M. KITAGAWA

Is it shame so few should have clim'd from the dens
in the level below,
Men, with a heart and a soul, no slaves of a four-
footed will?
But if twenty million of summers are stored in the
sunlight still,
We are far from the noon of man, there is time for
the races to grow.
Red of the Dawn!
Is it turning a fainter red? so be it, but when shall
we lay
The ghost of the brute that is walking and haunting
us yet, and be free?

TENNYSON

Problem of Understanding

Religion is a complex phenomenon, embodying within it diverse elements and different dimensions of relationship between man and the mysterious universe as well as relations among members of the human community. No one has as yet proposed a satisfactory definition of the term "religion" that is acceptable to everybody concerned, and obviously we cannot solve this matter in this article. However, the following assumptions pertaining to religion are generally accepted by

An abbreviated form of this article was presented orally under the title "Chaos, Order, and Freedom" at Grinnell College, Iowa, in 1965.

students of the discipline of History of Religions (*Religionswissenschaft*).[1]

First, religion presupposes "religious experience," however this term may be interpreted, on the part of *homo religiosus*. Call it the experience of the Holy, the Sacred, or the Power, it is that something which underlies all religious phenomena.[2] According to Joachim Wach, religious experience is (1) a response to what is experienced as Ultimate Reality; (2) a total response of the total being to Ultimate Reality; (3) the most intensive, that is, the most powerful, comprehensive, shattering, and profound experience of which man is capable; and (4) the most powerful source of motivation and action.[3] The notion that religious experience underlies all religious phenomena has a serious methodological implication in the study of religions. In this respect, Mircea Eliade rightly reminds us that "to try to grasp the essence of such a [religious] phenomenon by means of physiology, psychology, sociology, economics, linguistics, art or any other study is false; it misses the one unique and irreducible element in it—the element of the Sacred."[4]

[1] We are aware of the fact that not all the scholars of religions share our assumptions. For example, Wilfred Cantwell Smith is persuaded that the study of religion is the study of persons. He says: "The externals of religion—symbols, institutions, doctrines, practices—can be examined separately; and this is largely what in fact was happening until quite recently, perhaps particularly in European scholarship. But these things are not in themselves religion, which lies rather in the area of what these mean to those that are involved." (See his article, "Comparative Religion: Whither—and Why?" in *The History of Religions: Essays in Methodology*, ed. M. Eliade and J. M. Kitagawa [Chicago: University of Chicago Press, 1959], p. 35.) The same author elaborates this perspective in his *The Meaning and End of Religion* (New York: Macmillan Co., 1963).

[2] See Rudolf Otto, *The Idea of the Holy*, trans. John W. Harvey (London: Oxford University Press, 1923); G. van der Leeuw, *Religion in Essence and Manifestation*, trans. J. E. Turner (London: George Allen & Unwin, 1938); and Mircea Eliade, *The Sacred and the Profane*, trans. Willard R. Trask (New York: Harcourt, Brace & Co., 1959).

[3] See Joachim Wach, *The Comparative Study of Religions*, ed. J. M. Kitagawa (New York: Columbia University Press, 1958), pp. 30–36.

[4] Mircea Eliade, *Patterns in Comparative Religion*, trans. Rosemary Sheed (London and New York: Sheed & Ward, 1958), p. xi.

Second, religion is more than a system of beliefs, doctrines and ethics. It is a total orientation and way of life that aims at enlightenment, deliverance, or salvation. In other words, the central concern of religion is nothing less than soteriology; what religion provides is not information about life and the world but the practical path of transformation of man according to its understanding of what existence ought to be. That is to say, religion views social, political, economic, and all other aspects of life from the soteriological standpoint, and in this sense religion is concerned not only with what is usually regarded as "religious" dimensions but with the totality of life and the world.

Third, religions generally have three dimensions, to use Joachim Wach's schema, namely, (1) theoretical — beliefs and doctrines regarding the ultimate reality, the nature and destiny of man and of the world; (2) practical — rites of worship, sacramental acts, and forms of meditation; and (3) sociological — various types of religious groupings, of leadership, and of relations between specifically religious groups and society.[5]

These assumptions are descriptive statements, and they are not meant to be used as definitions of religion. They might enable us, however, to differentiate religious phenomena from pseudo- or semi-religious phenomena, such as communism and nationalism. On the other hand, with these characteristics of religion in mind, we may include in the category of religion such traditions as Confucianism, which is often regarded as a system of non-religious ethical teaching, and Buddhism, which is considered by some to be essentially a system of philosophy.

Even such a brief sketch of the assumptions which are generally accepted by the students of *Religionswissenschaft* already suggests some of the difficult hermeneutical problems involved in our attempt to understand the nature of religious experience and its expressions. The diversity of opinions proposed on this question of "understanding" reflect the nature

[5] See Wach, *The Comparative Study of Religions*, esp. chaps. iii–v.

of the discipline of *Religionswissenschaft* itself, which must hold within it both "historical" and "structural" approaches and methodologies. To be sure, most scholars agree that "historical" and "structural" approaches are closely interrelated, and they try to combine them in one way or another. However, in actual practice most of them tend to stress, either by temperament or by training and perhaps by both, one of the approaches at the expense of the other. Thus, historically oriented scholars are sensitive to the uniqueness of the particular religious phenomenon or the specific religious tradition. They are inclined to inquire about "what has actually happened" and the actual "becoming" of religions, and to deal with "religious data in their historical connections not only with other religious data but also with those which are not religious,"[6] even though they may resort to structural inquiry in their effort to delineate the meaning of "what has happened." Structurally oriented scholars, on the other hand, are sensitive to the universal characteristics of diverse religious phenomena. They tend to look for similarities, analogies, and homologies, and to deal with religious data typologically and cross-sectionally, disregarding historic contexts and religious traditions in which these data are found, even though they acknowledge the fact that religious data themselves must be provided by historical inquiry.

It goes without saying that the problem of "understanding," which is the central task of *Religionswissenschaft*, requires a hermeneutical principle which would enable us to harmonize the insights and contributions of both historical and structural inquiries, without at the same time doing injustice to the methodological integrity of either approach. This is easier said than done, of course. Indeed, most of the scholars in the discipline accept, reluctantly to be sure, the methodological schizophrenia in this respect. It must be noted, however, that there have been some significant efforts to integrate the historical and structural concerns of *Reli-*

[6] Raffaele Pettazzoni, *Essays on the History of Religions*, trans. H. J. Rose (Leiden: E. J. Brill, 1954), p. 216.

gionswissenschaft. Joachim Wach's concept of the "classical," for instance, is a case in point. According to him,

> There are, to give examples, among the religious leaders of mankind certain figures who stand out as classical founders; of the deities of vegetation known to us from various regions of ancient Western Asia, we can single out some as "classical" representatives; the seemingly infinite number of mystics of all times and places is reduced by choosing "classical" figures. There are classical forms of the institution of priesthood and classical patterns of sacrifice and prayer.[7]

In so stating, Wach, whose primary effort was directed toward structural understanding of religious experience and phenomena, attempted to preserve the historic character of religious data which are incorporated into his systematic, typological schema. Conversely, historically oriented students must also make serious efforts to integrate the insights of the structural inquiries into their perspectives and approaches. With this in mind, the present writer will attempt to depict three major types of religious experience and expressions that in some senses correspond to the historical development of religions of the human race. They are: (1) primitive religions; (2) classical religions; and (3) modern world religions.

Primitive Religions

The emergence of man upon earth is a fascinating problem, which, however, will not be discussed at length since it has no direct bearing upon the development of religion. The discovery of Zinjanthropus places man's origins at a date at least a million and a half years ago. The so-called erect ape man (*Pithecanthropus erectus*) and the Chinese man of Peking (*Sinanthropus pekinensis*) can be dated to the Middle Pleistocene epoch (around four hundred thousand years ago). Then, there was the long age of Neanderthal man (*Homo neanderthalensis*) before the appearance of *Homo*

[7] Joachim Wach, *Types of Religious Experience: Christian and Non-Christian* (Chicago: University of Chicago Press, 1951), p. 51.

sapiens somewhere in the Late Paleolithic period, which is roughly fifty thousand years ago. Although starting with the chance discovery of the cave of Altamira in Spain in 1879, several other prehistoric sites, such as the grotto of La Mouthe, the caves of Les Combarelles and Font de Gaume, the cavern of Niaux, the grotto of Tuc d'Audoubert, and the caves of Trois Frères, Montespan, and Lascaux, have been found and studied by scholars, our knowledge of the religious life of the paleolithic hunter is still very scanty. It is safe to speculate, however, that the development of agriculture—called "the food-producing revolution" by V. Gordon Childe—must have brought about a major change in the religious outlook of prehistoric man. Unfortunately, we cannot go into the discussion of prehistoric religion, except to depict some of the major characteristics of the so-called primitive religions.

The term "primitive religion" is often used to refer both to archaic religion, that is, the religion of precivilized societies, and to the religion of present-day primitive societies, partly because our knowledge of the former depends heavily on speculations based on the study of the latter.[8] Understandably, there are different kinds of religious beliefs and practices included in the broad category of "primitive religion." For example, the religion of food gatherers and hunters, characterized by belief in High-Gods, the Lord of Animals, and totemism, shows a marked difference from the religion of primitive planters, epitomized by the symbolism of the Great Mother. Nevertheless, there are enough structural similarities among them so that we can lump them together with some justification. Unfortunately, the term "primitive religion" connotes different things to different people, depending on their

[8] E. E. Evans-Pritchard, *Social Anthropology* (Glencoe, Ill.: Free Press, 1952), p. 7: "The word 'primitive' in the sense in which it has become established in anthropological literature does not mean that the societies it qualifies are either earlier in time or inferior to other kinds of societies. As far as we know, primitive societies have just as long a history as our own, and while they are less developed than our society in some respects they are often more developed in others. This being so, the word was perhaps an unfortunate choice, but it has now been too widely accepted as a technical term to be avoided."

preconceived notions of primitive man. In fact, one of the mysteries of our time is how our image of primitive man has changed from one extreme to the other. As Evans-Pritchard points out, "first he was little more than an animal who lived in poverty, violence, and fear; then he was a gentle person who lived in plenty, peace, and security. . . . First he was devoid of any religious feelings or belief; then he was entirely dominated by the sacred and immersed in ritual."[9] Likewise, some people tend to think of "primitive religion" as a qualitatively inferior religion of lawless savages, whereas others consider it to be a pristine form of religion practiced by our innocent ancestors just outside the Garden of Eden. Obviously, both views miss the point.

As far as we are concerned, the term "primitive religion" does not imply a qualitative value judgment. Rather, it stands for a special kind of religious experience and apprehension indigenous to the archaic and primitive societies. In this connection, the statement of Robert Redfield is worth quoting. He said that "the primitive and precivilized communities are held together essentially by common understanding as to the ultimate nature and purpose of life," for, in both cases, the society "exists not so much in the exchange of useful functions as in common understandings as to the ends given."[10] And it is our intention to suggest that the ultimate purpose of life was understood by the archaic and primitive men as participation in the act of creation of a "cosmos" out of "chaos" by imitating the celestial model, handed down in various kinds of myth.

The importance of myth and ritual in primitive religion cannot be exaggerated. Myths, it should be noted, are not tales concocted by the undisciplined imagination. "Myth," says Mircea Eliade, "narrates a sacred history; it relates an event that took place in primordial Time. . . . Myth tells us, through the deeds of Supernatural Beings, a reality came into existence. . . . Myth, then, is always an account of a 'crea-

[9] *Ibid.*, p. 65.

[10] Robert Redfield, *The Primitive World and Its Transformations* (Ithaca, N.Y.: Cornell University Press, 1953), p. 12.

tion'; it relates how something was produced, began to *be*."[11] In a similar vein, Charles H. Long states that myth, especially the creation myth, is an expression of man's cosmic orientation. "This orientation involves his apprehension of time and space, his participation in the world of animals and plants, his judgment concerning other men and the phenomena of the sky, the interrelationship of these dimensions, and finally the powers which have established and continue to maintain his being in the world."[12] In other words, the mythic mode, different from the rational and the scientific modes of apprehending reality, enables archaic and primitive men to grasp symbolically and simultaneously "man, society, and nature and past, present, and future" within a unitary system.[13] This accounts for the fact that to them the mythical world and this world interpenetrate to the extent that human activities are explained and sanctioned in terms of what gods, ancestors, or heroes did in primordial time.[14] To put it another way, by imitating the mythical accounts of supernatural beings, archaic and primitive men repeat and participate in the primordial act of creating cosmos out of chaos, which implies establishing and maintaining norms and forms as well as order.[15]

[11] Mircea Eliade, *Myth and Reality*, trans. W. R. Trask (New York: Harper & Row, 1963), pp. 5–6.

[12] Charles H. Long, *Alpha: The Myths of Creation* (New York: George Braziller, 1963), pp. 18–19.

[13] W. E. H. Stanner, "The Dreaming," in *Reader in Comparative Religion: An Anthropological Approach*, ed. William A. Lessa and Evon Z. Vogt (Evanston and White Plains: Row, Peterson & Co., 1958), p. 516.

[14] For examples of myths, see Long, *op. cit.*, and Joseph Campbell, *The Masks of God: Primitive Mythology* (New York: Viking Press, 1959).

[15] Eliade suggests that settlement in a new territory, for example, is equivalent to an act of creation. When the Scandinavian colonists took possession of Iceland and cultivated it, "their enterprise was for them only the repetition of a primordial act: the transformation of chaos into cosmos by the divine act of Creation. By cultivating the desert soil, they in fact repeated the act of the gods, who organized chaos by giving it forms and norms." He also suggests that "in Vedic India the erection of an altar dedicated to Agni, which implied the microcosmic imitation of the Creation, constituted legal taking possession of a territory." Mircea

The primitive mode of religious experience is dramatically expressed in rituals. The close interrelationship between myth and ritual has been suggested by many scholars. For example, according to Robertson Smith, myths are derived from ritual, and in turn "every rite is originally based on a myth."[16] It is also significant to note that, just as in the case of myth, every ritual in the archaic and primitive societies has a divine model. As Eliade states, man repeats the act of the Creation in ritual, "his religious calendar commemorates, in the space of a year, all the cosmogonic phases which took place *ab origine*. In fact, the sacred year ceaselessly repeats the Creation; man is contemporary with the cosmogony and with the anthropogony because ritual projects him into the mythical epoch of the beginning."[17] Thus, marriage rites are recognized as the repetition and continuation of the union of heaven and earth that took place in primordial time. The New Year rites signify on the one hand the return to chaos and the creation of cosmos. In the initiation ceremonies, death signifies a temporary return to chaos; "hence it is the paradigmatic expression of the *end of a mode of being*—the model of ignorance and of the child's irresponsibility. Initiatory death provides the clean slate on which will be written the successive revelations whose end is the formation of a new man."[18]

There are two main characteristics of the rituals or cultus of the archaic and primitive societies. First, rituals are corporate acts of the whole tribe or the community; in a real sense, there is no distinction between performers and spectators. For example, a few years ago, the writer had an opportunity to participate in the Bear Festival of the Ainus in Hokkaido, Japan. We were impressed by the fact that man and

Eliade, *The Myth of the Eternal Return*, trans. W. R. Trask (New York: Pantheon Books, Inc., 1954), pp. 10–11.

[16] Quoted in Joachim Wach, *Sociology of Religion* (Chicago: University of Chicago Press, 1944), p. 26.

[17] Eliade, *The Myth of the Eternal Return*, p. 22.

[18] Mircea Eliade, *Birth and Rebirth: The Religious Meanings of Initiation in Human Culture*, trans. W. R. Trask (New York: Harper & Bros., 1958), p. xiii.

animal, as well as invisible divine beings called *kamui*, played their respective roles in the great ritual. We then wrote:

> The *Iyomante* was a long ritual, and as it slowly moved from one stage to the next, there was a gradual heightening of religious feeling among those who took part. As the ritual approached its climax, one could not help being drawn into a drama, recapitulating a religious experience from the most remote past. The ecstatic expressions of those who participated in the singing, dancing, and praying gave one every reason to believe that for the Ainus, at any rate, the memorable experiences of their ancestors had become real again in the performance of *Iyomante*.[19]

Second, ritual is not isolated from other human activities as the only "religious" act in the archaic and primitive societies. Van der Leeuw reminds us that to primitive man every act is both ritual and work: "Song was prayer; drama was divine performance; dance was cult."[20] In this sense, the attitude of modern man toward life is grossly different from the attitude of the primitive man: "When we dance, we do not pray; when we pray, we do not dance. And when we work, we can neither dance nor pray. . . . The culture of primitive man is at the same time sport, dance, concert, and much more."[21] To be sure, there are apparent differences in human activities—farming, fishing, cooking, and fighting, as well as art, witchcraft, oracles, and magic. But they are interdependent parts of a whole, or interpenetrating circles sharing a mid-point, which is the meaning and purpose of life, namely, participation in the divine act of creating and maintaining cosmos (order).

In this connection, W. E. H. Stanner observes that the mode, ethos, and principle of the Australian aboriginal life are

[19] Joseph M. Kitagawa, "Ainu Bear Festival (*Iyomante*)," *History of Religions*, I, No. 1 (Summer, 1961), 98.

[20] G. van der Leeuw, *Sacred and Profane Beauty: The Holy in Art*, trans. David E. Green (New York: Holt, Rinehart & Winston, 1963), p. 11.

[21] *Ibid.*, p. 34.

"variations on a single theme—continuity, constancy, balance, symmetry, regularity, system, or some such quality as these words convey."[22] In such a situation, what life *is* as well as what life *can be* is determined, so that life is basically a "one-possibility thing," to use his expression.[23] Although the aborigines are endowed with intelligence and rationality, these faculties are directed primarily toward the maintenance of the "given order" of life, as apprehended by myths. In such a situation, if an accepted belief fails to correspond to a particular experience, "this merely shows that the experience was mistaken, or inadequate, or the contradiction is accounted for by secondary elaborations of belief which provide satisfactory explanations of the apparent inconsistency."[24] Essentially, primitive religion provides no real alternatives in life. There is no enlightenment, deliverance, or salvation in the usual sense of the term. The soteriology, if we may introduce such a term to the context of primitive religion, implies the primitive man's initiation into the ancestral orientation of his tribal or communal life that is expressed in the mythical apprehension of cosmos. It follows, then, that the *summum bonum* of primitive religion is continuity and preservation of this type of cosmic orientation, which holds the inner unity of ritual, art, interhuman relationships, and all the rest. Understandably, there is no room for individual freedom in the archaic and primitive societies. However, the primitive people, as a people, have managed to attain an ontological freedom of a sort by defeating and overcoming what Eliade calls the "terror of history."[25]

Classical Religions

Inasmuch as it is impossible to discuss all the historical religions of the world individually, we have adopted the two arbitrary and ambiguous categories of "classical religions" and "modern world religions" in order to portray, at least, certain

[22] Stanner, *op. cit.*, p. 522.
[23] *Ibid.*, p. 517.
[24] Evans-Pritchard, *op. cit.*, p. 99.
[25] Cf. Eliade, *The Myth of the Eternal Return*, pp. 141–62; and Stanner, *op. cit.*, p. 521.

differences in their religious perspectives. Under the category of "classical religions," we include religions of the ancient Near East, Iran, India, the Far East, and the Greco-Roman world, whereas more recent aspects of living religions are discussed under the heading of "modern world religions."

As far as archeological scholarship can ascertain, agriculture and stockbreeding developed as early as the eighth millenium B.C. in the Iranian plateau. This marked the beginning of the so-called food-producing revolution, which stimulated the rise of self-sustaining villages. The transition from the neolithic village pattern to a more advanced phase of the city and state was a long process. Around 3500 B.C., the first great civilization emerged in the Mesopotamian plain. Shortly afterward, other civilizations arose in Egypt, Crete, India, China, Mexico, Peru, and Palestine. All these civilizations were grounded in definite religious outlooks and orientations. Different though these religious traditions were, they shared these characteristics: (1) the emancipation of the *logos* from the *mythos*; (2) the negative attitude toward the phenomenal world and life coupled with recognition of another realm of reality; and (3) a high degree of sophistication and systemization of theoretical, practical, and sociological aspects of religion. In all these religious traditions, the existence of the cosmic order was taken for granted, variously known as *Ma'at*, *Themis*, *Ṛta*, *Tao*, and so on, although their understanding of the nature of the cosmic order varied greatly. Closely related to the question of the cosmic order is man's understanding of his own nature and destiny, which determines to a great extent the differences of various religious traditions, not so much in philosophical speculation as in soteriological outlook.

(1) One of the differences between the classical religions and the primitive religions is found in their attitudes toward myth. Earlier we pointed out that archaic and primitive men know only one mode of thinking, that is, the mythic, which enables them to grasp symbolically and simultaneously "man, society, and nature and past, present, and future" within a

unitary system. In such a unified system, everything in this world is endowed with life, so that every phenomenon appears to be a "Thou," in the sense in which Martin Buber uses this term. "'Thou' is not contemplated with intellectual detachment; it is experienced as life confronts life, involving every faculty of man in a reciprocal relationship. Thoughts, no less than acts and feelings, are subordinated to this experience."[26] In observing certain movements of the planets, for example, the primitive mind "looks, not for the 'how,' but for the 'who,' when it looks for a cause . . . he does not expect to find an impersonal law regulating a process. He looks for a purposeful will committing an act."[27] Thus, in the primitive religions, everything is "Thou," and every event is a concrete act by a certain "Thou." There is no effort to stand outside the world of myth and reduce different experiences to certain universal principles.

The classical religions, on the other hand, recognize the distinction among "man, society, and nature" as well as among "past, present, and future," although their interrelations are explained in terms of myth. In Babylonia and elsewhere in the ancient world, the correct performance of the New Year ritual was considered essential to insure good harvest, but the importance of agricultural skill was also recognized. The great rivers – the Nile, the Tigris, the Euphrates, the Indus, the Yangtze, and others – were no doubt believed to be living beings having their own will and temperament, worthy to receive gifts and sacrifices from the people. And yet, the regularity of their movements was observed in terms of mathematical calculations. Thus the classical religions retained the language of myth, but speculative inquiry into causal principles and universal laws was no longer inhibited and stultified completely by the mythic mode of thinking. In other words, there was a certain degree of emancipation of the *logos* from the *mythos*. For instance, the ancient Near Eastern man

[26] H. and H. A. Frankfort, John Wilson, Thorkild Jacobsen, and William Irwin, *The Intellectual Adventure of Ancient Man* (Chicago: University of Chicago Press, 1946), p. 6.

[27] *Ibid.*, p. 15.

recognized the problem of origin and the problem of *telos,* of the aim and purpose of being. He recognized the invisible order of justice maintained by his customs, mores, institutions; and he connected this invisible order with the visible order, with its succession of days and nights, seasons and years, obviously maintained by the sun. [He] even pondered the hierarchy of the different powers which he recognized in nature.[28]

(2) Probably, the difference between the primitive religions and the classical religions is most conspicuously demonstrated in man's own view of himself. In the former, there is no recognition of man apart from nature. Or, to put it another way, man is a part of society, which in turn is an integral part of nature and the cosmos. In the latter, however, man is recognized as something apart from society and the cosmos. Here again, various religious traditions developed different views of man.[29] Nevertheless, most of the classical religions accepted man as a psycho-physical-mental and spiritual being, a mortal endowed with memory, intelligence, and sexuality. There also developed speculations about the invisible inner self within man's physical being—atman, spiritus, anima, Seele, or pneuma. Undoubtedly the most sophisticated analysis of man was attempted by Greek thinkers,[30] although other religious traditions also provided theories and answers to the riddle of man and his destiny.

Most of the classical religions held a belief in the existence

[28] *Ibid.*, p. 8.

[29] Cf. Joachim Wach, *Typen religiöser Anthropologie: Ein Vergleich der Lehre von Menschen im religionphilosophischen Denken von Orient und Okzident* ("Philosophie und Geschichte," No. 40; Tübingen: J. C. B. Mohr [P. Siebeck], 1932); C. J. Bleeker (ed.), *Anthropologie Religieuse* (Leiden: E. J. Brill, 1955); and S. G. F. Brandon, *Man and His Destiny in the Great Religions* (Toronto: University of Toronto Press, 1962).

[30] Joachim Wach, *Types of Religious Experience: Christian and Non-Christian* (Chicago: University of Chicago Press, 1951), pp. 66–70; see also James Luther Adams, "The Changing Reputation of Human Nature" (reprinted for private circulation in slightly revised form from the *Journal of Liberal Religion* [Autumn, 1942, and Winter, 1943], pp. 7–10).

of some sort of cosmic order that provides ultimate meaning for human existence. However, the regulation of the relationships among the cosmic, social, and human realms was a difficult problem. Human beings, then and now, look for answers to the suffering, failure, and frustration of their existence. For example, according to Jacobsen, man in ancient Mesopotamia

> no longer permitted his world to be essentially arbitrary; he demanded that it have a firm moral basis. Evil and illness, attacks by demons, are no longer considered mere happenings, accidents: the gods, by allowing them to happen, are ultimately responsible, for only when an offense has been committed should the personal god be angered and turn away. Thus in human moral and ethical values man had found a yardstick with which he presumptuously proceeded to measure the gods and their deeds. A conflict was immediately apparent. Divine will and human ethics proved incommensurable.[31]

Caught by the discrepancy between human experience and the idea of a just cosmic order, various religions offered different explanations and solutions. Hinduism and the mystics of all religions are inclined to affirm the essential oneness of the human soul with God or the cosmic spirit, and Buddhism holds that problems of the human condition have no ontological reality. Ancient Greek and Babylonian religions, on the other hand, put the accent on the essential differences between the divine and human natures. Thus, the recognition and acceptance of human mortality was considered as the first order of wisdom. At any rate, these classical religions tended to take negative attitudes toward the phenomenal world and tried to locate the meaning of human existence in another realm of reality, however it was conceived.

In this connection, it is significant to note that some of the classical religions wrestled with the problem of time and history. One should recall that for the primitive religions the only time that was meaningful was the primordial time, so that

[31] Frankfort *et al.*, *op. cit.*, p. 213.

efforts were made to overcome and defeat the onslaught of empirical time and history. In a somewhat similar vein, a few of the classical religions adopted a cyclical view of time and taught men to live in an "eternal present." Some others like the ancient Egyptian and Chinese religions, on the other hand, stressed the normativeness of the golden past. It was the Persian religion of Zoroaster that interpreted the relation between the cosmic order and human experience in terms of a linear view of history. Accepting the cosmic dualism based on Ahura Mazdah and Angra Mainyu, representing Good and Evil respectively, Zoroastrianism viewed history as a battleground in which the divine will, order, and purpose are threatened by Evil. This concept of history had a profound significance for man in the sense that the individual was compelled to make a moral decision to join either the side of Good or that of Evil in a struggle that takes place in the temporal historical process without any thought for himself of "securing a good lot . . . in the *post-mortem* existence."[32] Zoroastrianism exerted a significant influence on Judaism, which stressed its god as the lord of the cosmic order who reveals his will through events in history. To the Jews, unlike the Egyptians and the Chinese, the locus of the meaning of history was to be found in its end (*eschaton*). No less important was the Christian view that amplified the Jewish notion of "history as the epiphany of God."[33]

(3) As to the third characteristic of the classical religions, namely, sophistication and systematization of theoretical, practical, and sociological expressions of their religious experience, we can discuss them only superficially.[34] Here again a brief comparison with primitive religions may be helpful. Earlier, we cited the view of Robert Redfield to the effect that the society of the archaic and primitive peoples—which he terms "folk society"—found its cohesiveness "in common understandings as to the ends given." It is significant to note that

[32] Brandon, *op. cit.*, p. 287.

[33] Cf. Eliade, *The Myth of the Eternal Return*, p. 104.

[34] For Wach's explication of this threefold scheme, see his *The Comparative Study of Religions.*

> the ends are not stated as matters of doctrine, but are implied by the many acts which make up the living that goes on in the society. Therefore, the morale of a folk society—its power to act consistently over periods of time and to meet crises effectively—is not dependent upon discipline exerted by force or upon devotion to some single principle of action, but to the concurrence and consistency of many or all of the actions and conceptions which make up the whole round of life.[35]

In other words, according to the comprehensive world view of the primitive religions, not only is there no distinction between theory and practice, there is only one unified order that governs cosmic law, ritual law, and social law, so that the course of nature, of human life, and of society was seen as one harmonious whole. In the classical religions, however, the distinctiveness of three domains of religion—theoretical, practical, and sociological—was recognized, even though a high degree of correlation among these domains was maintained. In most religious traditions, theoretical development centered around theological, cosmological, and anthropological concerns that are expressed in terms of myth, doctrine, and dogma, although certain religions tended to be more theocentric, others to be more cosmocentric or anthropocentric.[36] In some cases, philosophy and ethics grew out of theology and religious doctrine. It was the Greek thinkers who developed the notion of *theoria*, and as Wach points out, "we find in Aristotle's system a scheme for the organization of knowledge, evidencing the first beginnings of the pursuit of a theory for its own sake ('science')."[37] At any rate, with the develop-

[35] Robert Redfield, "The Folk Society," *American Journal of Sociology*, LII (January, 1947), 299.

[36] Wach, *Sociology of Religion*, p. 23: "The nature of God or gods, the origin and growth of deities (theogony), and their attributes, the relation of the deity to the world and its justification (theodicy)—all are delineated and expounded in theology. Cosmology is concerned with the origin, development, various phases and destiny of the world, while theological anthropology, including soteriology and eschatology, ponders over the origin, nature, and destiny of man."

[37] *Ibid.*, p. 24.

ment of the theoretical aspects of religion, oral traditions tend to be replaced by written traditions and professional or semi-professional interpreters of doctrines come into existence.

Side by side with the theoretical development, we find the gradual articulation of practical or cultic expressions of religion, such as ritual, symbols (images), sacraments, and various forms of sacrifices. In discussing the development of cults, it is well to remember that there is "the same continuous interplay between compulsion and tradition, on the one hand, and the constant drive for individual liberty, making for the emergence of new impulses and the creative activity of *homines religiosi*, on the other, which we observed in the development of thought patterns."[38] Equally important is the gradual stratification of religious groupings, leadership, and interhuman relations, based on the natural criteria of sex and age and/or the religious criteria of charismata, skills, knowledge, healing power, and training. In this connection it is to be noted that in the classical religions the structure of religious groups as well as their relations to sociopolitical order were believed to be based on, and sanctioned by, the cosmic order, whether it was understood to exist above the gods as in Hinduism or under a divine being as in the Judeo-Christian tradition. Moreover, various institutions such as the sacred king in the ancient Near East or the priestly cast in India came into existence ostensibly for the purpose of safeguarding the cosmic order from the destructive power of chaos. Thus, although there was some room for freedom and spontaneity exemplified by prophetic and reform movements, most classical religions were primarily concerned with the preservation of order in the cosmic, human, and sociopolitical realms. Inevitably, man's soteriological yearning was subordinated to an overwhelming concern for the preservation of order, so that salvation was sought either as the acceptance of order or as the rejection of it. The dichotomy between "this worldly ethics" and "otherworldly spirituality" confronted all the classical religions.

[38] *Ibid.*, p. 27.

Modern World Religions

The category of "modern world religions," as stated earlier, refers not to new forms of religion that have emerged in various parts of the world in recent decades but to the modern trends and ethos of historic religions that have been discussed in the previous section.[39] Unfortunately, the long and fascinating historical developments of the various classical religions cannot be discussed here. All we can do at this point is to remind ourselves that none of the historic religions has remained unchanged; each one has undergone numerous stages of transformation resulting from internal and external factors, even though some of the basic characteristics of each religion have been preserved.

Historians of religions today are greatly indebted to the structural inquiry of Gerardus van der Leeuw, who among other things attempted to depict the main characteristics of historic religions in terms of typology. For example, Confucianism and eighteenth-century deism are characterized by him as "Religions of Remoteness and of Flight," Zoroastrianism as "the Religion of Struggle," various forms of mysticism as "The Religion of Repose," certain features of Judaism, Christianity, and Islam as "the Religion of Unrest," a wide assortment of movements from polydemonism to polytheism as "Syncretism," some phases of Greek religion as "the Religion of Strain and of Form," Hinduism as "the Religion of Infinity and of Asceticism," Buddhism as "the Religion of Nothingness and of Compassion," Judaism as "the Religion of Will and of Obedience," Islam as "The Religion of Majesty and of Humility," and Christianity as "the Religion of Love."[40] Van der Leeuw also depicted three approaches of the religions to the world in terms of creative domination, theoretical domination, and obedience, and the three different goals sought by various religions as man, the world, and

[39] For discussion of individual religions, see Joseph M. Kitagawa (ed.), *Modern Trends in World Religions* (La Salle, Ill.: Open Court Publishing Co., 1959).

[40] Van der Leeuw, *Religion in Essence and Manifestation*, pp. 597–649.

God.[41] In all fairness to Van der Leeuw, we must bear in mind that his typological attempt, like similar efforts by other scholars, is not meant to portray historic religions in a monolithic and unidimensional manner. Each religion, at various stages of its historical development, often manifests contradictory features, as ably demonstrated by H. Richard Niebuhr in his discussion of the relation of Christ to culture, for example, Christ against Culture, the Christ of Culture, Christ above Culture, Christ and Culture in Paradox, and Christ the Transformer of Culture.[42]

What is significant from our point of view is that the modern ethos and trends in all major religions share, to a greater or lesser extent, (1) preoccupation with the meaning of human existence, (2) this-worldly soteriology, and (3) the search for "freedom" rather than the preservation of "order." These three features are closely interrelated, of course. Needless to say, we are not advocating these as religious ideals for our time; we are simply depicting them as significant characteristics of "modern world religions."

(1) Historically, the meaning of human existence (religious anthropology) has been one of the three main problems of many classical religions, the other two being the nature of Ultimate Reality or deity (theology) and the origin, structure, and destiny of the universe (cosmology). In various religious traditions, different doctrines have been formulated regarding these three major topics. In this connection we agree with Paul Tillich that all these doctrinal statements were formulated essentially as answers to "questions."[43] And the fact is that the traditional balance of the triple doctrinal formula is no longer meaningful to modern man, because his

[41] *Ibid.*, pp. 543–87.

[42] H. Richard Niebuhr, *Christ and Culture* (New York: Harper & Bros., 1951). See also Christopher Dawson, *Enquiries into Religion and Culture* (New York: Sheed & Ward, 1933); and S. Radhakrishnan, *Religion and Society* (London: George Allen & Unwin, Ltd., 1947).

[43] Thus he proposes for Christian theology the method of correlation that "explains the contents of the Christian faith through existential questions and theological answers in mutual interdependence." Paul Tillich, *Systematic Theology* (Chicago: University of Chicago Press, 1951), I, 60.

existential "question" is primarily concerned with the meaning of human existence and is rather indifferent to the topics of deity and the universe. In other words, the discussion of deity and the universe are meaningful only when they are related to the problem of man. This shift in accent or emphasis has profound implications for the ethos of modern world religions in the sense that various religious traditions can no longer preserve the traditional doctrinal formulations and the symbol systems intact however meaningful they may have been to premodern man. In this respect, the statement of Clement Webb is pertinent; that is, that "the idolatry of today is often the true religion of yesterday, and the true religion of today the idolatry of tomorrow."[44] In today's world, all religions are compelled to wrestle with modern man's question as to how man can realize his highest possibilities in the midst of the brokenness and meaninglessness of our time.

This does not imply, however, that traditional doctrines of man have become completely obsolete in different religious traditions. Modern Hindus still accept the ancient belief that man's inner self is an aspect of Ultimate Reality. Contemporary Buddhists would subscribe, just as most Buddhists of all ages have done, to the notion that man is ever "becoming" and that what appears as a self is therefore impermanent and basically unreal. And both Jews and Christians in our time still hold that man is "equipped with a reverence for the majesty of God who created him and endowed him with a sense of obligation as well as a longing for forgiveness. Man is a sinner not only in the sense of his finiteness but by an act of the will."[45] However, these doctrines are no longer accepted just because they have been sanctioned by religious traditions; they are meaningful to modern man only when these historic beliefs can be tested by experience and restated in a form of language that makes sense. Thus, Daniel Day Williams states the "question" behind the contemporary theological renaissance in the Christian world as follows: "What is

[44] Clement C. J. Webb, *God and Personality* (New York: Macmillan Co., 1918), p. 264.

[45] Wach, *The Comparative Study of Religions*, p. 92.

there in the Christian faith which *gives us such an understanding of ourselves* that we must assert our loyalty to the Holy God above all the splendid and yet corruptible values of our civilization?"[46] Similar observations can be made in regard to the serious effort of contemporary Jews, Muslims, Hindus, and Buddhists to discover the foundations of their faiths. Indeed, in today's world the primary concern of religious man, no less than of his secular counterpart, is man and the meaning of his existence.

(2) The second characteristic feature of modern world religions, namely, a "this-worldly soteriology," is closely related to the first. We might recall that all classical religions tended to take negative attitudes toward phenomenal existence and recognized another realm of reality, however differently it was conceived in various religious systems. Religious iconography in many parts of the world dramatically portrays the stages and grades of the heavenly state as well as of hell, purgatory, or the nether world. They were not invented merely to scare the ignorant masses as some skeptics and cynics think. To many adherents of the classical religions, the existence of other realms beside the phenomenal world order spoke with a compelling force. And man in his finitude was believed to be confined to this world which is permeated by suffering, sinfulness or imperfection. Thus, the religious outlook of the classical religions often had an overtone of "nostalgia for a lost paradise," to use Eliade's expression, or of longing for a heavenly reward in the afterworld. In this life, man was thought to be a sojourner or prisoner. In addition, there was a conviction that all these different realms of existence were either regulated by the cosmic order or dominated by an omnipresent personal deity. Thus, for example, the Hebrew Psalmist said:

> If I ascend to heaven, thou art there!
>   If I make my bed in Sheol, thou art there!
> If I take the wings of the morning
>   and dwell in the uttermost parts of the sea,

[46] Daniel Day Williams, *What Present-Day Theologians Are Thinking* (New York: Harper & Bros., 1952), p. 12 (my italics).

Even there thy hand shall lead me,
and thy right hand shall hold me.[47]

It is important to note that a radical change has taken place in this respect in the thinking of modern people, in that they no longer take seriously the existence of another realm of reality. To be sure, they still use such expressions as paradise, Pure Land, Nirvana, and the Kingdom of God. These terms have only symbolic meaning for the modern mentality. The colorful imagery of Dante, Milton, Bunyan, and their counterparts in the Jewish, Muslim, Hindu, and Buddhist traditions no longer convinces modern man that the present world is only a shadowy reflection of a more real world that exists somewhere else. To the modern man, this phenomenal world is the only real order of existence, and life here and now is the center of the world of meaning. The rejection of pluralistic realms of existence, however, coincided with the widening and broadening of the present world order and cosmos. The single cosmos of the modern man, despite superficial resemblances, has very little in common with the undifferentiated cosmos of the primitive and archaic man, since the modern cosmos is no longer a sacred reality for the experience of contemporary man. Increasingly the mystery of outer space has been diminished, and even the deities have been robbed of their heavenly thrones.

The loss of other realms of existence has compelled modern world religions to find the meaning of human destiny in this world—in culture, society, and human personality. Never has there been any period in the history of the human race when the relation of religion or faith to sociopolitical, economic, and cultural spheres has been taken so seriously as it is today. This does not mean that today we are witnessing another example of the phenomenon of the "ecclesiastification of culture," as in medieval Europe, or of the "secularization of religion," as in the days of rationalism. What we find now is an increasing realization on the part of modern world religions that, just as religious man must undergo the experi-

[47] Psalm 139:8–10 (R.S.V.).

ence of personal transformation or *metanoia*, culture and society must be renewed and revitalized in order to fulfill their vocation in the midst of the ambiguities and upheavals of this world. Thus, even in Theravada Buddhism, which has been regarded by some as one of the most otherworldly of the religions, advocates of a soteriology centered on this world argue that Buddhist leaders must pursue "not a will-o'-the-wisp Nirvana secluded in the cells of their monasteries, but a Nirvana attained here and now by a life of self-forgetful activity . . . [so that] they would live in closer touch with humanity, would better understand and sympathize with human difficulties. . . ."[48] Likewise, leaders of contemporary Judaism, Christianity, Islam, and Hinduism are deeply involved in the building of new nations and in various spheres of social, educational, political, and cultural activities because of their conviction that these areas of life are the very arena of salvation.

(3) As has become apparent, the ethos and trends of modern world religions reflect the questions and existential contradictions of modern man, whose concern may be characterized as an almost pathological search for "freedom" rather than as the preservation of "order." In today's idiom the term "freedom" has two different, but internally related, meanings. On the one hand, it refers to man's effort to be free from something, such as the established order of society, an outmoded standard of morality, or an archaic doctrinal system of religion. On the other hand, freedom refers to the aspirations of man in discovering novelty and creativity in art, philosophy, religion, and interhuman relations. Inevitably, modern man's search for "freedom" has resulted in the rejection of the foundation of the classical religions which believed that all aspects of the human, social, and natural orders were grounded in, and regulated by, the cosmic order. What was taken for granted by the classical religions was the notion of

[48] *The Revolt in the Temple* (Colombo: Sinha Publications, 1953), p. 586. See also Ediriweera R. Sarachandra, "Traditional Values and the Modernization of a Buddhist Society: The Case of Ceylon," *Religion and Progress in Modern Asia*, ed. Robert N. Bellah (New York: Free Press of Glencoe, Inc., 1965), pp. 109–23.

"order" or "law," not simply as a general descriptive formula depicting some specific complex of observable facts, but as a self-evident normative principle that governs all aspects of the universe. Thus, the effort was made by all the classical religions to preserve the "givenness" of the cosmic order as mirrored in the concrete structures of society and interhuman relationships. Such an understanding of cosmic order—its givenness and its normativeness—has been rejected by modern man and to a great extent by the modern world religions as well. In today's world, "order" simply means either a general descriptive formula or something man must establish in order to avoid chaos and disharmony.

The glory of modern man is his faith in his own capacity to transcend the limitations which premodern man had accepted as the "givenness" of finitude. To the premodern man, the dignity of man was found in his finitude, precisely because finitude was the gift of the gods. Thus, the ancient Psalmist could say:

> When I look at thy heavens, the work of thy fingers,
> the moon and the stars which thou hast established;
> What is man that thou art mindful of him,
> and the son of man that thou dost care for him?[49]

But today finitude is regarded as a source of embarrassment for man, who seems to be determined to create freedom, overcoming the limitations of time and space. But the glory of the modern man is at the same time the cause of his tragedy, for he is caught in a new existential situation which he has created. In the words of Eliade:

> He regards himself solely as the subject and agent of history, and he refuses all appeal to transcendence. In other words, he accepts no model for humanity outside the human condition as it can be seen in the various historical situations. Man *makes himself*, and he only makes himself completely in proportion as he desacralizes himself and the world. The sacred is the prime ob-

[49] Psalm 8:3–4 (R.S.V.).

> stacle to his freedom. He will become himself only when he is totally demysticized. He will not be truly free until he has killed the last god.[50]

Fortunately or unfortunately, the contemporary world religions are destined to address themselves to this tragic predicament of modern man, who is caught between his determination to gain freedom from the past with its transcendental sanctions, on the one hand, and his search for novelty, creativity, and freedom, on the other. In this connection it must be noted that bold reinterpretations of traditional doctrines have already been attempted by some theologians and philosophers in the various religious traditions. For example, according to a contemporary Christian philosopher, "the recognition that God requires the freedom of the creatures for his own life is the best way to insure against a false conception of omnipotence as suppressing that freedom. Divine power is an ability to deal with free beings, not an ability to suppress or avoid their existence or to manipulate them so thoroughly that they would not be free." [51] Similarly, a Buddhist existentialist philosopher, echoing the Kierkegaardian formula of "either/or," advocates the formula of "neither/nor" to reinterpret man's freedom for the Absolute Nothingness.[52] But for the most part, modern world religions have a long way to go before they can reinterpret their traditional doctrines in the light of modern man's existential situation.

The fact that the world religions are not adequately prepared to cope with the human situation today does not imply that the historic religions have become irrelevant or are dead. Undoubtedly, the challenge of the contemporary situation has released new energy that had hitherto been submerged in the tradition of the historic religions, as dramatically demon-

[50] Mircea Eliade, *The Sacred and the Profane*, trans. W. R. Trask (New York: Harcourt, Brace & Co., 1959), p. 203.

[51] Charles Hartshorne and W. L. Reese, *Philosophers Speak of God* (Chicago: University of Chicago Press, 1953), p. 234.

[52] Cf. Yoshinori Takeuchi, "Buddhism and Existentialism," *Religion and Culture: Essays in Honor of Paul Tillich*, ed. Walter Leibrecht (New York: Harper & Bros., 1959), pp. 291–318.

strated by the passive resistance movement (*Satyagraha*) of Mahatma Gandi in India, by similar movements on the part of Negroes in America, and by the active roles played by the Buddhists in South Vietnam and Muslims in Indonesia in social and political affairs. This energy is also evident in the dedicated efforts of adherents of other religions to establish a new order of society. However, the greater and a far more difficult task that confronts the modern world religions is that of relating modern man's search for "freedom," which demands an awesome responsibility on the part of man, to the cosmic source of creativity, novelty, and freedom—the Sacred itself.

3

Archaism and Hermeneutics

CHARLES H. LONG

Introduction: From History to Phenomenology

The study of archaic and primitive religious phenomena has always constituted a great part of the work of the historian of religion. E. B. Tylor's *Primitive Culture* was published in 1870, and Max Müller, the first modern historian of religion, published his *Lectures on the Origin and Development of Religion* in 1880. It is not surprising that a great deal of cross-fertilization went on between the young disciplines of comparative religion and anthropology. Both were interested in understanding the origins of human culture and its institutions, and to a great degree, both applied the same evolutionary theory to their data.

Because Tylor and Müller believed that they were dealing with the earliest human form of their data, the oldest forms of language and worship, and because both felt that they possessed a universal norm for culture and language, it was easy for them to arrive at normative statements regarding the meaning of religion. This position resulted in Tylor's minimal definition of religion as a "belief in Spiritual Beings" and Müller's definition of mythology as a "disease of language." In both cases one is able to see that these men arrived at their definitions of the archaic and the primitive because they saw their phenomena under the guise of a law exterior to their data. They thought certain structural and regulative principles were operative in the evolution of nature and mind which could be applied as an interpretive scheme for culture and history.

The door to the history and cultures of non-Western peoples

which they had slowly and timidly cracked burst wide open in the early part of the twentieth century. The disciplines of prehistory, archeology, ethnology, Sinology, Indian studies, Near Eastern studies, and so on, thrived, producing a mass of new data and methods.

As a consequence of this new development the theories of these two famous innovators were discredited. Tylor's definition of religion and Müller's theory of the development of Indian religion were corrected by subsequent research. In both instances they were, in fact, dealing with cultural and religious materials of a comparatively late period. In each case it was the data of history which obscured the answer to the question of origins.

The re-evaluation of these new religious materials from historical and ethnological study was accomplished by a complex relationship between the new methods of historical investigation and the employment of more systematic methods in the study of religion. The new tools of historical investigation, archeology, and the resulting technique of historical-cultural stratification brought to the attention of scholars remnants of cultures much older than any now existing (though still not the earliest) and allowed researchers to sketch out the broad outlines of the relationship between various forms of culture and specific techniques and discoveries. A universal history of mankind now loomed as a possibility. The differences between cultural stages could now be related to the discovery of a new technique or the acquisition of a new artifact from another culture. From this point of view, culture could no longer be encompassed within the dry and neutral definition put forth by Tylor. Tylor had defined culture as "that complex whole which includes knowledge, belief, art, law, morals, custom, and any other capabilities and habits acquired by man as a member of society."[1] Culture from this new perspective was now seen as the expression of man's creativity in history. It was through the medium of culture that man gave expression to those forms of life which defined him as a spiritual being. The difficulty of subsuming cultural

[1] E. B. Tylor, *Primitive Culture* (London: J. Murray, 1871), p. 1.

creativity under the abstract laws of evolution left the problem of the correct norm for cultural life open and flexible.

One of the early forms of the systematization occurs in Chantepie de la Saussaye's phenomenology of religion. He proceeded by placing together similar forms of religious phenomena to see if they revealed a coherent and internal structure. Here in the work of Chantepie we are able to discern one of the problems of the phenomenology of religion — does the same internal structure refer to an analogous structure of the human consciousness?

This early phenomenology sought the meaning of the historical expression within the expression rather than in general abstract laws. The watershed of phenomenological studies in the field is represented by Rudolf Otto's, *The Idea of the Holy.* Otto attacks the problem head on by describing the a priori religious category of the consciousness. Religious expressions and their peculiar modalities are manifestations of a *sui generis* religious consciousness.

Several objections may be raised to the position taken by Otto. First, Otto did not specify clearly the forms of the world through which the religious consciousness manifested itself. He was content to stress the modalities, the qualitative feelings of *mysterium fascinosum* and *mysterium tremendum.* This lack may be due to the fact that the model for his study was religious mysticism.

Second, his theory of the religious a priori operated as one of Kant's regulative ideas. The role of the historical subject undergoing or giving expression to experience in the world is therefore neglected. We therefore seem to be dealing with an explanatory *law* of religious experience and expression — a law not derivative from historical experience. The possibility of another subject's having or understanding such an experience and expression is mentioned only once and then in a polemical manner. Otto warns those who can never remember having had a religious experience but who can remember the last stomach ache to put the book aside for they will never understand it. Third, his phenomenology is an attempt to describe the fundamental nature of religious experience, and he discovers that this nature is non-rational. Although non-rational elements may appear in religious expression and experience, it is saying too much to equate religion with the non-rational. Despite these objections Ottos' work cleared the air and laid bare the problems with which the phenomenologist of religions must deal. It is evident from Otto's discussion of the religious a priori that he was trying to move beyond historicism. The religious consciousness did not come into being as simply an expression of historical experience; thus the expression and manifestation of religion could not be understood by limiting them to the categories of history. Otto's work cut through all the evolutionary theories of religion and provided a structure for all religious experience, a phenomenological structure of the consciousness which manifests itself in the same manner throughout the history of human culture.

But is this conquest of historicism a real victory? Otto's restatement and resolution of the problem on a level beyond historicism leaves us with many of the problems of historicism still unresolved. The meaning of the varying historical manifestations of specific religions remains a problem.

G. van der Leeuw takes up the problem from the side of religious expression and manifestation. His unique handling of a mass of religious data has made his *Religion in Essence and Manifestation* a classic in the History of Religions field. But, in the last analysis, Van der Leeuw refers all of the religious manifestations to one notion—power. He does not seem to have taken too seriously some aspects of his own phenomenological method. He states concerning the phenomenological method,

> Phenomenology, therefore, is not a method that has been reflectively elaborated, but is man's true vital activity, consisting in neither losing himself in things, nor in the ego, neither in hovering above objects like a god, nor in dealing with them like an animal, but in doing what is given to neither god nor animal, standing aside and understanding what appears into view.[2]

[2] G. van der Leeuw, *Religion in Essence and Manifestation* (New York: Harper Torchbook, 1963), II, 676.

Now it is clear from this statement that Van der Leeuw wishes to avoid all of the scholarly "isms" prevalent in the human sciences – historicism, naturalism, idealism, and psychologism. This avoidance is prompted by his desire to approach the human presence from a non-reductionistic perspective. He believes that the phenomenological method can be a valuable asset for historical study because it enables the investigator to deal with the "givenness" of human expression. The avoidance of the "isms" indicates that he refuses to make any one of the disciplines implied by the "isms" into a world view which would immediately categorize the data, but he fails to tell us just how one must deal with the background of interpretation, for in the last analysis these disciplines define to a greater or lesser degree the situation of the interpreter in life.

Van der Leeuw is aware of this issue, but his work does not reveal how he deals with it. He makes remarks concerning "the interpolation of the phenomenon into our lives,"[3] and he defines the phenomenon as "an object related to a subject and a subject related to an object."[4]

This note seems to be lost in the hermeneutic which Van der Leeuw applies in his work. Indeed, he seems to be "hovering above objects like a god." There is a disengagement of the subject from the historical object in his work which causes the phenomenon to lose its existential character. This may be required at a certain stage in any hermeneutic, but a complete hermeneutic cannot avoid the interrelationship of the historical subject and object. We must remember that the phenomenological method from its very beginnings with Husserl attempted to transcend the problem raised by the historical existence of the subject through the eidetic translation which changes the historical subject into a transcendental ego – a moment of consciousness which permits the perception of the essence of the phenomenon.

It may be that Van der Leeuw played down the role of the

[3] *Ibid.*, p. 674.
[4] *Ibid.*, p. 671.

subject, for if the systematic study of religion is ever to become a true science it must, as every other science, show that any cognition recognized by the interpreter as objectively valid must be recognized as being necessarily so for any other possible subject. This kind of objective rigor has allowed historians of religions to present with precision and clarity the structure and morphology of religious data. The problem presented by the interpolation of these data into our lives remains. It remains because phenomenologists of religion have not resolved the issue of phenomenology and history. If phenomenology is in truth "but man's vital activity," then the biases arising from its roots in Descartes and Husserl must be overcome before it can serve as a legitimate hermeneutic.

Husserl understood European (Western) culture as primarily and essentially an exfoliation of Greek forms. All of the modalities of experience are thus reduced too quickly and directly to a rational model. (Otto's designation of religion as a form of the non-rational is a protest against this tendency.) The fact that Husserl did not see the roots of the West in its Jewish-Christian religious heritage may account for his failure to deal adequately with the issue of rationality and historical contingency. It was only late in his life that he came to appreciate the problem of historical contingency.

Raffaele Pettazzoni, however, takes up the issue of phenomenological structure and historical contingency and poses a resolution.[5] Pettazzoni sees religious symbolism arising out of man's existential anxiety in history. The symbolism is thus a representation of man's "existential situation."

> Existential anxiety is the common root in the structure of the Supreme Being, but this structure is historically expressed in different forms: the Lord of animals, the Mother Earth, the Heavenly Father. All these structures have profound relations with different cultural realities

[5] See Raffaele Pettazzoni's "The Supreme Being: Phenomenological Structure and Historical Development," in *The History of Religions: Essays in Methodology*, ed. M. Eliade and Joseph Kitagawa (Chicago: University of Chicago Press, 1954).

> which have conditioned them and of which the various Supreme Beings are expressions.[6]

This statement explains at once too little and too much. While one must agree that particular symbols are discovered and predominate in particular cultural historical periods, is it enough to limit the meaning of the symbolism simply to a reflection of the world view of the period? And while existential anxiety may be a general characteristic of all human life, the modalities through which man expresses this anxiety take on different forms. What more than existential anxiety is expressed in religious symbolism? This question remains because of the wide variety of religious symbolism. Pettazzoni's resolution does not explain the persistence of the same symbolism in different cultural historical periods, neither does it suggest how it is possible to understand religious symbols or other times and places. In short, with Pettazzoni's marriage of phenomenology and history we regress to Dilthey's dilemma of world view.

All of the methods employed to understand the relationship of phenomenology to history have proven to be ineffectual for one primary reason. *All have made a direct relationship between historical expressions and a law or ontology.* This procedure has minimized the specific nature and structure of the historical expressions (all religious symbols are expressions of power—Van der Leeuw; all religious expressions proceed from a religious a priori—Otto; or all religious symbols express existential anxiety—Pettazzoni).

This section began with a discussion of the problem of origins in the history of religions. Origins were first sought in objective history and later with the advent of phenomenology in the human consciousness. I have been critical of the first attempts because they derived the meaning of their data from an exterior norm. I have leveled a criticism at the phenomenological method because it has tended to lead to one-dimensional interpretations of the variety of religious expressions

[6] *Ibid.*, p. 66.

and, in addition, has failed to deal with the interrelationship of the subject and his world.

In the last analysis both procedures are ineffectual, for their clarity has been obscured by history. In the case of Tylor and Müller, the historical shadows have come from the historical data itself, and in the case of the phenomenologists, the immersion of the subject in history as he seeks to understand history dims the clarity of Otto's religious a priori and Van der Leeuw's notion of power. The new historical methods and materials which served in part to disprove Tylor and Müller's theories revealed layers of history extending far back beyond existing cultures, for history at a certain point turns into archeology and cultural anthropology at a certain point turns into physical anthropology. If we couple this knowledge with the one stable meaning from our phenomenological analysis—that there is an enduring structure to religious experience and expression—we must conclude that the search for origins—the archaic in objective history—must now be complemented by a search for the archaism of the subject. The archeology of history and culture should be matched by an archeology of the subject. This archaism is no longer a search for origins in objective history, for, as we have seen, this poses an impossible task. This "new archaism" arises in relationship to the universal structure and intentionality revealed in religious symbols. We now wish to understand the meaning of the archaic as a constitutive element in man's understanding of himself and his world.

The Archeology of the Subject: From Phenomenology to Hermeneutics

There seems to be a rather natural affinity between phenomenology and the History of Religions. It was, we must remember, in the first real phenomenology of religion, Otto's *Idea of the Holy*, that the transfer of the problem of origins from objective history to the subjectivity of consciousness took place. I suspect that there is more than a simple clarification of method present here, for phenomenology, beginning with Husserl's *Cartesian Meditations*, was also concerned with first philosophy. With the obscuring of the problem of objective historical origins by history, it became clear that

> the significance of empirical history which seeks a causal explanation of events is ultimately based upon the "intentional history" which seeks to reveal the a-causal genesis of meaning and the advent of truth constituted by men's existential assumption of pre-objective meaning structures in the contingency of their situation.[7]

Husserl's early attempts to move beyond the empirical to the a-causal and thus to first philosophy involved the removal of the subject from history in the ultimate moment of understanding. This was possible, for the ego was conceived as a pure thinking subject. In his late work, *Phenomenology and the Crisis of European Culture*, he changes his views and admits that all experience begins with our corporeality. Prior to this, "reflection" had always meant a turning inward, not to the psychological activity of consciousness, but to the ideal act of consciousness which possessed an objective structure. In his late work he changes this conception and admits that there is an *Umwelt* or *Lebenswelt*—"a world in consciousness that has not been rendered 'thematic' which is simply taken for granted—it is the familiar world in which men perforce live."[8] Husserl goes on to admit that

> human spirituality is, it is true, based on the human physis, each individually human soul-life is founded on corporeality, and thus too each community on the bodies of the individual human beings who are its members.[9]

Here we see Husserl's admission that each thinking subject has a background and that this background must be taken

[7] Richard McCleary in the Preface to M. Merleau-Ponty's *Signs* (Evanston, Ill.: Northwestern University Press, 1965), p. xxiv.

[8] Quentin Lauer in the "Introduction" to Edmund Husserl's *Phenomenology and the Crisis of Philosophy* (New York: Harper Torchbook, 1965), pp. 67–68.

[9] Husserl, *Phenomenology and the Crisis of Philosophy*, p. 152.

into consideration if one is to develop a rigorous science of the consciousness.

Husserl's pupil, Heidegger, has undertaken an analysis of man's being on this level in his *Being and Time*. Neither Husserl nor Heidegger intended to reduce man to a function of his *Umwelt* or *Lebenswelt* with the introduction of this level of analysis. They intended, rather to demonstrate the modalities of being in relationship to this dimension of the human consciousness. Heidegger subsumes the problem of hermeneutics under his general analysis of Being. Comprehension is no longer a mode of knowledge but a mode of being—the mode of that being who exists in comprehending Being. In Heidegger's analysis historical knowledge is subordinated to ontological comprehension as an aspect of this type of understanding. For example, we have only to note Heidegger's attitude toward the use of ethnology in his discussion of the "Existential Analytic and the Interpretation of Primitive Being."

> But heretofore our information about primitives has been provided by ethnology. And ethnology operates with definite preliminary conceptions and interpretations of human *Dasein* in general, even in first "receiving" its material, and sifting it and working it up. Whether the everyday psychology or even the scientific psychology and sociology which the ethnologist brings with him can provide any scientific assurance that we can have proper access to the phenomena we are studying, and can interpret them and transmit them in the right way, has not been established. . . . Ethnology already presupposes as its clue an inadequate analytic of *Dasein*.[10]

Although this may be true, one should not avoid the disciplines through which the problem of being is stated. It is not, however, clear just how historical knowledge is in fact derivative from this ontological analysis. I prefer to see the

[10] Martin Heidegger, *Being and Time*, trans. John Macquarrie and Edward Robinson (New York: Harper & Bros., 1962), p. 76.

problem stated in the opposite manner. Ontological analysis should arise from historical understanding. This would mean that before one could undertake an elucidation of a historical ontology one would first have to understand the intentionality of both historical method and content. I propose to illustrate this procedure by taking my historical method and materials from the History of Religions.

The discipline of History of Religions seeks to understand, from a description and analysis of all of mankind's religious expression, the nature of religious experience and expression. Though one may begin by following a linear chronology of religious expression from prehistory to the present, this approach is not motivated by a search for origins as an objective history. Our first concern with this mass of data is, to quote Georges Dumezil, "le signe du *logos* et non sous celui du *mana* que se place aujourd'hui la recherche."[11] The *logos* nature of our task represents the attempt to order our materials so that they appear as a true structure of these phenomena—a structure which would appear true for any observer. Such an order may be seen in Mircea Eliade's, *Patterns in Comparative Religion.* Eliade in his explication of the modalities of the sacred implies that every religion can be considered as a variation on the themes he has outlined.

His analysis describes the pre-objective latent meaning structures of religious expression. For example, in speaking of sky symbolism, he is able to say,

> The transcendental quality of "height" or the supra-terrestial, the infinite, is revealed to man *all at once*, to his intellect, as to his soul as a whole. The symbolism is an *immediate notion* of the *whole consciousness*, of the man, that is, who realizes himself as man, who recognizes his place in the universe; *these primeval realizations are bound up so organically with his life that the*

[11] Georges Dumezil in the Preface to M. Eliade's *Traite d'histoire des religions* (2d ed.; Paris: Payot, 1964), p. 5. By *mana*, Dumezil has reference to the problem of the origin of religion which centered around this Polynesian term.

> *same symbolism determines both the activity of his subconscious and the noblest expression of his spiritual life.*[12]

This type of structuring of the primary religious expressions does not arise from the metaphysical desire to construct the world. The intent of this structure is a more modest one. Through this structure a pattern, a "language" of the sacred, is revealed, a language which describes man's immersion in life – in this case life as a confrontation with the sacred. It is through this language that he deciphers the meaning of the sacred in human history. This language or structure of the sacred is the medium through which the historian inserts himself into the historical being of others. The use of every structure, whether biological, aesthetic, or religious, points to the endeavor to find a common form for the self and the "other" which is the object of interpretation. Structure is thus a mode of communication.

Every adequate hermeneutic is at heart an essay in self-understanding. It is the effort to understand the self through the mediation of the other. By self-understanding I do not mean the reduction of the other to the dogmatic categories of contemporaneity. Self-understanding through the mediation of the other involves the principle of reciprocal criticism. It is this reciprocal criticism of self and other which permits the interpolation of the phenomenon into our lives.

Paul Valery once made an apt remark regarding this type of transaction. He said:

> There is no question in poetry of transmitting to one person something intelligible happening with another. It is a question of creating within the former a state . . . [which] communicates the intelligible something to him.[13]

[12] Mircea Eliade, *Patterns in Comparative Religion* (New York and London: Sheed & Ward, 1958), p. 39 (italics mine).

[13] Paul Valéry, *Collected Works of Paul Valéry* (Bollingen series, No. 45; New York: Bollingen Foundation, 1956) VI, 157.

This communication of the "intelligible something" (in our case religious structures) should lead to an opening of ourselves and permit us to order unexplored areas of our lives. Our return to the archaic and traditional religious forms does not express a desire to merely trace causal connections. It is a return to the roots of human perception and reflection undertaken so that we might grasp anew and re-examine the fundamental bases of the human presence.

Such a reorientation lies behind Heidegger's return to the pre-Socratics and Husserl's return to Descartes and the modern artists' return to primitive forms. Freud's exploration of the unconsciousness is a description of the archeology of reason.

This archaism or return to beginnings is predicated on the priority of something already there, something given. This "something" may be the bodily perceptions, as it is for Whitehead and Merleau-Ponty, or a primal vision of aesthetic form, as it is for the artist. In our case this priority and otherness is the history of those primary religious intuitions—religious symbols and their intentionality.

Now the return to the archaic modality does not mean a recapitulation to objective archaic history. We do not wish to live the life of the noble savage. As I have said above, it is a hermeneutical procedure. It presupposes modernity. It was Paul Ricoeur who rightly described our historical period as the moment of forgetting and remembering.[14] According to him, the forgetting of hierophanies of the sacred is a counterpart to the task of nourishing man and satisfying his needs through the technical control of nature. But it is just at such a moment that we have the dim recognition which prompts us to restore the integrity of language. He continues,

> For we moderns are men of philology, of exegesis of phenomenology of religion, of the psychoanalysis of language. The same age develops the possibility of emp-

[14] See Paul Ricoeur's article, "The Hermeneutics of Symbols and Philosophical Reflection," *International Philosophical Quarterly*, II, No. 2, 191–218.

> tying language and the possibility of filling it anew. It is therefore no yearning for a sunken Atlantis that urges us on, but the hope of a recreation of language.[15]

André Malraux reminds us that by a paradox of history it was left to the first agnostic culture that the world has known, "when it resuscitated all other cultures, *to recall to life their sacred works.*"[16]

These statements are examples of a critical phenomenology. They demonstrate the fundamental meaning of the *epoché*, the bracketing of experience in order to understand the givenness of the data to an observer. This *epoché* is not a "leap out of our skins." Through the *epoché* we try to find again through the phenomenon that link which establishes our existence with the world. By taking account of all the conditioning factors of our existence we are able to understand our life as a possibility among others. The *epoché* permits a meditation on our own existence—a meditation possible through the appearance of the "other."

Beginning and Reflection

Authenticity and clarity seem to be the twin norms of contemporary meaning. We are persuaded to accept the death of God, secularism, or some form of existentialism as the price of our modernity. Through one of these orientations we are to achieve a realization of our authentic selfhood. Each one of these orientations defines elements in our contemporary situation and from a positive point of view they express the desire for a new beginning. But as G. Van der Leeuw put it in his provocative essay, "Primordial Time and Final Time,"

> The riddle of time is the riddle of the beginning. We know that there can be no true beginning. Something has always gone before. In the beginning lies the whole past. The beginning is the past.[17]

[15] *Ibid.*, pp. 192 ff.

[16] André Malraux, *The Metamorphosis of the Gods* (New York: Doubleday & Co., 1960), p. 1 (italics mine).

[17] Van der Leeuw, "Primordial Time and Final Time," in *Man and*

We must therefore subject all of these orientations to the same judgment we applied to Tylor and Müller. The clarity of the beginnings is obscured by history, by the layers of humanness which lie behind them. The negative character of the orientations is expressed by the explicit need to cut the self off from the thickness of experience and relations. There is a certain iconoclasm present in the movements which tends to define the self as a lonely ego. A kind of heroic clarity and authenticity is thereby achieved. But in the words of Whitehead, we must seek clarity and then distrust it; or equally, as in the way of Merleau-Ponty, we must always take the phenomenon back into the shadows.

These aphoristic statements are more than slogans. They point to the pretension of the ego which tries to define itself in isolation. All of the cultural forms through which our experience is mediated have a prehistory. Every ontology of the self should begin with a comprehension of some particular aspect and expression of being before arriving at an ontological statement. It is only through the manifestations of being in the fullness of *time* and *space* that we come to know who we are.[18]

Time, Papers from Eranos Yearbooks, No. 3, ed. Joseph Campbell (New York, 1957), p. 325.

[18] There is a strand in modern philosophical and theological analysis which treats this problem. Heidegger's *Being and Time* and Whitehead's *Process and Reality* raise the problem in a formal manner. In Whitehead's *Science and the Modern World* some content is given to the formal categories in his discussion of the English romantic poets. I prefer the work of Merleau-Ponty and Paul Ricoeur, for they seem to be acutely aware of the historical dimension of this problem and for this reason their categories emerge in a different way. Both Ricoeur and Merleau-Ponty proceed from a critique of the Cartesian *cogito*. Ricoeur's philosophical analysis reveals that the Cartesian *cogito* is a vain truth. It is the positing of an ego which cannot be mirrored in objects, works, or acts and therefore cannot be judged by criteria which we apply to the aforementioned forms. It is in reality a void (*une place vide*) which is filled with a false *cogito*. The presumption of the isolated thinking subject always leads to a "bad conscience." (See Paul Ricoeur's, "Existence et Hermeneutique," in *Interpretation der Welt, Festschrift für Romano Guardini* ed. H. Kuhn, H. Kahlefeld, and Karl Forster [Würzburg: Echter-Verlag, 1965], pp. 32–51). Merleau-Ponty sees three possible meanings to the *cogito*: (1) There is the *cogito* as the psychic fact

The historical *cogito* is a *cogito* whose horizon and intentionality may be defined as memory—a mode of perception which anchors our life in prereflective experience. It is this horizon and its intentionality which has been overlooked by those who portray the subject as an ego isolated in contemporaneity.

Richard McCleary in his Introduction to Merleau-Ponty's *Signs* has defined the hermeneutical function of Western culture as follows:

> . . . Western thought and culture have a historically privileged position among men's creations. The West has invented an idea of truth which requires examination of all cultures in an attempt to incorporate them as aspects of a total truth, and a technology capable of one day sustaining a world culture. Consequently, it has the historical task of *re-examining all things* (*in terms of their source in the historical life world*) *in order to face up to the crisis of human culture by revealing its primordial unity and to achieve the new creations of effective cross cultural unity which are the only justification for its privileged position.*[19]

This program of re-examination and new creation cannot be carried out without the development of a historical memory. This historical memory must be commensurate with the

---

that "I think." This is an instantaneous constatation and is possible only under the condition that experience has no duration. I, therefore, adhere immediately to what I think and cannot doubt it. This is the skeptical understanding which cannot account for the idea of truth. (2) In the second way the "I think" of the *cogito* is combined with the objects which this thought intends. Both the "I think" and the things thought have in this context an ideal existence. (3) Finally, there is the third meaning, "the only solid one. . . . I grasp myself, not as a constituting subject which is transparent to itself and which constitutes the totality of every possible object of thought and experience, but as a particular thought, as a thought engaged with *certain* objects, as a *thought in act*; and it is in this sense that I am certain of myself." See Maurice Merleau-Ponty, *The Primacy of Perception* (Evanston, Ill.: Northwestern University Press, 1964), pp. 21–22 (italics mine).

[19] Richard McCleary in the Introduction to M. Merleau-Ponty's *Signs*, p. xxxv (italics mine).

forms of reality as these forms are delineated by modern disciplines. Such a memory must acknowledge its relationship with all historical forms, behaviors, gestures, objects, ideas. The new definitions of man introduced over the last one hundred years add to the designation *homo sapiens* supplementary or alternative descriptions of the human. Compare, for example, the following as descriptions of man: *homo geographicus, homo ludens, homo laborans, homo faber, homo religiosus.*

It was obviously common knowledge prior to the last one hundred years that man lived in a landscape, that he played, made tools, worshipped, and so on. But what was not so obvious was the importance and status of these dimensions of his life as a part of a total definition of his being. These definitions of man refer to his ordinary prereflective life. Man as *homo sapiens* is always rooted in some precise and specialized manner to the roots of knowledge. ". . . La ré flexion est pourtant toujours réflexion d'une réalité pré-réflechie."[20]

Historical memory is aided by a hermeneutic of the archaic in two ways. In the first instance, a hermeneutic of the archaic raises the problem of the constitution of the subject in the process of knowing. If it is the aim of historical knowledge to understand behavior and objects as well as ideas, the interpreting subject must be pushed back to a level of consciousness commensurate with the forms which he wishes to understand. This is the radical empirical level of meaning which is expressed in the forms of history. I understand, for example, Eliade's notion of religious symbolism as an expression of this primary prereflective experience.

The technical character of modern cultural life tends to dim this level of experience. We are able to be authentically and legitimately concerned with experience on this level as it is obscured in the "languages" of modernity—history, ethnology, linguistics, psychoanalysis, and so on. To prevent this level of experience from being subjected too quickly to the dogmatic categories of contemporaneity, we should try

[20] G. Gusdorf, *Traité de Metaphysique* (Paris: A. Colin, 1956), p. 62.

to understand it in culture and history where it is expressed as great cultural symbols. It is here that the History of Religions plays an important part. In the premodern cultures of mankind this symbolism has received a definitive expression.

This is not to say that primitive and archaic man expresses himself only on the symbolic level but that he is only consciously aware of the symbolic level of expression. It is clear from the work of anthropologists, for example, Godfrey Lienhardt, *The Religion of the Dinka* (London, 1960), and Claude Lévi-Strauss, *Structural Anthropology* (New York, 1963), that a logical structure is present in primitive symbolism. That which is obscured in their expression is the rational. On the other hand, that which is obscured in the expression of modern man is the symbolic.[21]

We must now ask how these symbols revealed in the History of Religions are to be interpolated meaningfully into the life of modernity. Paul Ricoeur is probably the only philosopher who has worked consistently with the meaning of religious symbolism as it is understood by historians of religions. Ricoeur accepts Eliade's understanding of religious symbolism: for him the symbol presents to us the possibility of a new hermeneutical meditation. Ricoeur goes beyond Eliade's morphology of religious symbols to philosophical reflection. His formula "Le symbole donne à penser" (Symbol invites thought) is the key to his philosophical reflection on symbols.[22] It is Ricoeur's contention that the symbolic level already contains everything. Like the Delphic oracle, it does not speak or dissimulate but signifies. The oracle must, however, be deciphered, and this is the task of rationality. Rationality for Ricoeur does not imply the reduction of the sym-

[21] For a discussion of religious symbolism, see Eric Dardel's analysis of the use of symbolism in the ethnographic works of Maurice Leenhardt, in "The Mythic," *Diogenes*, No. 7 (1954), and Mircea Eliade's "Methodological Remarks on the Study of Religious Symbolism," in *The History of Religions: Essays in Methodology*, pp. 86–107.

[22] Paul Ricoeur, "The Hermeneutics of Symbols and Philosophical Reflection," *International Philosophical Quarterly*, II, No. 2 (1962), 191–218.

bol to rational categories; rather, rationality is the tool which will unlock the enigma of the symbol.

Ricoeur illustrates this procedure when he deciphers the symbolism of evil, showing how Augustine, Kant, Spinoza, and Hegel have all delineated in their philosophies one or more of the elements in the symbolism. It is, however, only by reference to the primary level of symbolism that we are able to recognize the total intentionality of the problem of evil. The symbol is total and inexhaustible. A critique of the various theologies and philosophies of evil is possible when one subjects the more discursive form of thought to the basic intentionality of the symbol. By referring our rational categories back to their roots in the primary symbol, philosophical thought is renewed.

Eliade's procedure is more radical. Like Ricoeur, he too hopes that the philosophical tradition might be renewed through contact with situations and resolutions which have emerged from other cultures. But unlike Ricoeur, he is impatient with the model of Greek philosophical thought as the only possible way to do philosophy. Eliade believes that the religious symbols of mankind present to us a spiritual universe. Although these symbols may invite thought, the thought which they invite must not be restricted to the categories of the West. It may be that the symbols by their very nature invite different and varying types of thought.

Instead of deciphering symbols along the lines of Western philosophical thought, Eliade moves from his morphology of symbols to the level of comparison, criticism, and dialogue. The most extensive example of this process is found in his best-known work, *The Myth of the Eternal Return* (New York, 1954), where he compares and contrasts the differences between the archaic and modern notions of temporality. In his article, "Mythologies of Memory and Forgetting,"[23] he compares the modern notion of history with the older notion of *anamnesis*. He takes up this problem again in his essay, "Religious Symbolism and Modern Man's Anxi-

[23] Mircea Eliade, "Mythologies of Memory and Forgetting," *History of Religions*, II, No. 2 (Winter, 1963), 329–44.

ety."[24] Here he plays with the equation, modern historical consciousness equals the moment of death.

> It is, in many religions, and even in the folklore of European peoples, . . . at the moment of death [that] man remembers all his past life down to the minutest detail. . . . Considered from this point of view, the passion for historiography in modern culture would be a sign portending imminent death.[25]

In non-modern cultures death is not an absolute end or nothingness but an initiation which prepares man for a new life. Eliade hopes that historical study may also be an initiation, a therapy which will prepare our culture for a new beginning. A new beginning is possible if we take seriously that which is revealed to us through historical study. In his case, this is the religious world—man's confrontation with the sacred. I am never clear about the following point, since Eliade has not, as far as I know, made an explicit statement concerning it. It seems clear to me, however, from a reading of his works that he hopes to abolish the dogmatic categories which limit the meaning of man's life to its historicity through the study of history! He hopes to renew the West by seeing it within the context of a universal history as its past and a world culture as its present and future.

From this perspective the hermeneutical nature of our study is an absolute necessity. Through such a hermeneutic new levels of reality otherwise closed to us may be opened.

I have presented without critical comment two examples of the manner by which the religious phenomena may be interpolated into our lives. Both examples presuppose the historical subject as a being possessing an "archaic" structure. Through religious symbolism we might find a new and authentic basis for reflection. Reflection proceeding from religious symbolism has the merit of correlating the interpreter as he seeks to discover his being with a level of his-

[24] Mircea Eliade, *Myths, Dreams, and Mysteries*, trans. P. Mairet (London: Harvill Press, 1960), chap. ix.

[25] *Ibid.*, p. 234.

torical expression commensurate with this intention. The interpreter as he moves from symbolism to rationality will find that he must make another movement, back into the shadows of his ego and history, for he discovers that his being is mirrored in the reality of life and history and simultaneously created by him in the moment of comprehension.

4

History of Religions with a Hermeneutic Oriented toward Christian Theology?

KEES W. BOLLE

Simplicity Is Called For

In the topic to which I have committed myself, "History of Religions with a Hermeneutic Oriented toward Christian Theology?" there are three important concepts staring everyone in the face: History of Religions, Hermeneutics, and Christian Theology. One would not have to be malicious or unduly gloomy to suggest that there are too many unknown factors here to deal with in one session and that it would therefore be presumptuous to indicate their relationship or unrelatedness (or both). We might perhaps agree in the most general terms on what the History of Religions is: it is at least an academic discipline devoted to the study of religion in a responsible way. We might also find some minimum consensus on what Christian theology is: human reflection, as sound and coherent as possible, with its starting point in God's revelation in Jesus Christ. If we were more specific than that, we might invite confusion. Yet the most abundant source of confusion for the present discussion is in the third word: the hermeneutic of the History of Religions. What is at stake is the science of interpreting religious phenomena, that is to say, the very core of the religio-historical pursuit.

There are reasons for a historian of religions of the younger generation to be careful in broaching the issue. On the one hand, serious discussion of it seems to be carefully avoided by the vast majority of students of religion; that fact all by itself should make one think twice. On the other hand, the few who have mentioned it in earnest are the older and wiser ones, in whose company a representative of the younger generation is bound to feel like an ignorant beginner and whose circumspection in the matter must engender an awareness that he is slowly but inevitably getting lost in a labyrinth. It is Professor Eliade who concentrated his attention on hermeneutics *as a problem* in the opening issue of our Chicago journal *History of Religions*.[1] He has returned to the topic in a recent issue with even greater insistence and vehemence.[2] Then, ten years after Joachim Wach's death, it would be impossible not to think of the author of *Religionswissenschaft*[3] and *Das Verstehen*,[4] of him for whom the question of *understanding* religious phenomena prevailed in all discussions.[5]

These are some of the reasons why modesty will be becoming to me in bringing up the subject: the general apathy with respect to general statements about the manner in which we interpret religious facts, and the fear of being considered a dilettante—not just one who is sticking out his neck, but also one who is unaware of doing so. It would have been safer to have chosen for a subject one or two problems in Hinduism or Sumerian religion.

Having gone this far in self-disclosure, I might as well go

[1] M. Eliade, "History of Religions and a New Humanism," *History of Religions*, I, No. 1 (Summer, 1961), 1–8.

[2] M. Eliade, "Crisis and Renewal in History of Religions," *History of Religions*, V, No. 1 (Summer, 1965), 1–17.

[3] J. Wach, *Religionswissenschaft* (Leipzig: Hinrichs, 1924).

[4] J. Wach, *Das Verstehen, Grundzüge einer Geschichte der hermeneutischen Theorie im 19. Jahrhundert* (3 vols.; Tübingen: Mohr, 1926, 1929, 1933).

[5] For further literature on hermeneutical questions in the History of Religions, see especially G. van der Leeuw, *Religion in Essence and Manifestation* (New York: Harper & Bros., 1963), Vol. II, Epilegomena; J. de Vries, *Forschungsgeschichte der Mythologie* (München: Alber, 1961); F. Sierksma, *Freud, Jung en de Religie* (Assen: Van Gorcum, 1951); R. Pettazzoni, *Essays on the History of Religions* (Leiden: Brill, 1954), chap. xix; the contributions by G. Messina, S.J. ("L'indagine religiosa nella sua storia e nei sua metodi") and R. Boccassino ("La religione dei primitivi") in Pietro Tacchi Venturi (ed.), *Storia delle religioni* (Tornio: Unione Tipografico, 1949), Vol. I, esp. pp. 11–32, 47–77.

the whole way and add one more thing. The feeling of modesty turns into embarrassment when I realize the utmost simplicity of the ideas I can unfold about hermeneutical questions. However, I have a haunting suspicion that I am not alone in this realization and that this simplicity is in fact the weightiest reason why most historians of religions stay away from serious hermeneutical problems in public. If I may speak of a *common* embarrassment, we have a point of departure. For of one thing, there can be no doubt: when we speak as historians of religions about religion, no matter how specialistic we are and no matter how scientifically inclined, we do *interpret*. The most specialistic specialist has to identify cultic gestures, words, and things; the alternative would be complete taciturnity, which is ruled out under the present academic rules. Under the present rules it is not just advisable but mandatory to ask questions about the manner in which our identifications are guided and how they find their coherence. No specialist can hide his hermeneutical orientation or difficulties forever. There will always be others in the classroom who discover it from his casual remarks. Or worse, random observations may result in caricatures of his orientation among colleagues, pupils, and fellow students. Even when one does not consciously propagate a hermeneutical system, attitudes and choice of words are powerful interpreters. Since we cannot abstain from hermeneutics, we had better be as clear about it as possible. Unconsciousness or repressed embarrassment about our simplicity does not serve any scientific purpose. If we make mistakes, they will be less harmful if they are made in broad daylight.

If only a fraction of what I have said is true about the fear of revealing one's simplicity accounting for our hermeneutical malaise, it will be best to try no more than to raise a basic question. Hasty answers cannot help us. As in all humanistic studies, we should try to be fully conscious of the central problem of our discipline or, rather, to become fully conscious of it in each generation. Since everyone involved in the study of religion does engage (or dabble) in hermeneutics, even if only on the sly, according to the measure of his development and power, I too can only do this much: raise my question my way. Dealing with the question requires the manner of a meditation rather than a lecture. I do not expect to clear up all difficulties. But in presenting my question to fellow historians of religions, I do hope that you will be able to say of me something similar to what Wallace Stevens once said when he reflected on the inquisitiveness of a little grandson:

> His question is complete because it contains
> His utmost statement . . . .[6]

The burden of my topic is not on any one of the heavy words but on the question mark. No question is asked which will be answered by yes or no. The question mark must remain. To understand it is my assignment. First of all, the question mark is there, as I have indicated, because of an inevitable modesty and because of an embarrassment by which we as historians of religions recognize each other from afar. Where do we get by reflecting on our embarrassment? Let us try to visualize it for a moment.

I discover that some contemporary Indian deities have certain features in common with some deities of the ancient Near East: necklaces of human skulls, certain symbols that seem to have something to do with a calendar system, certain cultic vessels of a curious shape, and so on. With what questions am I faced and which ones do I consider most important? I may ask what historical factual relationship can be demonstrated. I may also ask what unity in human existence could produce such a similarity. I may also catalogue the data in detail and be sceptical about the possibility of indicating any meaning in them at all. I may concern myself with the psychological unity of man. I may even find one more occasion to harp on the theme that God has at no time left himself without witness. The peculiar thing is that each question could be defended as most important. Or should we rather say that the questions do not have enough in com-

[6] Wallace Stevens, "Questions Are Remarks," in *The Collected Poems* (New York: Alfred A. Knopf, 1961), p. 462.

mon to be put side by side and compared in significance? At any rate, *I* select. Or, more precisely and more disturbingly, my attitude with respect to religion in general is of decisive importance for my treatment of the subject in each case. Even if I should like to be silent about this personal element, it is almost impossible to ignore one's temperament when at any point of the exposition a student may say, So what? Thus one is involved in hermeneutics. And is it permissible to leave the matter there to be decided by temperament alone?

By temperament we can arrive at some sort of *philosophia perennis*, sometimes of a sublime form, too often a pale rationalistic reflection, the trouble being that it is *only* form and lacks all specific contests. Some arrive at such a universal compass of religion without even having considered the possibility of some specific sense in their own tradition. Because of its lack of content alone, it can easily embrace all manners and ways, of Islam, of Confucianism, and of the Eleusinian mysteries. Any generous *philosophia* of this sort could take on Christianity as well (including any number of the most recent language-analytical theologies. If I have understood anything of the subject, the last mentioned would be particularly eligible for inclusion, lacking as they are themselves in specific contents, and obsessed as their creators are with formal, logical defense mechanisms directed toward the evil and—thank God—rather uninterested world). From the point of view of the historian of religions, the basic mistake in these temperamental endeavors to arrive at universality is that they all find a support in only one factual observation and that they recognize that too hastily: the observation that no people has ever been non-religious. This fact may be well known, but as a cornerstone for a foolproof, all-embracing hermeneutics it fails. No religion ever occurs in a non-specific way. The word "religion" itself indicates a multitude of things of which we sense a unity, but this unity we can neither express nor demonstrate. Any self-styled universalism dependent on no more than a pure conceptualization bypasses the actual phenomena of religion and even that universality which is given with the specificity of religious symbols. A cosmic tree is not universal because I observe that cosmic trees occur all over the world (and because I can add this kind of evidence to my other evidence and conclude that religion in general is universal) but because any specific example is in some sense *the* cosmic tree. As we may come to see later, it would not be out of place to ask the eager rational universalist where *his* cosmic tree is situated. The temperament which rationalizes prematurely has not become any rarer among us since the eighteenth century, and it is not to ridicule others but to point to a temptation among ourselves that I mentioned it first.

Temperament alone can still help us a great deal to get a foothold in some sort of *crisis*-theology. Such theologies tend to present themselves as full of content and enable us to stand fast with zeal and certainty in the midst of an ocean of religious phenomena. The immensity of the ocean does not disturb that central zeal and certainty. Immensities generally stop being threatening there. Only particular situations count. For purely temperamental reasons we can like the idea of the church's saying its word about this or that moral problem rather than dealing with the whole immensity of human morality. Everything becomes specific in the great light and there is no reason to belittle this, for the endeavor to deal with specifics implies an endeavor to overcome the sterility which goes with the formalism of hasty perennial philosophers. Vis-à-vis religious problems, it takes some courage to speak of specific contents and specific confrontations. In Delhi, in the midst of traditions with cosmic symbolisms, the church speaks of the cosmic Christ. Elsewhere, although not exactly in time, yet as a result of specific problems, the church speaks of the fact that the Jews cannot really be accused of Jesus' death. Temperamentally, we may well sympathize with these and other appraisals of specific religious problems. We may recognize wholeheartedly that we cannot make truly general pronouncements.

Thus I have tried to depict two temperamental attitudes. They are both possible, yet diametrically opposed to each other. With respect to religious facts both are equally curious. Whereas in the former case tribute was paid too hastily and too formally to the observation that no people has ever been non-religious, in the latter case it is as if that observation does not mean anything at all. Along the lines of the crisis temperament, it has become possible to pronounce such words as secularism and secularity as if they were a battle cry, a summons to make us recognize the real state of things. It is nevertheless necessary to hold ourselves back for a moment and admit that "secularity" cannot mean anything, is indeed non-sense, except in contrast with and complementary to "religion." With the crisis temperament there is a soft adage ringing constantly in the background: ultimately, it does not mean anything that no people has ever been non-religious. For with this temperamental attitude as with the former, the religious *phenomena* are no more than a foil. For all their contrast, the two attitudes are strangely similar. Radically critical or perennially philosophical, the two resemble each other, in spite of their quibbles about details.

For the historian of religions, there are in the first place religious materials asking for interpretation. Neither of the two temperaments mentioned nor any other temperament can suffice. The History of Religions, compared with hasty harmonization and a theological determination to deal with specific situations, is quite chaotic. To put it in a more scholarly fashion, the History of Religions, to the extent that it deals with materials that are hard to arrange, is always inductive rather than deductive, empiricistic rather than aprioristic. As in all disciplines of knowledge, ultimate questions interfere with our work, but they should be allowed later in the course of that work. The temperaments discussed are examples of premature interference in our work by metaphysical and theological determinations. In one case the unity of religious structures is posited and thereby the unity of man's image. In the other case the idea of the situation (or this secular moment) is hypostasized.

As historians of religions we do not want to be naive and suggest that we do our work without presuppositions. Yet, the common character of our work and the natural order of it demand that we do our serious reflection on such matters later and abstain at all times from confusing the course of our work with the settling of final problems. In this sense we are like a biologist, for instance, watching the behavior of a turtle long before he gets around to asking the question, What is life? If we ask such crucial questions too soon, we obscure our observations and start babbling. Penetrating questions are essential to an understanding of our presuppositions in the History of Religions as in biology. But as a biologist in his field work is not helped by a metaphysician or a theologian, so we are not helped by either of them in most of our doings. When a theologian introduces a term like "ultimate reality" and habitually uses it in the singular, I am at a loss in the reading of the Tantras and a great many other Indian documents as well, because something that would qualify well as ultimate reality occurs in fact in the plural and in various ways at the same time. This is a problem that might still be open for discussion. Most instances of interfering theologians are much worse. What should be done with one who insists on the necessity of a theological hermeneutic in the History of Religions and yet plays a demonstrably false game with the evidence of Hinduism or Buddhism? The case is so common that one could not think of listing all the instances.

Let us admit that all difficulties of this nature are in the first place matters of temperament. It may be disappointing to do so; it seems almost impossible sometimes not to get excited. But the admission may save us much unnecessary trouble. Scholarly temperaments are human temperaments and can be understood. When Basham casually refers to the *lingam* as a phallic emblem,[7] some of us who know about the world-establishing and liturgical value of that symbol may get very upset. Surely a genetic hint could not illumine much of Saivism? When Laurens Vanderpost in his beautiful writings on the Bushmen sees his own nostalgia for the

[7] A. L. Basham, *The Wonder That Was India* (London: Sidgwick, 1954), p. 308.

first spirit side by side with the myths about "the early race," others will get equally upset. However, does not our excited reaction itself usually depend on temperament?

I may seem to have spent a long time on a very trivial subject. Still I feel certain that this subject of individual, almost whimsical decisions in establishing a vantage point deserves some consideration, much more consideration than it is usually given. Many a theoretical exposition is built on no more than an impulse of an individual and confuses the discussion hopelessly by smuggling in a metaphysic which is not a good metaphysic or a theology which is not a good theology. The problem of what is true is not broached only by the freshman, immaturely and too soon. In a way which is often much harder to detect the same thing is done by the adult scholar who is obliged to say *something* on religious phenomena.

Hermeneutics and Education

But does everything depend just on temperamental impulses and individual whims? Everyone would like to make an exception for his own branch of excitement. I for one am convinced that one focus of hermeneutics is of the greatest importance to all and that, indeed, many of our individual temperamental predilections and reactions, no matter how inadequate by themselves as hermeneutical principles, find their justification in it. Whatever else can be said about the History of Religions, it certainly has its focus in *education*. It is a matter of teaching and learning; it is not so much a matter of more and more knowledge as it is a process of human orientation and reorientation.[8] Of course,

[8] It is in this sense that I like to think of our longings for a "new humanism." Such a humanism, as a new orientation taking into account and recognizing humanistic traditions other than those of our own classical heritage, might well take as its motto the upanishadic enumeration of various duties as they all find their meaning and purpose in their alliance with "study and teaching" (*svādhyāyapravacane*): "The right order of things *and also study and teaching*; a true concern for things as they are *and also study and teaching*; asceticism *and also study and teaching*; self-control *and also study and teaching*; calm *and also study and teaching*; keeping the sacrificial fires *and study and teaching*; bring-

individual predispositions also play a role here. I cannot conceive of a method which would abolish temperament, but there is no necessity for letting it rule supreme. The process of education, even at its average level, has a way of curbing unhealthy individual predilections, such as the mere exhibition of facts (objectification and no more) and a boundless romantic assimilation of speaker and facts (*Einfühlung* and no more).

The crucial question in the educational process is more than an individual affair: What is the image of man? This question cannot be repressed forever in the humanities. It is an inevitable question of education in the History of Religions. Hardly anywhere can it be posed so directly as in our field. It should be admitted that this central question is of a *normative* character. I would like to underline this, because there is much loose talk about the task of the History of Religions as first and foremost descriptive and as separated from Philosophy of Religion for that very reason. There may be a grain of truth in this, and there may have been a time in which this grain required full attention. But it seems to me that in our period of hermeneutical abstinence such a separation should not be talked about too glibly, as if our aloofness from philosophical (and also theological) questions all by itself should make our field acceptable in a modern academic framework. Wach pointed out time and time again that hermeneutical theories worth the name developed only in a few areas of study and were born from the necessity to establish a *norm* for man's life and behavior (in theology, jurisprudence, and also classical philology, with its expectant search for an *ideal* of human existence).[9] An unqualified separation between our field and the systematic disciplines which deal with normative ques-

ing the prescribed (Agnihotra-) sacrifice *and also study and teaching*; welcoming and entertaining guests in the traditional way *and also study and teaching*; doing one's duty toward men *and also study and teaching*; raising a family *and also study and teaching . . .*" (Taittirīya Upaniṣad 1, 9 [my translation and italics]).

[9] See especially J. Wach, "Zur Hermeneutik heiliger Schriften," *Theologische Studien und Kritiken*, CII (1938), 280–90.

tions would result in the death of our hermeneutical concern and in fact bring our discipline to an end. Religious phenomena would become at most "interesting stuff," and it would not make much difference whether we took it or left it. Is it necessary to say that such a development is not hypothetical? In most of our institutions of learning the History of Religions is in fact given the place of an ornament full of "interesting" angles, a decorative addition to an already overloaded program. In a way the statement that the History of Religions is a matter of education is itself normative. It says how it should be; I do not describe a universally recognized phenomenon. This, however, is a problem which relates in the first place to the outsiders and their views: university administrators and publishers may still look on the History of Religions as a field for dishing out cute or interesting facts about outlandish people—with or without the varnish of greater mutual understanding of live specimens. For the History of Religions as a discipline things are different.

Education is the necessary form in which the rules of hermeneutics are tried out, practiced, and established. What is at stake in it is not merely interesting facts but, indeed, the final image of man. One cannot write a history of religion in the same manner in which one writes a history of medieval beer breweries or even a political history of the world. As the final imagination of man is presented in religious phenomena, a concern for man's final image is a methodological requirement. This "final imagination" always presents itself in specific forms. Accordingly, education as functioning in the History of Religions is more than a reflection on man's general need for orientation. I have already indicated that the actual process of education—one could say, the normal classroom situation—curbs excesses in interpretation. This is an almost physical law: there are usually some students who "talk back," to the benefit of the speaker, whether they know it or not. However, a general consideration of our subject matter may bring us a step farther and closer to the heart of our hermeneutical problem. Religious phenomena are our subject, and they set certain limits to the rules of our hermeneutics. Religious phenomena, as we know them, certainly do not follow individual whims. They change in the course of their history, but not arbitrarily. They are assimilated to other phenomena, but not whimsically or at the instigation of an individual effort. The most nobly conceived rationalistic, interpretive universalism falls in the category of individual efforts. The treacherousness of such rationalistic efforts lies in the fact that they take only a fraction of the phenomena into account. A rational interpretive scheme can only be the construct of an individual in a manner in which no religious phenomenon ever is. Of course one cannot object to the fact that individual attempts at understanding are made. How could it be otherwise? But these attempts cannot be used to decide essential questions of interpretation of religious phenomena, as if they could be viewed *from above*. Religious phenomena are never just intellectual propositions or just individual affairs. Hence neither can the manner in which religious phenomena are approached have its center in logical investigation and a resulting synthesis of general laws alone, even if the individual following this method is a master in the fields of logic and anthropology.[10]

The question arises: Is it possible at all to study religious phenomena *without* setting oneself up as a judge over these phenomena in some individual way or other? Even if we are fully aware of the hermeneutical work which we are doing willy-nilly, and even if we are aware of the form of our work as a process of education, and even if we have attained a good measure of self-control and have become critical of our own temperaments—how can we study without judging individually? The question is not as impossible as it

[10] The opening remarks in Claude Lévy-Strauss' wonderful book on mythology, *Le cru et le cuit* (Paris: Plon, 1964), are hard to evaluate positively. He speaks of the purpose of his book as "to demonstrate how empirical categories . . . can nevertheless serve as conceptual tools to disclose abstract notions which are to lead to propositions." He expects that his findings in the myths of certain primitive societies "will be of general importance" and "show the existence of a logic of perceptible qualities" and he even speaks of the "laws" that will become evident (p. 9).

seems to be. After all, many have recognized and tried to answer the essential question of how to deal with religious phenomena without in the end becoming guilty of reductionism, realizing that religious phenomena are always more than intellectual or emotional or psychological or sociological propositions and facts. The serious answers that can be suggested are in a way all disappointing in that they are not presented on the level on which the question is usually raised, and besides, they are very different among themselves. It should be clear that the answers should not be mere individual answers. Furthermore, they should not reduce the phenomena but do justice to their universal character as well as to their changing form. Is any hermeneutical stand conceivable that answers these requirements?

Three types of answers may be indicated, which can be conveniently distinguished in the following way: Catholicizing hermeneutics; Marxism; spiritualism.

There are, in the first place, a good number of scholars in our field who, by birth or choice, adhere to some form of Catholicism. The hermeneutical importance of such adherence for our field should not be underestimated. The wide embrace of which all catholic traditions are capable is twofold: With respect to religious phenomena, a positive evaluation is fostered (no matter how it is worked out in philosophical detail), and with respect to the investigator, an attitude may be fostered which is intent on explaining phenomena not just in terms of *some* coherent system but in terms of a living tradition.

Procedures of interpretation which have been inspired by Marxism with all their shades and varieties posit a *sense* to the historical course of things and hence assign also a place to religious phenomena. The objection may be raised that in this direction one cannot expect much of an evaluation of religious phenomena *qua* religious phenomena. That does not take away from the fact that the methods advocated in this type of hermeneutics are more viable than many an "individual" effort. The latter makes the mistake of positing or implying a rather arbitrary break between the materials studied (the *homo religiosus*) and the student. The former works with one criterion: the same dialectic applies to the formation of "ideologies" in all times, at least in principle.

A third type of answer may be suggested with the word "spiritualism," for lack of a better word. Under this heading I should like to refer to those who cannot be understood in the first place as adherents of an organic tradition or a party and yet point in an unmistakable direction. The catchword is "human creativity" or "cultural creativity." It is realized that no religious symbol can be "translated" adequately into any of our fashionable jargons. The only thing to be done is something creative: carrying the symbol over into a new life, our own. The word "creative" here has its full meaning: it does not mean something arbitrary; it is not the urge of a modern disoriented individual to "express himself." It is rather more artistic than that; it is the establishment of human order out of chaos on the basis of the (re)discovered coherence of a symbolism.

I do not think that I am wrong in assuming that Professor Eliade would like to reserve the title "creative hermeneutics" for this last type mentioned. Yet all three types have features in common. In the first place, all three are able to deal with the entire problem of religious phenomena. In their light we can detect the principal weakness of all merely "temperamental" efforts. This weakness consists in what I should like to call not just an "objectification" but a "quantification of the spirit"; it is the activity by which spiritual matters are not allowed any possibility of a structural unity of their own but are piled up and divided up as if they formed only a sum of measurable parts. All three types of hermeneutical orientation concur in some awareness of a totality of religious phenomena which cannot be manipulated but is made manifest. In the second place, all three go beyond individual explanation in their intent. At the same time, all three interpret phenomena in relation to the wider tradition of the investigator. Further, a clear distinction can be kept between the religious phenomena studied and the tradition (or system or culture) in relation to which the interpretation takes place, for the simple reason that in all three cases this tradition is held in full consciousness. (This is not to say that in actuality no borderline cases are possible; I am thinking rather of "ideal types.") This implies a tremendous advantage in the educational process, for it avoids the *confusion* of the actual study of symbolism and some "ultimate" commitment.

What I consider most important is that the type of interpretation in each of the three cases, each with its own direction, *cannot be forced upon anyone* in the process of education. No hermeneutic ever rises up by its own accord out of the subject material. The more viable, the purer, a hermeneutic is, and the more justice it does to the phenomena, the more obvious this truth is. Or, to put it in other words, a viable hermeneutic—which is an activity rather than a system—excludes quantification of the spirit.

I am not suggesting that the types of viable hermeneutics I have sketched are the only ones. There are many sorts in between, above, and below the ones mentioned. One more, altogether different, type might be named: that of the thorough, skeptical, historical-critical scholar. This type is supremely admirable because of its indefatigability. It goes on in endless researches, sometimes with the greatest subtlety; it goes on in interminable dialectics, without ever committing itself to any form or dialectic in particular. It may be called a tradition, too, nourished above all in Western learning. But it is a tradition of the very few and strong. In its wake the weaker ones tend to find themselves eventually in a particular dialectic, viz., dialectical materialism; or even worse, they end up quantifying and computerizing things to their individual hearts' content.

Quantification is the immediate result of suspending one's own religion or rather of the illusion that one's own tradition can be suspended. Suspending one's own tradition is indeed an impossibility and a hermeneutical hoax. Whatever we mean by *epochē*, we cannot mean this. To advocate such a suspension in order to enable oneself to "get at" another religious tradition is like saying that the best way to get acquainted with an other person is to divest oneself of one's own personal presence.

The excesses of objectification and quantification are ruled out by viable types of hermeneutics. The interpretation of religious phenomena with reference to the living tradition of the investigator is very much to the point. I would like to make a case for this, because I believe that what is *generally* considered as scientifically sound is just conformism to the fads of our day and is often not to the point in our field. The *ethos* of our discipline makes it impossible to comprehend religious materials in terms of something *beyond* religion. This follows from a reflection on the nature of religious phenomena. Symbolism and mythology have an authority beyond which no higher authority can exist. If such an authority is nevertheless posed, the phenomena are not understood for what they are in their total claim. Our reason can analyze and explain parts and sections but not the totality which is essential to religious symbolism and mythology. For instance, I can see why lower-class women function in the ritual of the Tāntrikas: they form a "naturally" given contrast to the educated and "pure" Brahmin. A pair of opposites could not be expressed more emphatically than by these data of an analyzable social order. But I can give no explanation on the same methodological level for the absolute unity reached through the ritual. All I can adduce to support by comprehension is my knowledge of such a unity or a similar unity in my own tradition; or, simply, my awareness that I too am religious.[11]

As an academic discipline all study of history "should preserve its ministering and subservient function within our frame of historical perspectives by contributing to our ex-

[11] It will be noted that in this whole discussion the words "religion," "religious tradition," and simply "tradition" occur side by side. Marxism can be considered "a new Tao," as R. C. Zaehner has done, and put side by side with the "recognized" religions. See R. C. Zaehner (ed.), *The Concise Encyclopaedia of Living Faiths* (London: Hutchinson, 1959), pp. 402–12.

istential orientation."[12] What can be said of general history certainly must be said of the History of Religions. However, we should be clear that contributing to our existential orientation cannot easily be made into an object of academic research. Contributions of this order are more like astonishing and unexpected gifts. We cannot make the interpretations of the multitude of religious phenomena with reference to our own life and tradition into an applicable system. The discovery of the sense of a symbol as *making sense* for ourselves is indeed astonishing. It "rectifies" us and may even humble us or judge us. Such orientations and reorientations could not be an "object" in the common meaning of that word. In view of the hermeneutical task of the History of Religions, there is indeed reason to speak of a subservient function.

The function of recognizing and—if we may use this word—assimilating religious phenomena can be underlined in another, different manner. There is no empirical way to find out about *the* origin of religion and thus establish a pristine, pure form. Every religion that we know about is a *syncretism* in the most literal sense of the word.[13] Apprehension of alien religious elements did not have to wait for considerations of modern Western scholarship. Religions with a great vital power have all absorbed numerous cults, symbols, and myths. Such absorption is not to be understood in the sense of the addition of alien elements to an existing tradition. There has always been an apprehension which was indeed more than a quantification process. The "assimilated" forms continued to live and were often even intensified because of the power of the assimilating tradition. Such a process of understanding can be called "transmythologizing." The word was coined by R. Panikkar to convey the proper means of understanding religious phenomena, that is, not by reducing, but by renewing, their sense of orientation within the process of understanding which itself functions as a

[12] P. J. Bouman, *In de ban der geschiedenis* (Assen: Van Gorcum, 1961), p. 84.

[13] See J. Wach, *Religionswissenschaft*, p. 86.

cross-fertilization of traditions.[14] It should be admitted that a transmythologizing is indeed what is commensurate with the form of the religious phenomena as we know them, viz., their historical form. The term seems excellent to me. It is clearly differentiated from "demythologizing," which suggests an activity without support in historical phenomena; moreover, "demythologizing" suggests the possibility of expressing at a certain moment non-mythologically what was said only mythologically until that moment; when that moment is or was remains enigmatic and is largely a decision of an individual temperament.[15]

Transmythologizing, then, is more than translating; it is more than linguistic know-how; it is more than identifying the Latin *deus* with *god*. The work of hermeneutics is not limited to a thorough understanding of the structure of another religious tradition. It is at the same time a matter of recognizing the shape and the power in our own—its shape being revealed in the sudden light thrown on it by the other tradition; its power manifesting itself in providing vital resources in places where we had not even expected life. What I am describing here is not only a hermeneutical vision of the future. Having its prototype in the life of religious phenomena themselves, it is a human experience that has never been totally absent, even in the darkest pages of evolutionism. E. B. Tylor will live on in scholarly memory not just as an evolutionist but as a man who recognized something basic in all human existence. The fact that it was his own well-to-do bourgeois England, in which the anxiety for the soul's survival seemed the one ultimate concern left, that supported him in his construction of "animism" does not subtract from but rather adds to his glory.

[14] See R. Panikkar, "Unmythologisierung," *Kultmysterium in Hinduismus und Christentum* (Freiburg: Alber, 1964), pp. 176 ff.

[15] The term "transmythologizing" is also better than the more mechanistic term "remythologizing," for the simple reason that symbols and myths change in the course of history without ever returning to their "original" meaning. The term "remythologizing" might perhaps be reserved for the activity of interpreters who *think* that they render the original sense (certain types of depth-psychology and sociology).

To sum up, I have in the first place argued that none of us can be freed from hermeneutical involvement and that individually conceived interpretive schemes tend to fall short of the goal; I have suggested that many theories which are offered with the intention of presenting a philosophically or theologically solid vantage point are in fact no more than whims. Second, I have endeavored to indicate that the actual locus of hermeneutics, education, does not demand a foolproof system but a direction; such a direction can be found in certain viable types of approach, but none of these can be made obligatory.

I am under the impression that all the points made so far are clear or, at least, could be made so through discussion. From now on, it is uphill all the way.

Theology?

Without reservations I want to come back to that problem which goes against the very grain of our "scientific" mentality. Something is true. Is it still the freshman's premature exclamation? Is not, in all seriousness, something to be considered certain by me before I can honestly adhere to my own tradition, that is to say, to that on which my hermeneutics hinges? I do not propose to say that my certainty lies in the circumstances and contingencies which caused me to be educated in a certain tradition. I do not want to say that the last word of hermeneutics is assimilation or, more precisely and more threateningly, assimilation (understanding with respect to my own tradition—which is itself an assimilation) of an assimilation (a religious symbol) of an assimilation of an assimilation *ad infinitum.* The recognition of the existence of structures rather than merely genetically conceived assimilations (or in Wach's spirit, the "genius" of a religion rather than its "syncretism"[16]) is no consolation, for, as we know now, the very interpretation of a structure does not show "what actually happened" but should be a "transmythologization" if it is to be anything at all. The question then is basically, What is the identifiable "stuff" of this

[16] Cf. Wach, *Religionswissenschaft*, pp. 86 ff.

transmythologizing? Every advocate of a viable hermeneutic who knows what he is doing, and who also knows that his hermeneutic is unenforceable, has to make some philosophical decision. Since this philosophical decision is implied in his tradition, the danger of reductionism in the study of religious phenomena continues to raise its head again and again. The danger may seem most conspicuous along Marxist lines of interpretation. If religious structures are to be seen like ideologies resulting from social and economic conditionings, what chances could be left for an interpretation rectifying the tradition of the investigator? The implied philosophical decision seems bound to make a veritable transmythologizing impossible in the end: injustice is done to the phenomena and no new light is shed on the scholar's tradition. Thus on closer investigation the only virtue of the viable hermeneutic is that it fulfils some minimum requirements: it presents more than the scope of an individual and applies the same criteria to the other tradition and one's own. The same thing needs to be said of every viable hermeneutic. It is even true with respect to those traditions which emphasize human cultural creativity. Speaking of human creativity seems to be no more than a confirmation of an empirical fact: man, in all his religious receptivity, always re-creates. The point is that a hermeneutic of this order also implies a philosophical stance: man's cultural creativity is posited as the center of our rediscovery of *homo religiosus.* All viable hermeneutics seem subject to the danger of reducing phenomena and misleading students because of a philosophical vantage point demanded and implied by the investigator's tradition.

The doubts levelled against the viable types of hermeneutics should not be exaggerated, for there is no serious alternative choice. The Christian faith may be called an interesting topic from a technical hermeneutical point of view since it presents a vantage point which is not given with a tradition and thus might seem to solve our fundamental problem. Nevertheless, it would be erroneous to identify a Christian theological perspective as an alternative hermeneutical choice. If a Christian theological orientation can be suggested, it has at least this much in common with the viable hermeneutics mentioned—it does not solve the problems on the level on which they are raised. Moreover, the subject cannot be broached painlessly.

I suppose that every Christian working in the History of Religions must be fascinated at one time or another by the great figure of Giambattista Vico. He was not only one of the first modern men to discover that there was a certain order in human religious history and at the same time to posit a structural unity in man and thus make comparison of religious phenomena in different times and places a viable enterprise—he was also a devout Christian. How did he do justice to the *homo religiosus* and to his own confession? Whatever interpretation of Vico's *oeuvre* is preferred, the answer will have to take into consideration Vico's peculiar use of the concept "Providence." In some contexts of the *Scienza nuova,* it seems to refer to the guidance by God and thus to be in harmony with common Christian tradition. In other contexts, however, it refers to the line of development, the very pattern of human cultural and religious history, which is "natural" to man's structure and capabilities and which can be detected by scholarly investigation. This concrete way of dealing with *homo religiosus* and one's own tradition at the same time seems to be confusing. Yet, it is in principle the same method which is followed by the "Catholicizing," the "Marxist," and even the "spiritualist" attempts. The point is that, in order to deal with man's religious phenomena in a sensible way, something sensible about man's structure must be assumed. This sensible something must be in harmony with one's own tradition. Compared with other viable hermeneutics, Vico's work is still among the best. The ambiguity of his vantage point, "Providence," does not diminish but rather increase its value.

The real problem of transmythologizing, necessary as it is in all viable hermeneutics, comes in with the category of faith. Faith after all cannot be equated with a religious tradition. As is well known, Van der Leeuw raised objections to such an equation; Van der Leeuw did not consider faith a phenomenon.[17] Theologically — that is to say, according to the discipline that should decide what can legitimately be said about faith — "faith" can certainly not be identified with "religion"; theologically, faith (*fides quae*) is a gift which may bring about great things — even move mountains — but it can not be put side by side with a group of religious phenomena and, together with that group, be directed by something else, no matter how sensible that something else is. Theologicaly, it is out of the question to substitute our Christian tradition for faith, no matter how subtly the substitution is proposed: via a consideration of outdated world views, changing ideas in the earliest (prototypical?) Christian churches, the empirical registration of changes in all religious consciousness, or what not. The Christian faith is not a general or generalizable something. It is as specific as the task of theology itself is inalienable and irreplaceable by the History of Religions.

The dangers thus presented are legion. The one danger that must appear most frightening to a Christian historian of religions may be called by the simple name, provincialism. The existence of religious man poses a question. How should the theologian answer this question without becoming provincial? The uniqueness of God's revelation in Jesus Christ, the *sine qua non* of faith, cannot be given up. At the same time, there is the inescapable problem of "the pagan." If the uniqueness of God's revelation is stressed, it is often couched in incomprehensible jargon, which has little in common with the *skandalon* of the cross and yet is also quite strange to its surroundings; it is very much like the provincial dialect of self-identification, if not of smugness. If the existence of the "others" enters into the picture, it is too easily broached in condescending terms which are worse than any of the methods advocated by the worldly but viable and sensible hermeneutics.

What can be done to put this unwieldly "Christian princi-

[17] G. Van der Leeuw, *La religion dans son essence et ses manifestations* (Paris: Payot, 1948), sec. 110.2.

ple" to hermeneutical action? This is indeed the question which has been raised a number of times. Purposefully I render it in this wooden manner. It is this wooden objectifying manner more than anything else which explains the terms which were invented and implied and are still operative. The pecularity of these terms is that they take for granted a difference between "the others" and "ourselves." Some of these terms, which are at the same time categories of thought, are as follows:

"the others"	"we"
paganism, heathens	the true religion
natural religion	revealed religion
substructure	superstructure
nature	spiritual perfection
potentiality	actuality

No matter how different these (and other) contrasts are, they are all contrasts. Actually, when it comes to the problem of *homo religiosus*, the consideration that the vast majority of Christians, with a significant exception in the early church, are in a real sense "heathen" has never received as much attention as these contrasts. Moreover, the best of these contrasting terms are condescending; this is also true of the most subtle pair, potentiality and actuality. The attitude behind this pair is the same as that which must have given rise to an institution like the "Vatican Secretariat for Non-Christian Religions." It may be good for some practical purpose; but just as a religion would not be qualified sufficiently by saying that it is "non Christian," so it is also not qualified by saying that it is *potentially* something.

No hermeneutic can be introduced along the line of such categories since they do not even come up to the level of ordinary human understanding.

The comedy of the concerns laid down in lectures and books on such topics as "Christianity and the other religions" or "Believing and being religious" is usually twofold: The "others" are not understood for what they are (with all their universal claim and intent and validity) and the Christian faith, in the end, is not revealed as what it really is but as an object of a simple, rational scheme which is itself extraneous to the Christian faith. The external assumption of a contrast leads to the confusion of phenomenology (as the endeavor to demonstrate the structure of religious phenomena) and theology; such confusion is the order of the day. One would not suspect Barth of this sort of confusion, because the "triumph of grace" in his theology seems to exclude all reliance on extraneous contrasts and thus all feverishness about the rescue operation of Christianity—in short, all provincialism. His anthropology (*Kirchliche Dogmatik*, III, 2) has as its real center Jesus Christ. Strictly theologically, all anthropological notions from extraneous sources are irrelevant. But it is a good horse that never stumbles. Thus we can also read in Barth's anthropology about the meaning of man's fear of death in the light of God's Word; we are told that the nothingness with which man is confronted "is not any ordinary type of nothing by which we are threatened in death"; and then we are presented with the following elucidation:

> . . . It is not that nothing of which Buddhism and all its sympathizers have always dreamt, viz., a nothing which is harmless, neutral and in the final analysis even enjoyable, but on the contrary that nothing which is quite dangerous and painful, which goes with our nothingness in the sight of God.[18]

Whose interests are served by such an exposition? Only those who have already decided that Buddhism is somehow inferior in some exterior scale of values can get a boost out of it. Is any aspect of God's word in need of being set off in such bold relief against an aspect of Buddhism? It is hard to believe. In fact, such an opinion would go against the grain of Barth's theology. The quoted exposition is indeed a rare exception in it. The point I am trying to make is that the very best modern theologians have a hard time avoiding the inclination toward uncalled-for contrasting. Somewhere a little phenomenological tirade—of a rather textbookish

[18] K. Barth, *Kirchliche Dogmatik* (Zürich: Zollikon, 1948), Vol. III, Pt. 2, p. 739.

nature—about some religious tradition pops up and the threat of provincialism is realized.

It is only with the greatest hesitation that I offer a suggestion. The only justification for doing so at all is the fact that in a real sense *homo religiosus* has been discovered very recently. He is not like a new continent or a new planet that has been discovered and mapped out and whose charts are right there before us, proving that our universe is thus and so. No, he is like every subject in the humanities—someone we will have to live with for a considerable time before any reorientation becomes generally recognized *and evaluated in terms of what we already know for certain.* My suggestion is that the lack of true respect for "the other" is immediately related to the Christian's lack of humility in himself before God. I mean this both in a very concrete, practical way and with respect to the formation of hermeneutical theories.

There is the most illuminating and very encouraging example of Father Wilhelm Schmidt and his school. It is well known that with him the first serious attempt was made to send out missionaries who were trained ethnologists to the culturally least-advanced peoples of the earth. It is also well known that in that school the expectation that pure ideas concerning a "high god" would be found among the most primitive peoples formed a great stimulus. Moreover, it was assumed that the occurrence of a "high god" would have something to teach us about the earliest religion of all mankind. Schmidt has been criticized severely for his method, but that does not concern us here. I should like to point to the astounding number of good ethnological materials that have been collected by a whole group of people who were not just faithful Christians *but who expected to learn something of the utmost theological importance from the peoples they studied.* What is more natural than that this expectation to be educated gained them the confidence of many and that for that reason their work has been so fruitful? It would be picayune at this point to say that the theology that was spelled out in the background of this movement was somewhat too scholastic and mechanical or that a word like *Uroffenbarung* was utterly wrong. It *worked*, and this fact should give every historian of religions substance for thought and should certainly raise a serious problem for theology. It could be that the question of "the others," "paganism," or whatever it is called, has usually been broached on too high a level. Or, more precisely, it could be that especially within the framework of theology we should become aware of the temptation to "solve" the problem prematurely, with the dubious help of extraneous contrasts that serve our vanity rather than the Lord. Let us not forget that in a very concrete manner our problems of hermeneutics are problems of life and death. Many primitive tribes have become extinct or are heading for extinction now because we have found ourselves incapable of understanding them; we cannot imagine a cure for their decreasing self-respect and for the physical decline that goes with it. Their death is linked up with our own spiritual death. Here is a religious problem and a theological problem in one. To transmythologize requires indeed more power than we can command in a hermeneutical system. It is a ghastly symptom that some modern Christian theologians, paying attention to religious man, can consider the subject closed with a few lines on Buddhism and Hinduism, the only concern being to safeguard the Christian faith on an intellectual plane by comparing it to other, superficially conceived religious notions. Indeed, the search for a hermeneutic is a matter of life and death, for ourselves as well as for "the others."

I wish to present the second part of my suggestion, no matter how vulnerable it may be, as follows: What the general historian may be forced to admit by experience with his subject matter — that he must serve man by contributing to the orientation of his own world — should be self-evident for the historian of religions who has any inkling of theology. His occupation, which from a certain perspective may seem an assimilation *ad infinitum*, is a servantship with a sense. It is not just a task that is insuperable but one that is delightful. If any contribution to our orientation takes place — it is a serious affair, and admittedly we expect to contribute something — it takes place as if by chance. I think that it is still responsible to say out loud why this is so. It is because of a servantship that turned out to be different from what was generally expected — a servantship that until this very day is hard to systematize, no matter how hard we have tried to give the foot washing an acceptable liturgical form. There are still encouraging "loose ends," such as the meeting of the Lord with the Syrophoenician or Caananite woman who turned out to be able to cause surprise to the Lord himself. There are also encouraging surprises in the lives of the disciples. There is the one apostle who was taught to set aside his rule of contrasting his own and the other tradition and who entered the house of the centurion Cornelius. What is significant is that the apostle learned his lesson without taking refuge in any "higher" extraneous contrast. He only raises a question: Thus I have learned and now I want to ask you, Why did you send for me? This is, I think, the question the historian of religions might well ask his subject material. Paul's mission to the gentiles begins with the vision of a *man* who beckons him. It is my hope that historians of religions might come to see the people of their subject matter inviting them and even that they might have dreams in which some man beckons them.

Is faith indeed not a phenomenon? Perhaps it really is not, but who cares at this point? The only thing to watch out for is that no theologian gets hold of such a phenomenologically intended statement and uses it to perform a rescue operation on "his own tradition." I do not know exactly what happens to faith when it gets mixed up in this, that, or the other tradition or how many other things it may run into that look like copies or even models of itself. For all I know a religio-historical hermeneutic which sees "cultural creativity" as its final and highest goal may express our common concern most precisely. Yet, neither cultural creativity nor any goal of the viable hermeneutics mentioned is theologically decisive. In spite of all gropings for words, the study of religious man requires a constant remolding and sacrificing of things we were sure of. What we call transformation of religious symbols in their history is a matter of dying and being born again. This is also true for our hermeneutics. What is and remains the issue at stake is the image of man. Whatever one's theological framework is, it seems to me that waiting until one is beckoned can best be identified as comprehensive and painstaking research. There are voices in the History of Religions that advocate an exclusion from our researches not only of primitive religions but also of the great ancient religions because they are of no immediate relevance to the great cause of ecumenicity and of profound worldwide understanding. This is not just shortsighted in general, it is a sin against every sound hermeneutic. Yet I should like to object not so much as a historian of religions and hence someone professionally interested in hermeneutics, even less as a historicist, but as a conservative theologian. Did not Jesus Christ descend to hell principally because he was interested in ancient *homo religiosus* as well as in modern ecumenicists? It may be doubtful theology to speculate on the details of His service down there; but that He did not go down as the risen, triumphant Lord—but just a little earlier—adds one more encouragement for the study of the general History of Religions with a sound and subservient hermeneutic. It is theologically sound to say that if He had not gone down He would not have risen. I know that in speaking of resurrection I touch on something that I really should leave wholly to the theologian; but at the same time, if the final shape of human orientation—along any of the lines of any viable hermeneutic—depended on our work, our situation would be far from delightful.

The demand for a deprovincializing of Christian theology is neither extravagant nor new. No theologian worth his salt has ever made it his task to limit human communication. Deprovincializing has always been a proper theological concern, in the sense of breaking the chains of categories that could no longer be used because they had begun to hinder the theologian in his proper task. This proper task includes proper reflection on the *universal* relevance of God's Word.

It could be that the resistance to extraneous contrasting—to the one sin of quantification which seems so heinous to the faithful among historians of religions—is part of all theologizing. However, there were certainly several Christian thinkers in the past in whose work the contrasting categories do not play a role. I should like to mention three of them: Nicholas of Cusa (1401–64), Soren Kierkegaard (1813–55), and J. G. Hamann (1730–88). It is particularly instructive to think of these three as examples, since they illustrate the *diversity* of character of theologies that are not privincial with respect to our problem. For the great mystic theologian, the idea of universality is crucial. What is important for our context is that within the framework of his thought—no matter how easy it is to see "non-Christian" historical roots—this idea of universality is never apart from the Christian faith. At the same time it is revealing in the structure of his famous trilogy, *De docta ignorantia*, that the name of Jesus Christ functions significantly only in the last volume. In the case of Kierkegaard, it is well known that many of his crucial statements and teachings are put in the mouth of Socrates. An extraneous contrast between the "pagan" and the "Christian" does not come up in the major arguments. The case of Hamann is unique. It could be said that his whole work was devoted to the struggle against fallacious distinctions and premises. Moreover, this struggle took place in the arenas of humanistic and theological concern and usually at the same time. The difficulty (or even obscurity) of his style is due in part to his simultaneous occupation with *humaniora* and *theologoumena*. However, this is not just a matter of stylistic artificiality. Hamann entitled one of his writings *Kreuzzüge des Philologen* ("Crusades of a Philologist") because he was quite conscious of his dual interests as a "lover of literature" (and therefore a philologist) and a "lover of the Logos" (and therefore also a philologist).[19] One could hardly advocate such a style of double understandings to uproot all provincialism. Yet, the

[19] See the remarks by E. Jansen Schoonhoven in his brilliant study *Natuur en genade bij J. G. Hamann* (Nijkerk: Callenbach, 1945), p. 69.

major root of this procedure can and should be understood as related to the parables in the gospel itself. There are ways in which the commonly known fact that "revelation does not put an end to mystery" can be made concrete. The gospel does not yield a bifurcation for provincial purposes but clarifies, without giving an analytical answer to anyone's analytical question. Hamann's *Konxompax,*[20] taking as its point of departure the Eleusinian mysteries, is a discussion of "pagan" mystery and of God's mystery at the same time.

One could object that these three examples are all on the fringes of the "mainstream" of Christian theology. That may be true, but it should be admitted that it is always on the fringes that the most enlightening visions are seen, in Christian theology as well as in any given religious tradition. Furthermore, I should like to make clear that deprovincializing is a perennial concern and that my own predilection for servantship is not a new key to open the door of the world, to show things in their true secularity, or a means to take outdated mythical garments off the "real thing." An emphasis on *diakonia* is no more than a feeble attempt to be freed from unnecessary bonds that are pressing us today. This attempt has many predecessors of greater scope and more consequential design.

In conclusion the significance of the question mark in the title of this paper must be underlined again. It may be a great gain to recognize that no viable hermeneutic in our field can be enforced. This is not a weakness but a strength. It indicates that our discipline is by nature a discipline of orientation and reorientation, of study and teaching. A fitting Christain theology, fruitful to the extent that it is deprovincializing according to its kind, cannot be enforced either. This, too, is not a negative result but a great gain.

[20] This treatise has been included in its entirety and explained in Jansen Schoonhoven's work mentioned in n. 19, pp. 172–204.

5

The Death of God and the Uniqueness of Christianity

THOMAS J. J. ALTIZER

Religion

An ironic dilemma of contemporary theology arises from its increasing insistence that Christianity both transcends and negates religion at the same time that theology refuses to open itself to an understanding of the actual nature or the historical phenomenon of religion. The persistent calls for a "religionless Christianity" can have little meaning so long as religion is conceived merely as a false righteousness or a shallow piety. All too clearly such conceptions of religion are reflections of the lifeless body of a dead Christendom, and although ultimately they may well derive from the historical actualization of Kierkegaard's prophetic judgment that the Christianity of the New Testament no longer exists, the problem of the relation between Christianity and religion remains and has now become both inescapable and overwhelming. Immediately we must recognize that this problem has a historical ground: Christianity is losing its ancient body; no longer can it find life in its traditional form, and to the extent that it speaks its former language, its witness becomes empty and silent. Faith must now find a trans-Christian language—that is, a language substantially if not wholly different from its previous speech—if it is to exist and to live as faith. Not only must it abandon its own language, but it must likewise move beyond all the meaning which Christianity once shared with the universal community of belief.

Despite the fact that the last two hundred years has seen the birth and the flowering of the historical discipline of the

History of Religions, the historian of religions has not been notably successful in meeting the problem of the uniqueness of Christianity. Few Christians doubt the genuine distinctiveness of Christianity, but this distinctiveness has for the most part been formulated in terms adapted from the general culture of Christendom, and that culture is now in process of disintegration or transformation, thereby leading to the bankruptcy of the established conceptions of the unique and particular nature of the Christian faith. Strangely enough, the theologian has had little interest in the relation between Christianity and the non-Christian religions, largely confining himself to extravagant claims bearing little relationship to the non-Christian religious world. If only because Christian theology has for the most part attempted to establish an impassable gulf between Christianity and the non-Christian religions, it would seem that an elucidation of the genuine and full uniqueness of Christianity might unveil its deepest faith; but this is a challenge which continues to go unanswered. Moreover this challenge cannot be met apart from a confrontation of Christianity with the highest expressions of religion. Of course, there are higher forms of religion that seemingly resist all comparison with Christianity—the Olympian religion of ancient Greece and the Confucian tradition of the Far East quickly come to mind—just as the religious forms of Judaism and Islam are so close to that of Christianity that they can scarcely provide the necessary perspective for an assessment of the full distinctiveness of the Christian faith. It is rather in the purer forms of Oriental mysticism that the Christian theologian must seek out the deepest challenge of the non-Christian religious world.

Obviously this study can do no more than make certain general observations about the relationship between Christianity and Oriental mysticism, but they are nonetheless deemed essential to our theological goal. If we can point to a root and fundamental difference between Christianity and the forms of Oriental mysticism, then this difference will have a significant bearing upon the problem of the authentic meaning of the Christian faith and can serve as a basis for a liberation of Christianity from an inessential and now archaic religious form. We must first arrive at some sense of what these various mystical forms have in common, assuming that here we may indeed find a true manifestation of religion. Granted that any effort to capture the common form of such an exceedingly complex phenomenon as Oriental mysticism will eliminate much of its richness and power, this is a price which must be paid for our particular purpose. Inevitably we must view Oriental mysticism from the vantage point of our own historical situation, confessing that it will have meaning to us only from our own point of view, even if such a perspective must necessarily lead to what the Oriental religious mind would judge to be a false conception. Yet by choosing the higher expressions of the Oriental religious vision as the arena in which to confront Christianity with the non-Christian religions, we may safely assume that we are taking up the full challenge of our problem.

Our initial judgment about Oriental mysticism must be that it is a way of radical world-negation. Directing itself against the ordinary contents of consciousness and all those forms of experience and perception resulting from an individual self's encounter with both the interior and the exterior worlds, it is a form of religion that seeks an absolute negation of the immediate and actual reality which is manifest in the world. Oriental mysticism sets itself against the autonomy of that which appears before it, seizing upon the actuality of that which happens to exist or to be at hand as the initial springboard for its own movement of negation. However, this movement of radical negation is inseparable from an interior recovery of a sacred Totality, a primordial Totality embodying in a unified form all those antinomies that have created an alienated and estranged existence. Transcending the mythical and ritual forms of a communal and cultic religion, the higher expressions of mysticism in the Orient culminate in an interior epiphany of the primordial Totality. Whether this Totality is symbolically known as Brahman-Atman, Nirvana, Tao, or Sunyata, it always becomes manifest in a mystical form as the original identity of an unfallen cosmos. Yet the primordial Totality, which is known here as Ultimate Reality, can only appear and be real to the mystic by means of an absolute and total negation of the fallen forms of the world. True, Eastern ways of negation differ substantially from one another; a difference particularly to be noted between the gradual way of the various forms of Indian yoga and the spontaneous and immediate way of Taoism and Zen. So likewise the form of the negation differs insofar as these are distinct and singular mystical ways, leading to widely different apprehensions of the relation between an original Totality and the fallen or apparent forms of the world. Nevertheless, it remains true that the Oriental mystic can only reach his goal of total redemption by means of a radical negation of *all* that reality which is present to an individual and isolated human consciousness.

Now despite those critics who insist that this negative movement of Oriental mysticism sets it wholly apart from the prophetic faith of the Bible or the Judeo-Christian-Islamic tradition, we must recognize that all expressions of religion in some measure share such a negative movement. Religion must necessarily direct itself against a selfhood, a history, or a cosmos that exists immediately and autonomously as its own creation or ground. Thus Hegel believed that religion is identical with dialectical or true philosophical understanding insofar as both must negate the Given: "For religion equally with philosophy refuses to recognize in finitude a veritable being, or something ultimate and absolute, or non-posited, uncreated, and eternal." [1] We might also note that critical definitions of religion in all their variety show that the sacred or the religious life is the opposite of the profane and the secular life.

What is important from our Christian point of view is to realize that the negative movement of Oriental mysticism is a *backward* movement to the primordial Totality. The Oriental mystic, whether Hindu or Buddhist, Far Eastern or

[1] G. W. F. Hegel, *Science of Logic*, trans. W. H. Johnston and L. G. Struthers (New York: Macmillan Co., 1929), I, 168.

Indian, reverses ordinary life and consciousness so as to make possible a return to the paradisiacal Beginning. He seeks a repetition of an original paradise in the present moment, a repetition effecting an absolute reversal of a fallen or profane reality and moving, whether suddenly or gradually, through a total inversion of the concrete processes of time and history. Remembering that Kierkegaard identified recollection as the pagan life view, we might conceive the negative movement of Oriental mysticism as a process of involution. Here the mystic reverses the fallen order of history and the cosmos so as to return to an unfallen Beginning. Whereas the prophetic faith of the Old Testament and the primitive faith of Christianity were directed to a future and final end, and thus are inseparable from a forward-moving and eschatological ground, the multiple forms of Oriental mysticism revolve about a backward movement to the primordial Totality, a process of cosmic and historical involution wherein all things return to their pristine form.

The Westerner would be grievously misled if he were to think that the backward movement of Oriental mysticism is confined to Eastern religion and occupies no role in the religious forms of his own tradition. Very nearly all forms of cultic or priestly religion, including those of Judaism and Christianity, revolve about a concrete renewal or a re-presentation (*anamnesis*) of a sacred time of the past. We should rather think of Oriental mysticism as bringing to its purest and most interior expression a movement of reversal and return that is universally present in religion. Moreover, it is of vital importance to realize that when this negative movement of return achieves its highest expression in Oriental mysticism it is indissolubly linked with an apprehension of the sacred as an original or primordial reality. If only because the Oriental mystic carries this religious way of involution and reversal to its radical and inevitable conclusion, he reaches the final goal of a movement of return: the original and unfallen Totality of the Beginning. Accordingly, the higher Oriental symbols of the sacred give witness to an eternal, an inactive, or a quiescent Totality, and a Totality that only truly appears with the disappearance or inactivity of all motion and process. Just as this very *dis*appearance or *in*activity repeats or resurrects the original Totality, it could also be said that the Oriental mystic must understand that the advent of motion and process is the beginning of the Fall, despite the fact that here neither motion nor process can be judged to be ultimately or finally real. Underlying all forms of Oriental mysticism is a cosmic and interior process of regeneration, a fully mystical process which either annuls or dissolves both spatial location and temporal duration, leading to the epiphany of a precosmic or pretemporal Totality. Hence the Oriental seer invariably speaks of this Totality as a timeless eternity, a nothing, or a void.

Too frequently we Westerners attempt to translate the symbols of Oriental religion into the language of our own Western ontology. Whereas the Western thinker has an almost invariable tendency to place a positive and even absolute evaluation upon existence and being, the Eastern mystical thinker begins with the conviction that actual or existing being must be abolished or reversed to make possible an epiphany of Being. Both the Chinese and the Indian Buddhists paradoxically employ words whose immediate and literal reference is to non-being and to nothingness when they wish to speak of Ultimate Reality. So likewise we cannot understand the Hindu symbols Brahman and Sat if we imagine them to represent a Being existing in continuity with the world of actuality. The language of Oriental mysticism is consistently and fully dialectical: it can speak of the sacred only by inverting the meaning of the profane, and its symbols of the sacred always refer to a total dissolution or reversal of an actual and immediately existent being. Finally, the language of the Oriental mystic is the language of silence. He can speak only by inverting or reversing all common and established meaning. But this practice must culminate in the cessation of speech. Total silence is the only appropriate witness to an absolutely quiescent Totality, just as the mystic who embraces this highest of religious ways must finally abandon all symbols, all language, all discipline, and all meaning. Why should the Oriental mystic concern himself with language when finally he knows that the truest communication takes place by way of silence? Such silence is beyond all possibility of realization wherever there is the presence of action, movement, or process. Thus here lies the necessity for mystical ways to abolish all actual or wilful movement, whether by way of the *wu wei* or inaction of Taoism and Zen, or the yogic discipline of emptying the contents of consciousness, or even the purposeless action of the Bhagavad-Gita. All such ways finally carry the mystic to that total quiescence which is an absolute inversion of everything that the Western ontological tradition has known as Being.

It is precisely because the Oriental mystical way revolves about a negation of all that reality which the Western mind knows as Being that it must appear to us as a way of radical world-negation. Yet Oriental mysticism, like all of the highest expressions of religion whether in East or West, follows a dialectical way. It seeks a total negation of the "being" which is manifest in the world as a means of transforming time into eternity or of unveiling the fallen form of the world as the elusive mask of an unfallen Totality. Here, in the higher forms of Oriental religion, what would appear to us to be a simple negation of the world is at bottom an epiphany, a renewal, or a repetition of the Totality of the Beginning. Dialectically, an absolute negation of the profane is identical with a total affirmation of the sacred. Consequently, the symbol of the *coincidentia oppositorum* lies at the center of Oriental mysticism. All too naturally we employ a Latin phrase in speaking of the "coincidence of the opposites." For it is none too clear whether *coincidentia* is a coincidence, a harmony, a unity, or an identity of the opposites. But with this ambiguity the meaning of the opposites themselves is obscured; and we cannot arrive at a theological understanding of Oriental mysticism so long as we remain unclear as to the opposition which it initially posits, and then finally removes, between the sacred and the profane. What is that "being" whose absolute negation issues in an epiphany of a cosmic Totality? What meaning can we give to a seemingly fallen profane reality which the mystic ultimately comes to know as total bliss? How can a world which is judged to be an arena of turbulence and suffering finally become manifest in a wholly sacred form as absolute quiescence?

Certainly the Oriental mystic reaches his goal of absolute quiescence by means of an inversion of human consciousness and a corresponding reversal of the cosmos. However, when the negative movement of religion is wholly a reversal of the profane, which is effected by way of a backward movement or return, the sacred must inevitably appear as an original or primordial Reality. It is the total repetition of this primordial Totality which reveals the sacred identity of the profane. We might even say that a purely mystical repetition annuls the possibility of profane existence, reversing its form and structure so as to make possible its manifestation as the original sacred, thereby definitively and finally abolishing the profane or fallen form of the world. Therefore a *coincidentia oppositorum* in this sense must identify the opposites by abolishing their opposition – an abolition effected by an absolute negation of the profane – and here *coincidentia* must finally mean a non-dialectical "identity." If by one means or another all forms of Oriental mysticism culminate in an identification of *nirvana* and *samsara*, then this is an identity in which the opposition between the sacred and the profane has wholly disappeared. No longer does either the sacred or the profane bear a polar or dialectical meaning, for with the abolition of the profane consciousness all human or worldly meaning has vanished. Now silence reigns triumphant; an absolute quiescence has become all in all; the sacred has returned to its original form and thus has ceased to exist in opposition to the profane. When the Oriental mystic insists that ultimately the "way" of mysticism must be abandoned, he is speaking of a transcendence of religion, a transcendence of the movement of dialectical negation. His goal is the cessation of all movement and process, including the movement of religion, and with the realization of that goal, every individual identity returns to its primordial source.

May we allow this understanding of Oriental mysticism to represent the true meaning of the negative or mystical movement of religion? Granted that it does violence to the complex historical phenomena of the higher religions of the Orient, does it apprehend a meaning of the ground of religion that is relevant to the contemporary Christian goal of the negation of religion? If religion is understood to be a backward movement or return to an original sacred, does this give us a proper basis for assessing the uniqueness of Christianity? Surely it gives us insight into the presence of universal religious forms within the historical body of Christianity: a nostalgia for a lost paradise, a quest for an original innocence, a cultic representation or recollection of a sacred history of the past, a conception of faith as contemporaneity with an ancient or long-distant epiphany of Christ, a belief in a primordial God whose very sacrality annuls or negates the existence of the profane, and a longing for an eschatological end that will be a repetition of the primordial beginning. At all these points and others we find religious forms within Christianity that belie its claim to uniqueness. Assuming that the true center of Christianity nevertheless remains unique, what is the relation of that center to these universal religious forms? Can it fully appear or become truly manifest apart from a negation or transcendence of these forms? The call for a "religionless Christianity" can mean no less than this, nor can it have real meaning apart from a resolution to abandon the whole religious body of Christianity, even if that body should prove to comprehend very nearly everything which Christianity once knew as faith. Above all a reborn and radical Christian faith must renounce every temptation to return to an original or primordial sacred, or to follow a backward path leading to an earlier and presumably purer form of the Word, or to seek a total silence in which both Word and world will have disappeared.

Word and History

Having seen that a pure form of religion knows the sacred as an original, an immobile, and an impassive reality, can we conceive the uniqueness of the Christian Word to lie in the fact that it is a dynamic, a living, and a forward-moving process? It is seldom remarked that theology, in its distinctively Christian form, is a unique creation of Christianity. Christian theology is a thinking response to the Word that is actively present upon the horizon of faith, and thus it is neither a systematization of a mythical vision nor a metaphysical or mystical system. The Christian Word appears in neither a primordial nor an eternal form: for it is an incarnate Word, a Word that is real only to the extent that it becomes one with human flesh. If we are to preserve the uniqueness of the Christian Word, we cannot understand the Incarnation as a final and once-and-for-all event of the past. On the contrary, the Incarnation must be conceived as an active and forward-moving process, a process that even now is making all things new. Unless we are prepared to allow the Christian Word to recede into an impassive and primordial form, we must acknowledge its occurrence in the present, no matter what form that present may assume to the believing consciousness of faith. There are times, and certainly ours is not the least of them, when the darkness of history would seem to impel faith to seek an earlier and even primordial form of the Word. Then theology is tempted to conceive the Word in an abstract, an inhuman, and a nonhistorical form. Yet we must confess this to be an anti-Christian temptation if we are not to succumb to a regressive and backward movement of the religious form of faith, a form that ever threatens a true witness to the Incarnation.

Christian theologians and historians of religion are united in asserting that the uniqueness of Christianity derives from its proclamation of the Incarnation; thus Archbishop Söderblom has judged that uniqueness to lie in the fact that here revelation has the form of a "man." However, a movement of incarnation, of the transition of spirit into flesh, is not unique to Christianity. Already we have observed an act of repetition in Oriental religion in which flesh is transformed into spirit in such a way that flesh loses its own apparently intrinsic form and spirit ceases to exist in opposition to flesh. What is distinctive to Christianity is a witness to an incarnation in which spirit becomes flesh in such a manner as to continue to exist and to act as flesh. Such a movement is both active and real, because here we do not find an unveiling of the illusory form of flesh but rather an actual movement in which Spirit decisively and truly becomes flesh. Christian theology has never thought through the full meaning of the Incarnation if only because it has remained bound to an eternal and primordial form of spirit. When spirit is apprehended in this religious form, it obviously can never be known as becoming fully incarnate, and consequently the Christian doctrine of the Incarnation has thus far only been able to posit a Word that is partially flesh and partially Spirit. Despite the Nicene formula, the Word cannot be fully God and fully man if, on the one hand, it continues to exist in an eternal form and, on the other, it is unable to move into the present and the full reality of history.

Throughout its history Christian theology has been thwarted from reaching its intrinsic goal by its bondage to a transcendent, a sovereign, and an impassive God. Once having absorbed a Greek metaphysical idea of God as an eternal and unmoving Being, and having refused Paul's proclamation of faith as freedom from a moral law and a priestly cultus, Christian theology found its ground in the God who alone is God, the awesome Creator and the distant Lord. No way lay from this transcendent and wholly other God to the Incarnation, the act of the Word's becoming flesh, apart from a transformation of the Incarnate Word into an eternal Logos and a mysterious Lord. Blake's Albion, a symbolic figure representing a cosmic and universal humanity, while dying under the weight of sin and darkness, curses the Christian God—"God in the dreary Void dwells from Eternity, wide separated from the Human Soul"—and then he laments the disappearance of the merciful Lamb of God:

> O Human Imagination, O Divine Body I have Crucified,

> I have turned my back upon thee into the Wastes
> of Moral Law.
> There Babylon is builded in the Waste, founded in
> Human desolation.
>
> . . . .
>
> The footsteps of the Lamb of God were there; but
> now no more,
> No more shall I behold him; he is clos'd in Luvah's
> Sepulcher.[2]

Luvah's sepulcher, most simply interpreted, is the repressive body of the Christian church — as Nietzsche remarked, Christianity is the stone upon the grave of Jesus — for Blake, like many radical Christians before him, believed that the resurrected Lord was an epiphany of the wholly other God who had been left behind by the movement of the Incarnation. Like the Krishna who appears to Arjuna in the Bhagavad-Gita, the resurrected Christ of Christianity is a monarchic Lord and cosmic Logos. Despite the efforts of modern theologians to formulate a kenotic Christology, a doctrine of the incarnate Lord resulting from the emptying of the power of God, an understanding of a fully kenotic Christ continues to elude the theologian, who at best has reached Karl Barth's ironic and antikenotic conclusion that God's omnipotence is such that it can assume the form of weakness and in that form can triumph.

The problem which the theologian refuses to confront is the inevitable incompatability between the primordial Christian God and an incarnate or kenotic Christ, a refusal arising from a new epiphany of the primordial Godhead in Christian history. Even as Christianity almost immediately came to worship Christ in the image of the Hellenistic mystery gods, the Christ of Christianity has almost invariably appeared in the form of a high god or heavenly deity, which is found almost everywhere in the history of religions. Certainly the

[2] *Jerusalem*, 24:23–25, 50–51, in *The Poetry and Prose of William Blake*, edited by David V. Erdman (New York: Doubleday & Co., 1965).

Christ who is fully God is not unique to Christianity, except insofar as he bears some sign of a concrete descent of God into human flesh. Such a descent cannot be truly meaningful unless it is understood as a real movement of God Himself, a movement which is final and irrevocable but which continues to occur wherever there is history and life. So long as the Christian God continues to be known as transcendent and impassive, or as a primordial deity who is unaffected by the processes of time and history, He cannot appear in His uniquely Christian form as the Incarnate Word and the kenotic Christ. Thus the radical Christian reverses the orthodox confession, affirming that "God is Jesus" (Blake's Laocoön engraving) rather than "Jesus is God." Before the Incarnation can be understood as a decisive and real event, it must be known as effecting a real change or movement in God Himself: God becomes incarnate in the Word, and He becomes fully incarnate thereby ceasing to exist or to be present in His primordial form. To say that "God is Jesus" is to say that God has become the Incarnate Word; He has abandoned or negated His transcendent form, or rather, He remains present and real in His original form only where faith itself refuses to become incarnate.

A religious form of Christianity resists this forward movement of the Incarnation, regressing to a pre-incarnate form of the Word and by this means dualistically isolating flesh from spirit. Only in radical Christianity do we find a fulfilment of the incarnate movement of the Christian Word, and here alone do we discover a "religionless Christianity." The radical Christian identifies religion with a repressive opposition to the Word of life because in its Christian form it effects a reversal of the Incarnation. Thus Blake prophetically denounces natural religion in his address "To the Christians" in *Jerusalem*:

> I stood among my valleys of the south
> And saw a flame of fire, even as a Wheel
> Of fire surrounding all the heavens: it went
> From west to east, against the current of

> Creation, and devour'd all things in its loud
> Fury & thundering course round heaven & earth.
> By it the Sun was roll'd into an orb,
> By it the Moon faded into a globe
> Travelling thro' the night; for, from its dire
> And restless fury, Man himself shrunk up
> Into a little root a fathom long.
> And I asked a Watcher & a Holy-One
> Its Name; he answered: "It is the Wheel of Religion."
> I wept & said: "Is this the law of Jesus,
> This terrible devouring sword turning every way?"
> He answer'd: "Jesus died because he strove
> Against the current of this Wheel; its Name
> Is Caiaphas, the dark preacher of Death,
> Of sin, of sorrow & of punishment:
> Opposing Nature! It is Natural Religion;
> But Jesus is the bright Preacher of life
> Creating Nature from this fiery Law
> By self-denial & forgiveness of Sin." [3]

We must not imagine that such a condemnation of religion is directed at the non-Christian religious world. It is rather Christianity that has reduced human existence to sin and guilt, confronting a broken humanity with a wholly other God who demands a total submission to His numinous and judgmental power. Religion assumes its most repressive form in the Christian religious tradition, because only here — and in its historical antecedent, the Book of Job — may one find a God of naked and absolutely sovereign power, a God who was evolved out of a reversal of the movement of spirit into flesh, and who now for the first time becomes abstract, alien, lifeless, and alone.

The solitary God of the Christian religious tradition certainly embodies a measure of uniqueness: no other religious tradition has so isolated deity and humanity, and all too naturally He finally appears under the forms of Blake's Satan,

[3] *Jerusalem*, 77:1–23.

Hegel's abstract Spirit, and Melville's Moby Dick. Nevertheless, even this most awesome of the forms of God illuminates the unique process of the Christian Word, for it is an evolving Word, a forward-moving Word, a Word that only exists and is real in the concrete life of history. Christianity is an historical faith, not simply because it is grounded in a sacred history of the past, but more deeply because it celebrates the human reality of history as an epiphany of the Word. An incarnate Word embodying a real transfiguration of spirit into flesh cannot be sought in a heavenly beyond, nor can it be reached by a backward movement to primordial time; it is only in the actual and contingent processes of history that spirit fully becomes flesh. Here, spirit never truly appears in a pure or eternal form, nor does it simply appear as spirit, except insofar as it is known apart from its movement into flesh. Moreover it is only a regressive and religious form of Christianity that would confine the Word to its biblical and past historical expressions. When the Incarnation is known as a dynamic process of forward movement, then it must be conceived as a progressive movement of spirit into flesh, even if it should succeed in evoking a religious reversal of its own movement and process. Each historical expression of the Word will bear its own peculiar and distinct reality, and although no clear path may be seen to lie between one and another, faith must ever seek that particular form of the Word which acts in its own present.

Finally, we must conceive the Christian Word as being directed to the eschatological goal of the absolute reversal of flesh and spirit. Ever since its establishment in the second century, Christian theology has chosen one of two paths: either it has adapted the language of a purely rational and non-dialectical thinking, a thinking that wholly isolates theology and faith, or it has become partially dialectical and has thereby attempted to ground its language in the reality of faith only insofar as it has repudiated an eschatological goal. In either case, theology has refused a thinking that would incorporate the apocalyptic ground of the proclamation of Jesus, just as it has turned aside from any attempt to understand the full meaning of an eschatological end. Consequently, Christian theology has never sought to unveil the meaning of an apocalyptic *coincidentia oppositorum.* It is no accident that radical expressions of Christianity have invariably assumed either a dialectical or an apocalyptic form. Apart from a dual and dialectical movement of flesh and spirit into each other, there can be no actual process of incarnation; here, an original sacred must "descend" and become flesh, just as a fallen flesh must "ascend" and become spirit. Yet this process cannot be real apart from an actual transfiguration of flesh and spirit: flesh must cease to exist as flesh in becoming spirit, even as spirit must wholly perish as spirit in fully becoming flesh. The Incarnation can culminate in a truly apocalyptic or eschatological end only by effecting an absolute negation of the original identities of flesh and spirit. Thereby the given and intrinsic forms of flesh and spirit are totally reversed so as to make possible a final movement of each into its respective other. Inevitably, the radical Christian believes that the end of the world, whose immediate coming was proclaimed by Jesus, is the total transfiguration of the fallen form of the world, the end of a flesh which is isolated from Spirit and so likewise the end of a spirit that is isolated from flesh.

At first glance an apocalyptic *coincidentia oppositorum* would appear to be identical with its mystical counterpart in Oriental religion. Both embody a total dissolution of the "being" of a fallen or profane world, just as each is the fulfilment of a movement of absolute negation, a negation shattering or dissolving an autonomous selfhood, a repressive history, and an exterior cosmos. But does an apocalyptic *coincidentia oppositorum* abolish the opposition between the sacred and the profane by annihilating the reality of flesh or old aeon? True, the religious forms of Christianity have celebrated a Kingdom of God that is wholly Spirit and lived in hope of the disintegration of the world and the flesh. Even Paul was unable to believe in the resurrection of a fallen flesh, for he posited a wholly negative relationship between flesh and spirit; and the Gospel of John, which unlike

Paul abandoned the original apocalyptic ground of Christianity, betrayed its own symbol of the Incarnate Word by envisioning the Kingdom of God in the form of pure spirit. Let us fully recognize that so to conceive the eschatological destiny of the Word is both to abolish its incarnational form and to renounce the reality of the Incarnation. Furthermore, we must observe that a religious expression of eschatological faith differs at no decisive point from the purely mystical way of Oriental religion – except for the all too significant fact that eschatological religion has yet to receive a pure expression in history. A truly or radically Christian *coincidentia oppositorum* must pass through an actual transfiguration of flesh and spirit; each must dialectically move into its own other, as spirit moves kenotically and historically into flesh and flesh is transposed into a new and final form of Spirit.

Fall and Death

No myth has been more persistent in Christian history, and no religious theme more pervasive, than the myth of the Fall, of man's expulsion from paradise and his consequent condemnation to death. In the perspective of the History of Religions, we can sense the significance of this motif by noting that no religion has so stressed the importance and the centrality of the Fall as has Christianity, just as no other religion has accepted the Fall as an ultimate and final event. Almost from its very beginning, moreover, Christianity has paradoxically if partially affirmed that the Fall was a fortunate occurrence, a *felix culpa*, a finally blessed and even necessary event apart from which there could be neither Incarnation nor full redemption. This bitter if liberating knowledge of the loss of paradise is integrally related to the eschatological ground of the Christian faith. Only when the paradise of the Beginning has finally been lost, thereby dissolving the very possibility of a true nostalgia or longing for primordial time, can faith fully give itself to the forward movement of the Christian Word. The Christian may lament the loss of an original paradise, but he himself is banished from its garden.

As we discover the points at which Christianity transcends the universal movement of religion, reversing its intrinsic direction and ground, we can only look with amazement upon the obvious fact that throughout its history Christianity has almost invariably appeared in a religious form. Perhaps nothing else could so forcibly demonstrate the theological truth of the historical reality of the Christian Word. Having never appeared in a pure or definitive form, the Christian Word is a Word in process of realizing itself. Inevitably, the Word has only gradually and partially become manifest, appearing in forms that are extrinsic and even antithetical to its own reality, if only as a means of accommodating itself to the actual contingencies of history. Of course, a religious Christianity will dogmatically insist that the Word has been given its definitive and final expression in the Bible. But we must hasten to observe that this is an intrinsically religious claim, exhibiting—insofar as it confines revelation to a past or primordial time—the backward religious movement or return. Nor does such a claim take account of the full and Christian meaning of the Fall. It seeks an unfallen form of the Word, a pure moment of revelation untarnished and unaffected by history, in which the Word is manifest only in its primordial and eternal meaning. Even a Christian belief in the possibility of a final revelation in history is a flight from the truth of the Fall. If Adam has been expelled from paradise, resulting in the advent of a truly profane history, then a final revelation cannot occur in history, apart from a dissolution or reversal of history itself.

In the Orient, where the religious movement of involution, reversal, and return receives its fullest and clearest expression, an absolute or final revelation is always known as occurring in the primordial time of the Beginning. Here, revelation is either wholly isolated from the profane reality of time or is visible in a fallen form only to the extent that it ceases to be absolute and accommodates itself to human ignorance and weakness. When revelation is so conceived, it will be historical only to the extent that it ceases to be revelation. As opposed to this purely religious form of revelation, a truly historical revelation can only occur in the contingent actuality of a profane history, and thus it must inevitably appear in a fallen rather than an eternal form. Therefore a historical revelation can be manifest in a sacred or eternal form only to the extent that it has not yet become or has ceased to be historical. Revelation can be historical only by means of a metamorphosis of the sacred into the profane, an actual movement of the Word from the sacred to the profane, reversing the backward movement of religion. Religious Christianity resists this movement of the Word, opposing its abandonment of an original and primordial sacred by resurrecting the Word in a religious form. Refusing the Word that appears and is real in the fallen reality of history, the religious Christian succumbs to the temptation of the past by fleeing to the primordial God of an unfallen Beginning.

A fully consistent or radical Christianity knows the totality of the Fall. Consequently, it condemns the religious quest for an unfallen sacred, repudiates the God who alone is God, and renounces all attachment to the past. Blake's prophetic hatred of memory, his realization that "Innocence" must become "Experience," and his subsequent attack upon innocence as a subhuman flight from the human reality of history all illustrate this antireligious ground of radical Christianity. Having been initiated into the totally fallen and historical reality of the world, the radical Christian knows that the original paradise is both lost and forbidden—lost, in the sense that it has wholly vanished from history, and forbidden, if only because a quest for an original paradise must reverse the reality of history, a reversal which can only be accomplished by abolishing humanity. To speak of the totality of the Fall is to recognize that there is no way in history to an unfallen innocence or a primordial Word. Once history has become truly manifest in its fully profane form, both an original paradise and a primordial sacred have been forever lost. Confronted with the advent of a totally profane world, faith has an inevitable temptation to flee to the past. Yet radical Christianity points the way to a new epiphany of the

Word: a Word that has died in its original and sacred form and is now manifest only at the center of the radical profane.

If we are to grant that the Christian Word is truly a forward-moving process, and moves by way of a metamorphosis of the sacred into the profane, then it can move only by negating its original identity, thereby passing through the death of its original form. Christianity has always celebrated death as the way to redemption, proclaiming that Christ's death inaugurated a new reality of joy and forgiveness and calling all men to a participation in His death as the way of salvation. Death, it is true, is a universal motif in the history of religions: man dies to his profane or fallen condition as a means of being reborn in the sacred. However, Christianity, and Christianity alone, proclaims the death of the sacred; and only in Christianity do we find a concrete experience of the factuality and the finality of death. At this point Buddhism presents an instructive contrast to Christianity, for here one discovers unbelievably complex systems of meditation centering upon the image of death but a death that is a way to the dissolution of the human condition and therefore to the abolition of pain and suffering. No other higher religion in the world calls its participants to a full experience of the pain and darkness of the human act of dying as the way to transfiguration and rebirth. Unique, too, is the call to share or to co-experience Christ's death, in which a sharing of the passion of Christ becomes a participation in the process of salvation. Underlying this Christian experience of death is a new openness to death as an ultimately real event. Nowhere else is death granted its simple if brutal reality, for nowhere else in history has man found life through the human event of death.

Once again, however, we must note that the historical forms of Christianity have thus far failed to embody the full and radical consequences of the Christian Word. Not only did unchristian ideas of immortality creep into the body of Christianity, but the very religious form of traditional Christianity has foreclosed the possibility of its acceptance of the finality of death. A belief in the resurrection of Jesus in the form of an eternal and primordial God must necessarily annul the reality of his death, either reducing it to a mere transition to a higher state or retrogressively conceiving it as an abolition of His human condition. Unlike the doctrinal expressions of orthodox Christianity, Christian meditation upon the passion of Christ has grasped His death as an ultimate and human event, a concrete but decisive event which has transformed the primordial relation between man and God. Despite its claim to be a historical faith, orthodox Christianity tenaciously clings to the primordial Creator, an eternal and unchanging Lord. Thus it is closed to the presence in Christ's passion of God Himself. Trinitarian forms of Christianity have inevitably dissolved the actual and the historical reality of the Crucifixion and the Incarnation, because in identifying Christ with an eternal Word they have eliminated the possibility of either actual death or real movement. Therewith, too, they have retreated from the factuality and finality of death, for death cannot be real in the presence of an eternal and primordial Word.

Only when the Fall is known as a real and decisive event does death assume its awesome reality. A religion which is innocent of the damning knowledge of the finality of the Fall cannot know the true reality of death, for insofar as an eternal and impassive Word is present to the religious consciousness death can pose no ultimate threat to the believer. Before death can become fully actualized and wholly real to consciousness, it must penetrate the realm of the sacred, not simply appearing there as an image of the profane, but rather affecting by the fulness of its own actuality the very form and reality of the sacred. Christian imagery of death, perhaps to the greatest extent in the New Testament, has ever tended to regress to a pre-Christian religious form, dissolving the reality of death in its vision of resurrection and thereby confining death to temporal contingency and fallen flesh. Such a reversal of the full meaning of death inevitably resists the finality of the Fall, isolating Word and Fall by clinging to an unfallen and imperishable Word and annulling the historical actuality of the Fall by positing its culmination in a pre-fallen Spirit. Moreover, when the finality of the Fall has been so reversed, the Incarnation and Crucifixion can no longer be manifest as fully historical events, because here the Word can only be present in a pre-fallen and hence non-historical form. No true movement is possible for a Word which is unaffected by its own action and process; accordingly, the real ground of religious Christianity is an impassive and unmoving Word.

Again and again we have discovered that Christianity has resisted the Word of its own proclamation by regressing to a primordial, an unfallen, and a non-historical Word. Above all it is faith's resistance to the Word's becoming fully actualized as flesh that has driven it to the backward movement of religion. Rather than open itself to the forward movement of the Word, with its intrinsic goal of undergoing a total metamorphosis in history, Christianity has given itself to a dualistic isolation of flesh from spirit, thereby imprisoning the Word in an inactive and lifeless form. Not until the Word has been liberated from its religious veil will it appear and be real to the Christian in its own intrinsic reality. Yet this can only occur when the Word is known as undergoing an actual movement into history, wherein the Word itself is affected by its movement, abandoning its original and primordial form as it becomes incarnate and moving forward to the goal of a new and eschatological Totality. An incarnate Word that truly and actually enters the profane reality of history not only must appear in a fallen form but must itself pass through the reality of Fall and death, thereby emptying itself of its original purity and power. The Christian Word itself is a fallen or kenotically emptied Word, just as the Incarnation is the truest witness to the totality and finality of the Fall. Now the Word is active and real *only* in the profane reality of a fallen history. In the Crucifixion the Word has finally died to its original form, losing its transcendent glory and its primordial holiness, while fully becoming flesh.

Only in the Crucifixion, in the death of the Word on the Cross, does the Word actually and wholly become flesh. Finally, the Incarnation is only truly and actually real if it effects the death of the original sacred, the death of God Himself.

6

The History of Religions and the Study of Hinduism

PHILIP H. ASHBY

In his *The Comparative Study of Religions* Joachim Wach quoted Friedrich Max Müller as follows:

> If the history of religion has taught us anything, it has taught us to distinguish between the names and the thing named. The names may change, and become more and more perfect, and our concepts of the deity become more and more perfect also, but the deity itself is not affected by our names. However much the names may differ and change, there remains, as the last result of the study of religion, the everlasting conviction that behind all the names there is something named, that there is an agent behind all acts, that there is an Infinite behind the Finite, that there is a God in Nature; that God is the abiding goal of many names, all well meant and well aimed, and yet all far, far away from the goal which no man can see and live. All names that human language has invented may be imperfect. But the name "I am that I am" will remain for those who think Semitic thought, while to those who speak Aryan languages it will be difficult to invent a better name than the Vedanta *Sakkid-ananda.* He who is, who knows, who is blessed.[1]

We are concerned with problems in understanding. It is appropriate, I believe, that at the beginning we should re-

[1] Granfel A. Müller (ed.), *Life and Religion: An Aftermath from the Writings of F. Max Müller by His Wife* (New York: Doubleday, 1905), p. 56, quoted in Joachim Wach, *The Comparative Study of Religions* (New York: Columbia University Press, 1958), pp. 41 f.

mind ourselves of the truism that understanding and language, comprehension and words, are closely related. The "thing" and the "name" given to it stand in relation one to the other. And, yet, understanding is impeded if we do not distinguish between the names and the thing named.

Among the many thinkers of history who have made this fact most clear to us, it is, perhaps, most appropriate for historians of religion to remember Nāgasena's reply to King Milinda's question, "What is your name?"

> Your majesty, I am called Nāgasena; my fellow priests, your majesty, address me as Nāgasena; but whether parents give one the name Nāgasena, or Sūrasena, or Vīrasena, or Sīhasena, it is, nevertheless, your majesty, but a way of counting, a term, an appellation, a convenient designation, a mere name, this Nāgasena; for there is no ego here to be found.[2]

In a much different context, W. Brede Kristensen along with many others has reminded us that from early religious cultures onward the meaning of the name as spiritual essence, power, or authority has been widespread. Origen contended that the name is the metaphysical designation of the essence. For Origen, names are not conventional designations of persons; rather they are sharers and bearers of the essence.[3] So also Van der Leeuw suggests that the "names of things subsist before they acquire a 'personality'; and the name of God is there even before 'God' exists."[4] It would appear that in the context of the *homo religiosus*, when he is apprehended as religiously believing man and not as intellectually, logically, philosophically, theologically reflective mind, the problem of nominalism and realism takes on a somewhat different coloration.

The historian of religion, phenomenologically oriented as

[2] H. C. Warren, *Buddhism in Translations* (New York: Atheneum, 1963), p. 129.

[3] W. Brede Kristensen, *The Meaning of Religion* (The Hague: Martinus Nijhoff, 1960), pp. 414 f.

[4] G. Van der Leeuw, *Religion in Essence and Manifestation* (London: Allen & Unwin, 1938), p. 147.

he so often is today,[5] is particularly concerned to ascertain what things are. As phenomenologist, the historian of religion seeks essence. In Husserl's terms this is an attempt to understand *being* in terms of *essence*. And it was his contention that that which appears can be set forth in words in a fashion which is adequate to the essence of the appearance. Essences can be known in their phenomenality, as they appear. The name, in Nāgasena's words, the "way of counting, a term, an appellation, a convenient designation, a mere name," is happenstance and of no import. However, the historian of religion, at least when he is phenomenologist, must separate himself from the last phrase of Nāgasena's sentence. For the phenomenologist there must be essence ("ego") present.

Our first point, then, is the reminder that in the search for understanding we are not centrally concerned with the name of a thing or an appearance, as if that name or designation were its paramount quality. A term of identification may or may not convey the quality, morphology, or value of an appearance. The investigator must consider carefully as he confronts the appearance and reflects upon its appellation.

However, as Van der Leeuw has reminded us, the history of phenomenological research is not to be completely separated from romanticism.[6] Although pre-phenomenological—as that term is used and understood today—the studies of religion under the influence of romanticism did nevertheless leave a legacy of significant importance for us. It was the growing recognition of the role of the religious man and the religious community. Gottfried von Herder's "voices of the peoples" was a significant insight into the centrality of the human reaction to, and appropriation of, the hierophany of the divine in the midst of the human.

"The voices of the peoples" do tell the historian of reli-

[5] See R. Pettazzoni, "The Supreme Being: Phenomenological Structure and Historical Development," *The History of Religions*, ed. Mircea Eliade and Joseph M. Kitagawa (Chicago: University of Chicago Press, 1959), p. 66: "Religious phenomenology and history . . . are two complementary aspects of the integral science of religion."

[6] Van der Leeuw, *op. cit.*, pp. 691 ff.

gion something; their words, their "names," reveal something. If it is not the essence, "the thing in itself," it may very well be something of equal or greater importance in the search to understand the history of religion, namely, a fuller comprehension of *homo religiosus* himself.

In his *The Idea of History*, R. G. Collingwood asks the question whether the historian can know the past.[7] And, his well-known answer is that the historian must re-enact the past in his own mind. History is the re-enactment of past experience, and by such engagement it is possible, so he holds, for the past to be "known."

Despite the many dangers inherent in this understanding of historical methodology—but then, what method does not have its dangers?—the historian of religion, seeking to understand both the past and the present of religion, must above all be engaged as an "actor." He must re-enact the past, engage in the religious longings of others now dead and of others who are his contemporaries. He must re-enact in his own being the religious striving, searching, and response of that which, as investigator, he seeks to understand.

It has become quite common for the student of culture to use the word "empathy" in reference to what we are now discussing. Certainly this is understandable in any student of Joachim Wach, who discerned so well the values of "fellow-feeling." For the student of culture who is a historian of religion, empathy is precisely the channeling of the voices of *homines religiosi* through his own mind until, in a sense, he himself becomes a part of that voice. This is not simply a legacy from romanticism or a lack of intellectual objectivity and rigidity to which some of us are prone. It is a basic demand placed upon those seeking understanding by the nature of that which they seek to understand. The "names" used must in the deepest sense become the "names" I use and reflect upon.

But this endeavor, of course, leaves the student open to many criticisms, some obvious and essentially trivial and

[7] R. G. Collingwood, *The Idea of History* (New York: Oxford University Press, 1956), p. 282.

others potentially shattering to the whole attempt at understanding. It is, obviously, not the name but that for which the name serves as a signpost that interests the observer. And there is no magic in the name itself by itself whereby I, if I use it and appropriate it to myself, gain unique powers of understanding. Further, and I do not believe this to be contradictory, in endeavoring to become a part of the voice which was originally foreign to me—and which, almost predictably, will remain ultimately foreign—I am not required to believe, to accept as true in an ultimate sense, that in which I am attempting to participate. Nevertheless, I must, as a seeker after understanding, have as a primary element in my own mind the recognition that there is value present in what I am observing and that this is precisely what makes my engagement significant.

If I must proceed on the assumption that ultimate truth is not necessarily present in that in which I seek to participate and also assume, for the sake of stimulus for my endeavors, that value resides in the data of the religious culture with which I am engaged, am I not caught in a dilemma which defeats or makes absurd my whole attempt to understand? In a very real sense it was, I think, this situation that defeated the work of many Christian "comparative religionists" of the past. They observed but could not participate in the religions of others, first, because they were convinced that ultimate truth was far removed from that which they were studying and, second, because the value of their endeavors was understood to be primarily, or only, the negative one of demonstrating the errors, perhaps demonic, of the *homo religiosus* when he is outside the context of the revelation in Christ.

But the seminal historians of religion of the past did attain a degree of participation in that which they studied and left us a legacy upon which we can proceed, in fact *must* proceed, in our participation with all religious men, living or dead. This legacy is the recognition that there is value in all religious phenomena, a value which we must discern if we are to understand. And that value is the worth of the religious belief, act, and community for the adherent committed to the phenomenon. Here there is absolute value, and we must recognize it as such or we completely misunderstand. Professor Eliade has urged that after all data have been gathered, the historian of religion should "make an effort to understand them *on their own plane of reference*."[8] Kristensen advised that "every religion ought to be understood from its own standpoint, for that is how it is understood by its own adherents."[9] We today know that every religion *must*, not ought to, be understood on the basis of its own fundamental and absolute presuppositions or it is not understood. And the unqualified certitude of the *homo religiosus* wherever found is, most certainly, that supreme value is present, is of the essence, of that to which he is committed.

Here, then, is the basis and the need for the participation which is essential to the historian of religion. Value, I would maintain, can be observed and, more important, encountered even when it may not be shared. I can feel—yes, even be intrigued and disturbed by—the values that sustain and motivate others even though they do not possess that quality or serve that function for me. I can participate, empathize, because I recognize the presence of value, absolute in its quality and intensity. And I am now on the way toward understanding. I have approached close to the other's "own plane of reference."

A further step in seeking understanding, in addition to the concern with an appearance and its name and empathetic participation whereby indigenous value is perceived, is made when the historian of religion (if his special area is not an archaic religion) is adequately aware of his role as contemporary historian. Our discipline, as we well know, has had and continues to have a problem in terminology and definition in describing itself. Such terms as Comparative Religion, *Religionsgeschichte*, *Religionswissenschaft*, Phenomenology

[8] Mircea Eliade, "History of Religions and a New Humanism," *History of Religions*, I (1962), No. 1, 4.

[9] Kristensen, *op. cit.*, p. 6.

of Religion, and so on, all have their values and their limitations.[10] The individual scholar may, and often does, limit himself to a specific role or task which is best defined by one of the many available terms. The nature of modern scholarship often correctly requires this, and the individual scholar and our discipline as a whole are enriched by such a self-imposed limitation.

Nevertheless, more and more historians of religion are conceiving their task, in whole or part, as one of involvement with *contemporary* religious man in his variety, diversity, and similarity. Here the search for understanding of the fundamentals and their appellations and the participation in the values of the specific presuppositions that are understood as absolute are united with an understanding of religion as a phenomenon of the present and of the future as well as of the past. It is most obviously contradictory to speak of a scholar as being now, in the present, a historian of the future. However, just as secular historians today are seeking to enrich history as living history by the means of "oral" history, so the historian of religion is challenged as contemporary historian to delve into present history as it unfolds into future history. He is compelled, if he seeks more adequate understanding, to engage in "oral" history, which becomes "dialogic" contemporary history in process. And in this engagement, not only is the present more fully understood and the past roots of the present more adequately perceived, but the dim possible, if not probable, outlines of the future are adumbrated.

In this event, if the historian of religion is even minimally prepared by his scholarship, personally disposed by his religious inclinations, and allowed by his colleagues to retain a reasonable professional standing, he is then called upon to enter into the dangerous area of the constructive and evolving theology of his own tradition of faith. Despite its frightening and perilous byways, in which descriptive scholarship so easily and almost inevitably becomes highly subjective

[10] See P. H. Ashby, "The History of Religions," *Religion*, ed. Paul Ramsey (Englewood Cliffs, N.J.: Prentice-Hall, 1965), pp. 3–49.

individual value judgment, some historians of religion, who are deeply involved in the problems of understanding, are embarking on this path. In so doing they are departing from the discipline as narrowly conceived and returning to the discipline as earlier understood by, for example, Max Müller and Archbishop Söderblom. In these circumstances, the appellation "historian" appears, to modern ears, to be misleading and, perhaps, when one applies it to himself deliberately, an attempt at deception. The "historian" engaged in "theologizing," despite the fact that he is seeking to construct his experimental thought structures upon solid history (empathized, relived, participated-in history) is inevitably, and rightly, suspected as historian and distrusted as theologian. Now the names, the appellations applied to him, to paraphrase Nāgasena, refer to no quality or ability which is present in the historian of religion who has turned participator in present and unfolding religious history.

Let us look, then, at these three modes or methods of approaching the problem of understanding by considering a leading religious tradition and community in the world today – Hinduism. In what way does continued grappling with the problem of name and form (*nāma-rūpa*), in relationship or identity with essence, contribute to more significant understanding? Are we, as sympathetic, empathetic, but nevertheless still foreign investigators, able to participate in Hinduism to the extent that we may speak even feebly with *the* voice of the Hindu religious man, so that his words become our words? And, finally, what understanding can we gain, tentative and subject to constant change though that understanding may be, of present Hinduism becoming future Hinduism and, perhaps, of present *homo religiosus* becoming the religious man of the future?

The beginning student of Hinduism, even at the textbook level, is immediately confronted by very significant problems as he seeks to comprehend the central themes of the Hindu philosophical-theological tradition. The more advanced scholar may believe himself to have attained adequate comprehension of these themes only to be advised by his Hindu friends, whose opinion is confirmed by his own intellectual confusion, that he has not yet comprehended.

Among the many concepts, *Brahman* is perhaps the prime example. I need not cite the numerous problems involved or the voluminous literature, Indian and non-Indian, upon the problem of Brahman. But here where we seek the "essential," we all too frequently indulge in a play of words and fail to take into account adequately the ethos, the mind-set, which continually informs the Hindu thinker as he uses a name, an appellation, to which we give a content and essence not at all meant by him.

Relativity is basic to Hindu philosophizing since all empirical phenomena are relative. Human speech, names, and so on, fall under this category. And though we are told this, we continually forget to remember it. Thus, as Betty Heimann has put it, "*Brahman* is the *coincidentia oppositorum*, the falling-together of all opposites."[11] Brahman is more than all empirical appearances or qualities; it is beyond the limitations of *nāma-rūpa* (name-form).

The foregoing is, of course, familiar to even elementary students of Hinduism. Nevertheless, it is incumbent upon the historian of religion who seeks understanding not simply to recognize it as a student and then only occasionally to remember it in his mature scholarship but to struggle with that which separates him as, for example, a Western Christian man from the Eastern Hindu *homo religiosus*. His awareness of Western negative theology will aid him, but it will not alone suffice. Corresponding or analogous structures of thought from his own intellectual environment are helpful but frequently misleading guides.

Of course, it can be maintained that Brahman is not an "essence," does not have the faculty or function of appearance, and is not in an ultimate fashion irrevocably bound to this designation or name. Then, why cannot the historian

[11] Betty Heimann, *Facets of Indian Thought* (London: Allen & Unwin, 1964), p. 146.

of religion dismiss the problem by holding that Brahman is merely a convenient Hindu designation for the Ultimate and let it go at that? If this is done, it will be obvious that little or no understanding of Hinduism has been attained. Not only will the problem have been ignored, but the ignoring will have contributed to misunderstanding.

In a brief introductory but scholarly discussion of Brahman, Heinrich Zimmer has indicated the value of discovering both the meaning of the term Brahman and the essential nature of the object to which it refers.[12] By an analysis of the vocables concerned, he leads the student into a recognition that, although the term Brahman may, by one method of approach (a rather superficial one, perhaps), be comprehended simply as a convenient designation, yet from another perspective (an essential one if adequate understanding is sought), the term's root forms and related contributive concepts open up a significance that no mere "name" would reveal if left standing as a simple, agreed-upon sign. It is true, as Zimmer puts it, that "Brahman as the charm, or sacred magic formula, is the crystallized, frozen form (the convenient, handy form, as it were) of the highest divine energy."[13] Nevertheless, the nature of this divine energy, its inherent and essential relationship to or identity with the ultimate essence of man, its paramount significance in the structure of Hindu anthropology — all of these and more are inextricably involved in the very etymology of the name Brahman and are revealed to us, understood in greater measure by us, only as we "participate" in the name used, in the "crystallized, frozen form" which continues to inform the sophisticated Hindu religious man.

It is well for us to note what our understanding of the Hindu comprehension of Brahman contributes to our perception of, for example, Hindu attitudes toward human existence. The well-known "world affirming, world denying," or "optimism and pessimism" categorization of Western and

[12] Heinrich Zimmer, *Philosophies of India*, ed. Joseph Campbell (Cleveland: Meridian Book, 1956), pp. 74 ff.

[13] *Ibid.*, p. 78.

Eastern attitudes toward the human situation provides a useful illustration. When the Western student of religion and culture seeks an understanding of this matter in India, for example, he is often and easily led astray if he does not recognize the inherent, necessary presence of opposites in Indian thought structures. For as Brahman is the source from which all things come (from which in some Hindu systems they never, in an ultimate sense, leave) and is also, and primarily, the "*coincidentia oppositorum*, the falling-together of all opposites" (given the Hindu understanding of existence) no such optimism-pessimism distinction can be made. Valorizations are to be made, of course. The empirically known and experienced is different from the transempirical and is ultimately less valuable. Nevertheless, such categories as value as over against disvalue are, as in the case of opposites in Brahman, complementary and related. As Betty Heimann reminds us so pointedly in her attempt to demonstrate the absolute necessity that we adopt Hindu criteria of logic when seeking to understand (though not necessarily evaluate) the Hindu estimate of the world, the pessimism present "is only a relativism of value."[14] Unfortunately, Western historians of religion and students of culture all too often continue to ignore or misunderstand the centrality of this relativism.

The relativism of a name, a designation, when viewed from within a *Weltanschauung* wherein all is relative and wherein the Ultimate encompasses all actual and potential opposites, takes on a different significance from the relativism of another culture in which there are different intellectual presuppositions.

Starting with Brahman (though, of course, no fundamental theme stands alone and, therefore, none can be conceived adequately in total isolation), the scholar seeking understanding of Hinduism is required to comprehend, if not accept, the name used, that to which it refers, and the significance of both for the religious orientation and intellectual stance of the Hindu person. If he does not attempt this, not

[14] Heimann, *op. cit.*, p. 152.

only is the appellation Brahman of little value to him, but perhaps of more importance, he almost inevitably misinterprets most if not all other matters related to Hinduism—he is unable to comprehend the words and actions of Hindus past or present.

In turning to a consideration of the second method of approaching the problem of understanding, we are involved with a matter which was of very great importance to Joachim Wach. He believed that it was absolutely necessary for the historian of religion to be so emotionally equipped that an affinity to the subject that was being studied could be established.[15] This "adequate emotional condition," as he put it, was not, as positivism maintained, to prepare the investigator to be indifferent. Rather, if adequately nurtured, it was to enable the student of a religion "to do justice to that religion's true nature." For many of us who were his students, it was precisely this faculty of sympathetic understanding of the varied forms of religious structures and expressions that constituted Joachim Wach's genius as a scholar and teacher.

When the historian of religion sets about the challenging task of understanding Hinduism—to pursue further the example we have chosen—he must endeavor to participate *in* Hinduism. And to "participate in" demands that one become as fully as possible at one with those who are Hindu by birth, environmental conditioning, training, and mature adult commitment.

If we examine, first, the fundamental stance of the contemporary Hindu intellectual who is religiously committed as well as intellectually intrigued by the tradition that surrounds him, we note very quickly that for him Hinduism is conceived and appropriated personally as a continuous, living, non-static organism. To be sure, he may, and often

[15] See J. Wach, *Das Verstehen* (Tübingen: J. C. B. Mohr [P. Siebeck], 1929), Vol. II; Wach, *Sociology of Religion* (Chicago: University of Chicago Press, 1944), p. 10; Wach, *The Comparative Study of Religions*, p. 12.

does, base his thought on forms highly dependent upon a particular document or intellectual tradition of the past. But close examination will usually reveal that his particular citation of authority, or its mode of expression, arises not out of exclusive allegiance to the source but, rather, from an awareness that this is for the moment the most appropriate documentation or form of articulation.

It is only as the historian of religion participates by reenactment within himself of the long continuous unfolding of Hinduism, and thereby comprehends something of the religious pilgrimage of the Indian people, that he can begin to understand the voice of Hindu religiosity. Perhaps the reenactment will need to begin with Mohenjo-daro–Harappa; most certainly it will become active and deeply involved by the time of the Ṛgveda; and from then on there is little, if anything, in the total Indian scene that can be allowed to escape attention. With the Hindu intellectual he must ponder the *upaniṣadic* ferment and participate in the transformations brought about by the Ajivikas, the Jains, and the Buddhists. He must call to mind the deep involvement of a people, their culture and their society, with a religious quest that has marked and molded them from the dawn of history. This may be historic romanticism, but it is also historic fact. The historian of religion who identifies Hinduism with any one of the periods or aspects of Hindu history and thought, to the exclusion of others, misunderstands because he limits the scope of his participation.

A similar degree of participation is required when one seeks to understand the less intellectual Hindu, the *homo religiosus* of the countryside, the village, and the large city slums of today. Hinduism as a continuous, living growth offers the same variety of riches to the humble as to the religiously committed intellectual, although in a somewhat different fashion. One must participate, become involved with *Dharma, Karma, Saṃsāra,* and so on, as humbly understood, as the "givens" of an existence perhaps naively comprehended, or the Hinduism of the masses will remain an unfathomable mystery.

However, on this level the seeker after understanding is required to perform an extremely difficult task for which most of us are not intellectually or emotionally prepared. The historian of religion is trained to investigate the thought forms of a religious culture, to describe the cultus, and to discuss the community that is inextricably involved with the first two categories. It is the rare one among us who is prepared religiously and emotionally to enter into what appears at first glance to be the rather limited intellectual horizons, elementary religious feelings, and unsophisticated cultic expressions of even our own religious tradition, let alone that of another religious tradition such as Hinduism. And how is it possible for us to penetrate into the sociological element, the community, beyond our own rather impersonal studies and those of the sociologists to which we are so greatly indebted? Obviously, in any ultimate sense, we cannot become *members* of the community.

Nevertheless, our understanding of Hinduism will continue to be greatly limited and subject to gross error if we do not work hard to overcome this handicap. It is here that study of, and involvement with, the theoretical must be supplemented by participation, a participation with the intellectual whose language is more our own and a cultivation of relationships with the so-called humble layman whose mind-set and expressions constitute barriers that are difficult but not absolutely insurmountable. Such a relationship has not been completely absent in the past (witness among others, Abbé J. A. Dubois around 1800), and today the historian of religion is beginning to take the opportunity to live among the people he is studying to a degree not known before. I think of one brilliant young Western scholar, for example, who before embarking upon his formal doctoral program spent a number of years in India, some of them as a student and one year as a resident in a low-caste village. The "voices of the people" on the level of interpersonal relationships began to be meaningful to him in the very early years of his scholarship. He and his generation of historians of religion, strengthened by the growing research of various disciplines of the humanities and social sciences, are coming into a sphere of closer participation with religious man as he lives, believes, and acts in communities of the countryside as well as in crowded urban centers. As trained investigators seeking understanding, many such scholars are particularly well suited for their search because they possess the "adequate emotional condition" for which Wach pleaded and are able "to do justice to that religion's true nature," which he reminded us was the goal of our discipline.

As is the case in most other areas where men seek to understand—to be at one with that which is not indigenously their own—our attainments can most probably be only proximate at best and never complete. Nevertheless, the historian of religion, although recognizing this limitation, must seek to overcome it in order to understand more fully.

In regard to our third method of approach, let us ask what insights can be gained by today's historian of religion when he focuses his attention upon contemporary Hinduism, its present strengths and weaknesses, its tendencies and its problems? What may he discern more clearly as a non-Hindu religious man among Hindu religious men? And if he is so inclined, what justification is there for him as a historian of religion to become involved in the theological endeavors of his own tradition because of his participation in present-day, evolving Hinduism?

The answer to our first question is, of course, obvious. The historian of religion may, as we noted earlier, limit himself to a particular period or problem. The history of religion, however, cannot be so confined. If it could, it would be the history of Buddhism, Islam, Hinduism, and the other religions, or the history or study of the sociology of a particular time, phenomenon, category, and so on. But even in these instances, it is clear that added insight is gained when the investigator can become involved with contemporaries who possess an inherited, and perhaps dynamic, relationship with his subject of study. In the case of our example, Hinduism (or any other living religion), the resources for such an involvement are abundantly present and can serve to make Hinduism a live and exciting subject.

In addition to a more revealing insight into Hinduism, what it has been and what it is, the historian of religion as a student of contemporary religious history is brought into direct confrontation with claims of religious faith that are viable in the larger religious world of which he is a part. If he ignores these claims and thereby neglects the viability of the religion with which he is concerned, he will not comprehend the role of religion today in the area he is studying, nor will he be sensitive to the appeal of the presuppositions of great numbers of religious people in his own time.

It does little service to human knowledge or to the discipline of the history of religion to dismiss quickly religious beliefs and fundamental religious themes and claims because they are not an inherent ingredient of the predominant cultural ethos within the present and evolving world culture. There is no guarantee that the culture's hegemony will continue. Nor should the fact that some religious traditions are not in all aspects alive, dynamic, and "modern" in our eyes be allowed to obscure their present and potential contribution to the place of religion in the lives, societies, and affections of men. Above all, the historian of religion when he is involved as contemporary historian is failing in one of his primary responsibilities if he does not bring these claims to the attention of fellow scholars of his own faith.

In his richly suggestive essay on "The Place of the History of Religions in the Study of Theology," Wach contended that it is the function of the historian of religion to provide "a comprehensive but articulated inventory of the varieties of expression" of the religious experience.[16] He went on to say:

> Discussion of the claims of non-Christian religion does not fall within the competence of the historian of religion as such. Inasmuch, however, as the facts provided by him

[16] J. Wach, *Types of Religious Experience: Christian and Non-Christian* (Chicago: University of Chicago Press, 1951), p. 28.

remain without meaning for us if not evaluated in a normative context, such evalution has to be essayed.[17]

Here the historian of religion is confronted with the responsibility of providing knowledge on which the theologian may base the fulfilment of his task in the twentieth century. The historian of religion, to the degree that he has re-enacted the past of religion in his own being and participated in the present ethos of religious men of great variety, is perhaps far enough along the road to understanding to bring his scholarly involvement with its resulting comprehension into the arena of theological discourse and evaluation. There is little doubt, I should think, that such a task must be essayed and that this is increasingly becoming the responsibility of the historian of religion, hazardous as the venture may be.

The historian of religion in company with Hindus (or others he is studying) is required to ignore the advice of the sage Yājñavalkya in the *Bṛhadāraṇyaka Upaniṣad*:

> Gārgī, do not question too much, lest your head fall off. In truth, you are questioning too much about a divinity about which further questions cannot be asked. Gārgī, do not over-question.[18]

We seek to *understand*, and to do so we question, we re-enact, we seek to participate, and we are called upon to contribute our understanding to present and future religious man.

[17] *Ibid.*

[18] *The Thirteen Principal Upanishads*, trans. R. E. Hume (London: Oxford University Press, 1934, p. 114, Third Adhyāya, Sixth Brāhmaṇa).

7

A Note on Field Method in Historico-Religious Studies: The Vallabhasampradāya

CHARLES S. J. WHITE

The Problem of Understanding

Methodology may not be very clear in the mind of one who embarks on a voyage abroad for the purpose of coming to understand a religious faith and culture other than his own.[1] He and his guides may take more or less for granted that he has acquired a certain competence, that he understands a given body of methodological theory, that he knows or has begun to learn languages suitable to his study, or when all

[1] Methodology stands out as the single most important problem for the historian of religions. Let us be frank about it. There is no lack of material for our speculations. The researchers in the various linguistic and other humanistic disciplines have recorded an enormous amount of relevant *data* which, aside from whatever other uses they may have, apply to the work of the historico-religious interpreter as well. Without an adequate method for handling these materials, our uses of them become mere improvisations. This problem is particularly acute for someone who, besides being a historian of religions, with the implication that he is a generalist, aspires to be a specialist in some phase of man's religious history. Such a specialist is required to concern himself not only with the formal character of the religion described in the literature but with the lived experience of one religion in the midst of its cultural realization, if, indeed, it continues to be a living religious expression. Hence he enlarges the problem of method. He must know how to be a specialist against the background of, or in a way that contributes to, his function as a generalist. This small problem in the specialist's field method is thus related to the larger concern for an adequate general theory of historico-religious methodology. Our teachers and colleagues, Mircea Eliade, Joseph M. Kitagawa, and Charles H. Long, have shown us the way along the road toward such a methodology. Our own responsibility consists in contributing whatever further enlightenment we can.

else fails, that he has *savoir-faire* sufficient to launch himself rapidly and effectively toward the achievement of the goal that he has set for himself. Often at the outset neither he nor his guides realize fully that the level of his training may provide merely the barest outline for a project which, if it were fully realized, would encompass the greater part of a professional career. (Probably, he does realize something of the enormity of the task, but he says to himself that a beginning must be made somewhere!) At the same time, or besides, his goal in field study may not yet be sufficiently clear to enable him to say with certainty whether and to what degree he has achieved success. As a consequence, the beginning historian of religions may return from the field with a feeling of being unfulfilled—asking himself whether he will ever be able to accomplish enough to satisfy an ambition for understanding that has outgrown the limitations of the type of field work that he might conceivably undertake. Or he may long for the time when his specialized knowledge may take him to the core of a system of religious meanings that he wishes to perceive in depths where language and custom no longer hold anything back. Probably, for many, such an analysis in the aftermath of field study will produce a combination of two sharp pangs: one from realizing that one will never know the all, the other from the sense that one does not even yet know enough.

At best one must accept the fact that a first trip (or perhaps even a second or a third) into the field is likely to be tentative and filled with mistakes. One may be either too bold or too shy in one's efforts and in either case the consequences may be humiliating. By some standards, not entirely unworthy, just to have survived the experience is counted a total victory!

But after saying all this, let me really begin by affirming that I agree with Eliade that the desire of the historian of religions is for an understanding perhaps more grandly conceived than in the other scientific and humanistic disciplines in our time.[2] Surely the historian of religions does not wish less than to understand the whole religion of which he studies only parts (or the whole of the *religious* of which the religions are only parts).

And so when he goes to India, to refer to my personal experience, he at first views the religious world he is studying as an object that can be summed up in *x* number of temples and *y* number of ceremonies seen and/or photographed. His equation is complicated by language study, by interviews, by having to learn to move in and out of the circles of the various communities that he has to deal with, and by excursions far and wide through different social contexts. This initial phase can be an agonizing experience of glittering and ghastly surfaces that seem impervious to spirit. Even the flame of life may seem to burn low. Then when one has been working for a length of time, suddenly as if a light had gone on within, some inner reaches of the particular are illuminated and a sense seems to come to one of the whole.

As Schleiermacher and Dilthey knew,[3] the processes of understanding are tautologous. The whole and its parts continually examine each other, so to speak, and reshape each other. Perhaps it is untrue to say that the whole comes first;

[2] One could scarcely imagine a more exciting and challenging statement of the destiny that might be envisioned for historians of religions, if they accepted the responsibility of becoming universalists and synthesists again, than that presented in Mircea Eliade's article, "Crisis and Renewal in History of Religions" (in *History of Religions*, V [Summer, 1965]). It is difficult even to grasp the suggestive richness of all that he says there, let alone to prepare oneself, if possible, to act upon it. Nevertheless, if I have understood at least part of it correctly, perhaps it would be an implementation of his challenge to suggest that an attempt be made to enlarge the present general theories of historico-religious methodology to enable us to deal with religious cultures in detail as well as with systems of hierophanies, without necessarily revising the fundamental notions in Eliade's own methodological theory. I think that the theory of hierophanies already allows for such a usage if it were extended descriptively throughout a religious culture (for example, Hinduism). Of course it would be a major task.

[3] Friedrich Schleiermacher and Wilhelm Dilthey, a nineteenth-century theologian and philosopher, respectively, can be described as the modern founders of the science of hermeneutics.

rather it is the part conceived of as the whole and thus disinclined to relinquish its sovereignty in the confrontation with each new particularity. Hence the problem is to find the wholeness in the process of reappraisal that each new event brings with it. And ultimately, too, one does not hope to understand a mechanism only but a human expression. One may find the divine or the sacred without external human help, but in religions one finds those other dimensions of the self expressed in the forms and communities of religious life.

However, I do not wish to gloss over the difficulties I have experienced and described in my opening paragraphs. I hope you will forgive me if I have merely summarized well-known *dicta*. Let us leave the whole and the particular for the moment. As existentialists, let us gird for the encounter. Let us marshal our examples.

The Vallabhasampradāya

The essential purpose of this paper will be to present a model problem in historical religious interpretation within certain limitations. That is, I shall attempt to create the structure of a problem of religious interpretation and to show to what extent I have worked on it to provide a basis for interpretation. Then I shall propose the areas in which work remains to be done. Finally, I shall hope to draw certain relevant conclusions on the basis of this model problem that might be of use in working toward a functional theory of the method of the historian of religions as he undertakes field work.

The problem is as follows: to come to understand the Vallabhasampradāya (or Vallabha sect) as a religious form within Hinduism from the sixteenth century to the present day. The two primary elements for study are a certain body of sacred literature consisting in poetry and liturgical texts written in Braj Bhāśā, together with the philosophical writings of Vallabha in Sanskirt, and an extremely elaborate liturgical tradition that has been perpetuated down to the present day in the private temples of the sect leaders and the shrine rooms of the householder devotees.

According to Dr. R. G. Bhandarkar, the Vallabhasampradāya was founded as a consequence of a direct commission given by Gopāla-Kṛṣṇa to Vallabha while the latter was living in the sacred Kṛṣṇite country at Vṛndāvana and Mathurā.[4] Kṛṣṇa appeared to Vallabha on Govardhana Hill and told him to erect a shrine for himself as Śri Nāthjī and to institute a special method of worshipping him, without which a man could not enter upon the *puṣṭimārg*, or the path of divine grace—a term used to describe the philosophico-religious system that Vallabha founded. It seems that Vallabha equated his philosophical theory with a particular manifestation of the divine.

Philosophically, Vallabha was a follower of Viṣṇusvāmin, who accepted a dualistic interpretation of the Vedānta, namely, that God and *jīvas* are distinct. His special emphasis, and that of his follower, Vallabha, lay in conceiving of the relationship of God and his devotees as a process of mutual enjoyment. Without here explaining the more technical aspects of the philosophical statement of this point of view, one may summarize by saying that it held that Śri Kṛṣṇa is the sum total of the divine reality. The experiencing of the divine reality is possible through *bhakti*,[5] which has various

[4] R. G. Bhandarkar, "Vaisnavism, Saivism and Minor Religious Systems," in *Collected Works of Sir R. G. Bhandarkar* (Poona: Bhandarkar Oriental Research Institute, 1929), Vol. IV, pp. 109 ff.

[5] *Bhakti* is a term that has come to be applied to theistic religion in general within Hinduism but especially that type which produces an intense emotional response on the part of the devotee in which he has a feeling of dependence upon God for salvation. *Bhakti* derives from the Sanskrit root, *bhaj*, and has as one of its earlier connotations the meaning "to spread out," in the sense of to spread before the deity in worship. Various theories have been given as to the nature of the forms of *bhakti*. A simple division lists four types of *bhakti*, that is, ways in which the devotee is related to the divinity: (a) *vatsalyabhāva*, as a parent toward his child; (b) *madhuryabhāva*, as a lover toward his beloved; (c) *sakhyabhāva*, as a friend toward his friend; (d) *dasyabhāva*, as a servant toward his master. The Vallabhasampradāya follows the path of *vatsalyabhāva bhakti*.

levels that are attainable according to the ability of the devotee and the grace, or *puṣṭi*, of the Lord. The general consequence of following this path is the development of *premabhakti* or loving adoration of God, which at its highest pitch becomes *vyāsana*, or a haunting passion. *Vyāsana* leads to bliss and the rejection of *mukti*, final spiritual transcendence, in favor of the eternal service of Hari, who is seen everywhere and in everything. Mythologically speaking, this means being admitted to the eternal sports of Kṛṣṇa. "The Bhaktas join in these sports, assuming the forms of cows, beasts, birds, trees, rivers, etc. These eternal sports are like those which Kṛṣṇa went through when he became incarnate in Vraja and Vṛndāvana. Some of the devotees become, in the celestial Vṛndāvana, Gopas and Gopīs and join in the sports." [6]

So much then for the general theoretical background of the system. The poems of the poet Sūrdās are important material for the creation of the mythic scenario in which the divine sports of Kṛṣṇa are recapitulated in worship. Sūrdās was himself a devotee of the Vallabha sect and had been initiated by its founder. Following the pattern of stories of the *Bhagavata Purāna*, Sūrdās set out to create in vernacular form a compendium of hymns touching on the major theological issues of importance to devotees, but he was especially interested in the sacred events of the life of Kṛṣṇa in Vṛndāvana, which are largely contained in the tenth book of the *Bhagavata Purāna* and recapitulated in the tenth book of Sūrdās' *Sūrsāgar Sar*. Ultimately, the emphasis in Sūrdās and in the worship of the Vallabha sect was on the divine child of Vrindavana [7] rather than on the amorous adolescent who figures in the poetry of Jayadeva and in the practices of many Kṛṣṇite sects in the middle ages. One might note that this motif influences the Vallabha sect also but that it is not central to the myth and worship in themselves.

The sect is headed by a dynastic hierarchy descended

[6] Bhandarkar, *op. cit.*, pp. 113–14.

[7] The *bhaktas* identified themselves with Yaśoda and Nanda, the foster parents of Sri Krsna; hence the form of *bhakti*, known as *vatsalyabhāva*.

from the grandsons of Vallabha. Vallabha's only son Viṭṭhal is himself a leading saint of the sect and was a close associate of Sūrdās'. The primary shrine of the sect is at Nāthdwara in Rājasthan. Vallabhite shrines are not generally open to the public, whether Hindu or otherwise, and admission to them is reserved for devotees of the sect, who are members of the trading classes. However, in communities where the devotees live — Gujarat, Rājasthan, and Maharashtra as well as other areas of northwestern India — members of the Vallabhite hierarchy have their private temples to which initiates are admitted. In addition, many householders recapitulate the worship of the temple in their own private shrines with lesser or greater splendor, depending upon their resources.[8]

The Content of the Personal Encounter

I became interested in studying the Vallabhasampradāya as a result of research done for my dissertation on the subject of the devotional movement among Hindus in the Hindi-speaking area of North India. In addition to general study of the subject in the United States I began to read the poetry of Sūrdās in Braj Bhāśā and had read selections from several parts of the *Sūrsāgar Sār* before going to Inda. In India for several months, I continued to study the *Sūrsāgar Sār*, especially the opening section which emphasizes the theological beliefs of Vaiṣṇavas generally, of which the Vallabhites are a subsect. My personal encounter with the Vallabhite

[8] The worship itself is performed in fourteen movements, sometimes called *darśanas,* which ideally are enacted daily. "They consist of the following: (1) ringing the bell; (2) the blowing of the conch shell; (3) awakening of the Lord (Thākurjī) and offering morning refreshments; (4) waving of lamps; (5) bathing; (6) dressing; (7) Gopivallabha food; (8) leading the cows out for grazing; (9) the mid-day dinner; (10) waving of lamps; (11) after the last the screen is drawn up and the God cannot be seen; this interval is called *Anosara* or *Anavasara*, i.e., no time for seeing him; (12) the finishing up; (13) the evening meal; (14) going to bed" (Bhandarkar, *op. cit.*, p. 116). These *darśanas* are performed in sequence throughout the waking hours of the day. In addition there are special festivals associated with the sacred drama from one season to another and the devotees spare themselves no expense in performing the rites of the important festivals with unusual magnificence, although, again, they are conducted in private.

sect was made possible through an Indian acquaintance who was my music teacher, Śri Mahārudra Dhumal. He is a high-caste Hindu but not a member of the Vallabhasampradāya. Rather, he counts one family of Vallabhites as his close friends, particularly two older male children who have the responsibility of maintaining the family business of selling silver ornaments in a shop in Poona city.

After I had been studying with my teacher for several months and had learned that he was a devotee of various saints and deities although not particularly devoted to Kṛṣṇa, I asked him if he knew any members of the Vallabhasampradaya. My inquiry led to an invitation to visit the brothers' shop and subsequent invitations to visit their home.[9] One Sunday morning I made my first visit to their home in Maruti Cāuk and was received in the foyer of a huge rambling house that could only be called a mansion. The entire family, of perhaps thirty members, lived together, that is, all the married male children and grandchildren as well as a cousin-brother, an uncle, and so on. Their style of life was clearly traditional. There was little or no modern furniture in their home, and there was an air of spaciousness in their rooms that the average Hindu, living in cramped quarters, could not have emulated. The family looked back to days of grandeur when the British Resident in Poona had called upon their grandfather and had been received in the reception hall, where his photographic portrait still hung behind a long row of crystal chandeliers, gloomy in their dusty bag coverings. After I had drunk tea in one of the sitting rooms, I was taken to the shrine where the mid-day meal had just been offered to Lord Kṛṣṇa. The officiant at the first ceremony I witnessed was the son of the eldest brother among the children of the family. The father, although rather elderly and

[9] I should like to take this opportunity to express my deepest thanks to the Bharatiya family, whose kind hospitality I enjoyed in Poona and who allowed me to learn from them something about the life of devotion in the Vallabhasampradāya. My special thanks to Narayandās Raghunathdās, Ramanlal Narayandās, Mrs. Tarabai Ramanlal, Pravinchandra Ramanlal, Rasiklal Narayandās, Mrs. Padmabai Rasiklal, Ratilal Narayandās, and Rameshcandra Narayandās.

enfeebled, remained the head of the household in respect to his dignity, even though his children were responsible for the business in silver and such other affairs as the household worship.

The family situation was such that the eldest brother had been entirely relieved of any responsibility for earning the family living and spent all his days in offering the services in the household shrine. His own young son was also being trained to perform the daily worship and had been put to work the day of my visit because of his father's absence.

From that Sunday onward, for a period of two months or so before I returned to the United States, I experienced a very warm and happy friendship in the midst of this family. Through their help I was able to meet other members of the sect, although it was not possible in the brief time available to institute direct conversations with any members of the dynastic hierarchy even though at least one such person lives in Poona and functions as the leader of the religious community in his private temple.

I visited the family home several times on Sunday mornings and was allowed to witness various parts of the morning rituals of the deity, including bathing Lord Kṛṣṇa and his companions and dressing them in their elaborate silk costumes and jewelry and offering *Raj Bhog* and betel nut. At an appropriate moment in the service pleasant smelling attars were offered to Kṛṣṇa in the palms of the hands of the officiant, and the deity was shown his splendid countenance in a silver-bound mirror.

I was also shown parts of the ceremonial equipment that were used during the special festivals and was always invited to participate in the *prasād* or reception of the holy food offered before Kṛṣṇa in the shrine room. The figures of Kṛṣṇa and his companions were of miniature size and were enthroned on a small altar raised about four feet from the floor by means of gradine. The coverings of the altar and steps, which were in different colors, were changed daily. In addition, a small *punkhā* was suspended above the throne and was set in motion by vigorous pulls on a cord during certain parts of the ceremonial. The steps leading up to the altar were used for displaying the toys of Kṛṣṇa, including hockey sticks, balls, and chess boards. Some of these were made of precious metals, and others of wood. The shrine itself was inaccessible to any but the officiant who had bathed ritually before beginning the divine service in the morning. Other witnesses of the ceremony stood before the open doors of the shrine. I subsequently met the elder brother on several occasions. He was a very quiet man with a somewhat distracted air, as though even while walking about he were in meditation. He usually spoke only in the periods when he offered prayers in the shrine room, but he smiled often with a certain radiance.[10]

In addition to these religious activities with the family, I attended a yoga class which the brothers who ran the shop were interested in, and I entertained the same brothers at my home for tea. Their household was run on traditional lines to the extent that I never conversed with an adult female member of the family although they brought me refreshments during my visits. At one ceremony I witnessed the elder brother's wife helping him in the rituals in the shrine room.

The Future of the Encounter

As the previous material indicates, my study of the Vallabha sect was carried on within the two primary elements of the religious structure, that is, the literary sources and the liturgical tradition. Future work would have to include, first of all a deepening of the understanding of the literature. This problem is enhanced in the light of a comment made by a Vallabha pandit whom I visited, who declared that the

[10] The absorption of the devotees in the life of the deity is quite extraordinary. For them there is simply no separation from the sacred world in the midst of human life because the center of their home, the shrine room, is a Vṛṇdāvana in miniature. There Lord Kṛṣṇa recapitulates daily the charming life of the Divine Child and showers his devotees with blessings. It has become evident to the followers of Vallabha that Kṛṣṇa favors them because of their love for him. Kṛṣṇa makes them happy in a life of fulness, of material well-being and spiritual enjoyment.

poems of Sūrdās cannot be taken simply at face value since they are filled with allegories and cryptic meanings that can only be understood when one has studied with a teacher qualified to reveal their hidden side. If this is the case, then some measures must be taken to try to find the resources for such secondary interpretations, even though the superficial difficulties of accurately translating medieval *Braj* dialect are still being overcome. The liturgical books of the sect, which have been published and are in free circulation, constitute another special area of investigation. In addition, the philosophical teachings of Vallabha require further study. In this last area, the researcher is aided by the extensive work of translating and interpretation done by such scholars as S. N. Das Gupta and the Jesuits from De Nobili College.

With respect to the liturgical tradition, it seems evident that a considerable amount of time will be required to overcome the general reluctance of the Vallabhite hierarchy to be interviewed by a Westerner or to establish the kind of rapport necessary for easy movement among various levels or elements in the sect. Because of the aestheticizing tendency of the Vallabhite worship, it would be valuable to preserve the ceremonies of the various shrines, or their exemplary observances, in the form of colored slides, motion pictures, and so on. This is the more necessary because of the rapid decay of regular observance in the Vallabhite sect, a fact commented on by several members who lamented the decline of wealth, leisure, and trained persons to carry on the worship with the same splendor as formerly.

Somewhere between these two elements lies an area of what might be called the secular history of the sect; for example, its involvement in social issues in the nineteenth century. Before embarking on a study of this kind of material, one must decide whether it sheds light on religious structures within the Vallabhite movement, or on Vaiṣṇavism and Hinduism as a whole, or whether it is more properly the concern of other specialists.

As regards my friendships with members of the Vallabha community, several things might be said. First of all, for several months before meeting members of the sect, I had been searching about the temples and religious byways of ancient Indian cities and had always been taken for an observer and felt that all I did do was observe. If I did feel that I had shared an experience with a group worshiping in a temple, for example, I did so only to the extent of the contrivances of my own sensibility and Western background. Therefore, when a Hindu religious community welcomed me personally to participate to an extent in their religious life, in spite of our mutual strangeness, I felt that I had found a way to go behind the surface of things. But I shall have more to say of that in a moment.

Second, such relationships in addition to being "part of the business" have a character involving ethical decisions. I conducted my research with the full knowledge of my friends that I might use my impressions and the material of our discussions for scholarly purposes, and it seems likely to me that the future of such research involving personal relationships is even more promising for the India of tomorrow since the time is nearly here when the Hindu religious community will be as open to inspection as, say, the American Christian community is today. Nevertheless, there is a problem that needs to be studied concerning the lengths to which one may exploit such relationships for the purpose of acquiring additional quantities of information. Doubtless an ethic of interpersonal relations should operate in the method of the historico-religious researcher.[11]

From the over-all point of view it seems possible that India will follow the example of the West, where often the most revealing things about society appear in the form of certain technical and scholarly "confessions," of which the literature of sociology and cultural anthropology abound. No

[11] It seems obvious that an ethic of existential encounter is what is required. It is impossible, aside from hermeneutical technique, for a researcher in History of Religions to consider the religions which he studies (and the persons who embody them) simply as objectifications of culture. A common meeting before the sacred and the religious object must induce the perception in the researcher of a shared humanity, with its ethical corollaries.

doubt members of the Vallabhite and other communities will themselves institute studies that will greatly increase our understanding of presently obscure aspects of their society.

The Structure of Field Method and the Problem of Understanding

From the preceding delineation of the content of a model problem in historico-religious research, certain minimal conclusions may perhaps be drawn with respect to a method of approach that might be called field method. In the first place, let me reaffirm that I feel the poignant tension that exists between the desire to know the whole of Hinduism and the necessity of having to live, in a scholarly sense, from moment to moment at some deeper level of one of its aspects. The illustrative problem in this paper is one of several that might have been developed on the basis of excursions abroad throughout India in an attempt to acquire some visual, perhaps even tactile, conception of the total religious being that is Indian religion. For any researcher in the field there will be opportunities to go for a brief time, a day or even a week, for research on a wide variety of subjects. But even after several of such widely varied types of experiences, filled with illuminating moments and creating intriguing possibilities, one will have to concede that one has only troubled the surface of mysterious waters. In practice the researcher will have to settle down finally to go below the surface—on a voyage that involves labor.

His work, it seems to me, will consist of certain interlocking progressions.

(1) In the first place, if he is studying in an area where he needs additional, even consummate, linguistic competence, he will have to continue to study languages in a more or less formal sense.

(2) Directly related to the first is the usual necessity of having to carry out textual analysis in order to have materials with which to pursue research. At this point additional technical help is often required in the form of specialized tutoring by native speakers who are also scholars.

(3) He will have to consider the source materials in their fullest extent. He will have to read previous interpretations, examine new sources, and work with a wide variety of subsidiary interpretive materials, including anthropological and sociological field studies and the relevant comments of other types of historians. Much of this work, to be sure, may be saved for periods of research at home, in libraries in the West, and so on. Nevertheless, an adequate conception of the available source materials is often impossible without firsthand investigation of specialized libraries in the field. Often, too, the required sources are more easily obtainable in the field.

(4) It becomes necessary, given the incomplete development of other techniques, to enter at some stage into personal contact with representatives of the religious community as well as to devote time to examination of iconography, temples, and paraphernalia and presentation of worship. It is my contention that religious expression is a product of human experience and that it unfolds its meanings when one learns to understand (if possible, to recapitulate) the experience of another. The difficulty of such interpersonal relations in foreign lands, especially in the area of religious faith, should be obvious, but they are as worthy of conscientious work as any other aspect of one's total field method. How else shall one come to know the human reality of particular expressions of religious faith? Much can be learned in the same way from observing the uses of art and ritual in worship, as exemplified in the motifs of religious expression.

(5) Of course it is taken for granted that the researcher, as a historian of religions, acknowledges the uniqueness of the religious experience and its expression within the total realm of human possibility, and so his field method must involve accurate and sensitive reporting. What is seen and heard, what is lived or endured, must be applied directly to the exposition of the structure of religious faith. Historical and other materials will attain new measures of life under the stimulation of the researcher's lived and recorded experience.

These five points, which are drawn from experience in

handling a specific area of study in the field, are not in any measure intended to exhaust the total method of historico-religious interpretation. But let me advert to a final, perhaps meritorious, aspect of the method here preliminarily conceived. It implies a commitment on the part of the researcher to a specific religious expression to the limit of what phenomenologists mean by understanding. From the vantage of such commitment, the researcher may look forth upon the whole religion of which he intensively surveys only a part and begin to see clearly its whole meaning. The experience is analogous to the experience of what is called commitment in Christian faith. From their discrete vantages on the many articulations in the Christian body, Christians can perceive the whole with gradually developing clarity. May we not say, axiomatically, therefore, that the maturation of our total understanding comes from particular understandings, given their subsequent and continuous intercombinations with the whole?

8

The History of Religions and the Study of Islām

CHARLES J. ADAMS

The purpose of this paper is to offer for discussion some remarks on methodological problems that arise in the effort to understand certain aspects of Islām. Specifically, this essay will explore the relationship between Islamic Studies and the History of Religions in recent days. What follows shall to some degree be autobiographical. The reader's indulgence is requested for approaching the subject through the avenue of personal history and experience, but such a method has seemed the best and easiest one for delineating the problems to be discussed. In any event my purposes are serious.

Since leaving the University of Chicago some years ago to pursue specialized training in Islamic Studies, I have often had occasion to reflect upon developments and trends in the study of History of Religions in relation to the field of specialization I had chosen. Having been infected with some of the enthusiasm of Joachim Wach and imbued with respect for his comprehensive and systematic approach to the study of religion, I advanced into the Islamics field with the expectation that a deeper knowledge of what scholars had done and were doing in the History of Religions would prove to be among the most valuable of resources for the work that lay ahead. I understood my growing interest in the religious life of the Muslim community as a specification of a more general interest in the religious life of mankind as a whole. It seemed appropriate — indeed, imperative — if one were to progress far, or ever to speak with any authority, to equip oneself with the tools, methods, and content of technical scholarship in some one special field; but the concern for greater depth of knowledge of one historical religious tradition was in no sense a renunciation of the broader aims of History of Religions. Quite the contrary; my expectation was that greater involvement in the study of Islam would bring me ever closer to the more universal interests of historians of religions. Or put the other way around, it was anticipated that the growing insights and developing methods of the History of Religions would prove a major guide to an expanding and deepening grasp of Islamic religiousness. Basing my expectations on the example of the illustrious Wach, I though to gain from my colleagues in the History of Religions the conceptual tools for an ever sharper analysis of the Islamic tradition and for a more lucid understanding of the relationships among its diverse elements as well as of its structural connections with other traditions.

These expectations have not been realized. As time has gone by, it has proven increasingly difficult to see a direct and fructifying relationship between the activities of Islamicists and those of historians of religions. At first this fact was the cause of some uneasiness for me personally. I suspected a gross intellectual failure to be at the root of my inability to make a connection. On the face of things, it appeared obvious that the broad objectives of History of Religions to arrive at an understanding of religious phenomena qua "religious" should play directly and immediately into the concerns of one studying the tradition and forms of Islamic religiousness. But it was not so. Instead, the desire to follow both areas of study resulted in my being pulled in two diverging intellectual directions. As an Islamicist, I did not find that the scholarly work in History of Religions compelled an avid interest because of its bearing on my own peculiar concerns in the field of Islamics. Eventually, though reluctantly, I came to accept the conclusion that the main thrust of scholarship in History of Religions in our day has little relevance, even little interest, for students of Islam. For the moment I am not prepared to argue that things should have been otherwise, only to record the conclusions of my personal experience and my impressions of the views of my colleagues in the Islamics field.

There are, it would seem, two principal factors in the situation. First, there is the fact that historians of religions, as such, have dealt but little with Islamic data and made only a relatively small original contribution to the growing store of knowledge about the Islamic peoples and their religious tradition. The burden of work in this field has been borne by Arabists, Iranists, Indianists, and so on working as historians and philologists in a relatively restricted area of concern.[1] Exceptions there are, to be sure; one thinks immediately of such persons as Tor Andrae in the previous generation of European scholars or Helmer Ringgren and Anne Marie Schimmel in the present one. For the most part, however, it is almost as though the body of Islamic materials that might serve the cause of the historian of religions had been ruled out of consideration on some a priori basis, so little is the attention given to it. It is well known and often commented upon that Islam and the Muslims have attracted far fewer students in the West and on the whole received a far less enthusiastic and sympathetic treatment by scholars than have other important religious traditions, such as those of India, of the Buddhists, of classical antiquity, and of the ancient Near East.[2] The reasons for the normally negative attitude of scholars, even professional Islamicists, toward Islamic piety and the relative neglect of things Islamic would be interesting to explore if we had the time. Whatever the reasons may be, recent historians of religions, as historians of religions, have largely ignored Islam to work in other fields and have had very little, indeed, to say that would stimulate, provoke, or contribute to the interests of students of Islām. As Ismā'īl al-Fārūqī has put it with only slight exaggeration: "So little is the Western historian of religions nowadays equipped in Islamics that the discipline, to which he has hardly contributed anything, does not seem to

[1] In recent times behavioral scientists have also given attention to the Islamic tradition and peoples, and are beginning to make substantial contributions to the store of knowledge in the field. For the present, however, it remains true that both the greatest accumulation of knowledge in the past and the greatest advances of the present have been contributed by those working within historical and philological rather than social scientific perspectives.

[2] For example, see Marshall G. S. Hodgson, "Islām and Image," *History of Religions*, III (Winter, 1964), 223 ff.

need him."[3] It is not true that Islamicists do not need the insights of historians of religions applied in their field, but it is true that they are not now having the benefit of such insights.

More important, however, is the second factor: that the great themes which have dominated the horizon of historians of religions in recent decades have not been such that would throw light on the Islamic experience or speak to the problems occupying Islamics scholarship. As the phenomenological approach, or some variation on it, whatever it may be called, has gained ever more adherents — until today almost every historian of religions is a phenomenologist — the tendency has been for scholars to seize upon certain especially exciting results of phenomenological analysis and to exploit the fields which have gained new illumination from these results. One would be foolish to criticize the course of this development. Such is the manner in which knowledge grows and scholarship advances to the conquest of new worlds. As a result of the phenomenological method and the scholarly emphases it has thrown up, our awareness of many areas of man's religiousness is vastly expanded; similarly, the phenomenological mode of thinking has served to clarify the task of the historian of religions and make it easier. Of the advance achieved through phenomenology there can be no doubt, and the historians of religions have laid a debt upon all thinking people for their contribution. But so far as understanding in the field of Islamics is concerned, there has been but small gain flowing from the preoccupations of the leading scholars. It may even be said that these very preoccupations or themes of scholarship are a principal reason for the failure of historians of religions to give attention to Islām as we have noted above.

Without going into detail, let us recall some of the more important themes around which scholarly investigation in the History of Religions has revolved in the past several decades. I am speaking now largely of Europe, since the History of Religions has been slower to develop elsewhere and in other en-

[3] Isma'il Ragi A. Al Faruqi, "History of Religions: Its Nature and Significance for Christian Education and the Muslim-Christian Dialogue," *Numen*, XII (1965), Fasc. 1, 2, p. 40.

vironments has taken a somewhat different course. One of the earliest and most fruitful themes was the inquiry into the relationship of myth and ritual. Perhaps the greatest gain from pursuing this line of work has accrued in biblical scholarship, but it has been followed in a number of other fields as well where the results achieved are impressive. Scholars have been stimulated to study the nature of myth as never before, and there now exists, as the direct outcome of this preoccupation, a considerable literature describing, analyzing, classifying, interpreting, and probing the significance of mythologies of peoples in diverse places at diverse times. From the same element in scholarly thinking has also come an emphasis upon religious cults — the study of rites and ceremonies which are at the same time the vehicle and stimulus of religious experience and one of its most important expressions. Efforts of scholars have been heavily concentrated upon the significance of rites in recent years. It is no accident, but rather an indication of where scholarly capital is invested, that the officers of the International Association for the History of Religions chose to focus the attention of the last Congress[4] of the organization upon the discussion of a certain type of rite. Intimately related to the interest in myth and ritual is the study of sacral kingship, which has been another of the great themes of historians of religions and which was the focus of the IXth Congress of the International Association for the History of Religions, held in Rome in 1958. More recently the development of studies in the field has led to a concentration upon symbolism. There is an obvious connection among these emphases as they have emerged, a connection that is both intrinsic and genetic. The development has been logical; one thing has led to another as scholars have moved out from a central body of insights.

For the student of Islām, however, the succession of emphases and the direction of development in the History of Religions has had little direct meaning. None of these emphases evokes an immediate and avid response as offering a tool to probe deeper into the Islamic tradition and forge more adequate understandings of it. The historical stuff of Islamic

[4] Held in Claremont, California, in September, 1965.

religiousness is extraordinarily, one may say almost perversely, impervious to significant analysis along the lines which the majority of historians of religions have followed and are following. At the points where History of Religions has had some of its greatest successes, it has been irrelevant to the work of Islamicists, and Islamicists have in consequence exhibited very little interest in what historians of religions have to say. Though both are students of man's religiousness, they sometimes appear to inhabit different worlds between which communication is difficult and infrequent.

The lack of communication comes about because the mainstream of the Islamic tradition is not notably rich in mythological expression, in cultic development, or in the proliferation of symbolism. As for sacral kingship, there is simply no Islamic exemplification of this phenomenon known to me. One may find some material for discussion by considering religious implications and aspects of the Khilāfat or by reflecting on the influence of old Iranian concepts of kingship on the understanding of the Khilāfat, and so on . . . but the field of research opened up by investigation of sacral kingship among the Muslims is sharply limited. There are, of course, mythological elements and ritual practices in the historical stream of Muslim religiosity. There is data for the investigator in these realms to consider, but in comparison with the Hindu tradition or that of the ancient Near East, it is very much less in both quantity and significance. In this connection it is important also to realize that some of the most elaborately developed and structured ritual activities of the Muslims — such as those surrounding the Ḥajj — are survivals from pre-Islamic times. The prospects are no more optimistic for the approach to Islām through myth and ritual. Study of the relation of these two does not seem to offer access to the heart of *Islamic* experience as it has in so many other cases. With respect to studies of symbolism, the prospects for Islamicists to profit significantly from the researches of historians of religions are much greater. In at least its Ṣūfī and Shī'ah components, the Islamic tradition has enjoyed some richness of symbolic expression, notably in poetry, and there are scholars, especially among the French students of Ṣūfism, who are alive to its significance. By contrast, Sunnism, especially as expounded, upheld, and preserved by the fuqahā', is markedly rationalist in its self-expression and determinedly iconoclastic. Its principal mode of apprehending, responding to, and expressing the sacred has been ethical. Sunnī Islām has been much more a matter of living out an ordained pattern of life than of anything else.

The problem for Islamicists in coming to terms with trends among historians of religions was dramatically exemplified in the discussion sections devoted to Islam at the XIth Congress of the International Association for the History of Religions. A group of scholars, including some of the most able and productive people now in the field, was gathered to discuss "guilt and rites of purification" among Muslims. After listening to a paper on the *wuḍū'* in which the author came to the conclusion that the ablution preceding the ritual prayer is not primarily stimulated by or classically explained in terms of feelings of guilt, the group heard another paper giving a semantic analysis of the various Qur'anic words for sin, transgression, wrongdoing, and so on. In the general discussion following, there was no more success than in the papers in speaking directly to the topic. The effort to explore the theme eventually led the group into talking at length about aspects of the doctrine of man in Islamic thought; in terms of Islamic materials and the attitude of the Islamic religious mind, the group could make no closer approximation to the theme it had been asked to consider. The conversation was valuable, but it became so as it departed from the topic to discuss Islamic concerns in an Islamic frame of reference. In that frame of reference, guilt and the ritual purification of guilt do not occupy a fundamental place. Had the group included more and better students of Ṣūfism, or had it concentrated on the ritual of the pilgrimage,[5] the discussion would perhaps have taken a different turn; I cannot say. The matter of importance is that a theme which seemed crucial to the scholars organizing

[5] There was a paper read on this subject by Harry Partin of Duke University.

the Congress and which apparently was capable of stimulating interesting exchanges among other groups did not awaken a response from Islamicists.[6] It is of some importance to emphasize that the fumbling and groping to find the revelance of the subject to their own field of study was not the result of the group's having an insular character. Muslims and non-Muslims, Shī'ah and Sunnī, Easterners and Westerners, Europeans and North Americans, Arabists and Iranists, and still others, were all represented.

In my opinion the fundamental reason why the great themes of the History of Religions in recent years have had little appeal for students of Islām lies in the fact that historians of religions have exhibited a marked preference for certain levels or types of religiousness as the objects of their study. I am speaking here still of trends in Europe more than of those in America. During the nineteenth century there were students of religion who consciously held to the theory that the so-called primitive religions were purer and more genuine representations of the human religious drive than the more complex traditions. They reasoned to this conclusion, as everyone knows, from the assumption that the "primitive" religions were closer and more faithful to the original "simple" religious responses of our earliest ancestors. As everyone also knows, this theory has long since been given up as untenable, and at least in principle it has been accepted that all religious phenomena, from whatever tradition and from whatever period of time they may be drawn, stand on an equal footing as materials for the historian of religions in his effort to understand the religious. It has also been recognized that "primitive" religiousness is by no means so "simple" and easily understandable as earlier generations had thought. In spite of the fact

[6] It would be wrong to assign too great significance to the subjects chosen for the regular meetings of the International Association for the History of Religions. The officers must select topics that will evoke a broad interest among the members, and the fact that discussion topics over a period of years show a clear relationship does not exclude the possibility that many members are interested in quite different matters. By the same token, however, the fact that the topics chosen are of interest to a number of scholars sufficient to support an international gathering shows their force in scholarly thinking.

that no contemporary scholar would be likely to subscribe to the old nineteenth-century view when speaking of methodology in the abstract, in the practice of their investigation a significant number of leading historians of religions show a bias toward primitive religions and the religions of antiquity. If one examines the standard manuals of phenomenology or the numerous studies on particular forms of the religious life, one finds that the vast majority of the material considered has been taken from primitive or ancient religious practice. There are manuals that take account of the "higher" religions, but the overwhelmingly greater emphasis in this type of literature falls upon archaic material. In deed, if not in theory, such material appears to be affirmed as richer and more important for the understanding of religion than any other. Now, there may be very good reasons for this state of affairs; I wish only to call attention to one of its consequences, that it has resulted in difficulties for those with interests outside the primitive or ancient fields — and the closer to modern times those interests come, the more imposing the difficulties — to profit from the development of History of Religions. The obverse, of course, is that the historians of religions in their turn have not realized the benefit they might have from the work of other students of religions.

To illustrate the point may I revert to the disquieting experience of the XIth Congress of the International Association for the History of Religions. The secretary, a distinguished scholar who holds his position precisely because he is a recognized spokesman for historians of religions, closed his address (to me a disappointing speech for reasons that have to do with the last section of this essay) with the admonition that we must endeavor to bridge the gap separating antiquity from the classical world and so learn truly to understand the archaic. There was, however, no corresponding emphasis on the importance or difficulty of studying more recent periods of religious history. My point is not to criticize what was said but to call attention to what was not said. It is true that we moderns have particular difficulty in penetrating the world of the archaic; it is true also that an understanding of the antique and archaic is vitally important for a comprehensive grasp of man's religiousness. My uneasiness arises only because the archaic and antique have been singled out as uniquely important areas of study. There is implied an order of priority and significance that would turn (and, in fact, has turned) scholarly attention away from a large area of man's religious experience. In spite of their richness and immediate relevance to our own lives, the more developed traditions, and especially their contemporary evolution, seem to have been relegated to a background position. Other delegates also expressed themselves, as the congress proceeded, as being suspicious of the genuine scholarly character of any study of religion in the recent past, not to speak of the living present. Those who have been closest to the development of History of Religions throughout its various phases since 1920 are distinctly uneasy with scholarship directed to any but remote periods. Excepting "primitive" religious phenomena that some scholars still seem to consider to have a timeless quality, data for the study of religion appear to gain in respectability and worth with their distance in time from the modern world.

Such an attitude is not characteristic of North American and Asian scholars or of many Englishmen, but the older generation of Europeans who have formed and led studies in the History of Religions hold it almost unanimously, if one may judge by their reaction at the Congress of the International Association for the History of Religions.

For many Islamicists there is little of encouragement or stimulation in the quest of their colleagues to unlock the mystery of the archaic view of the world. Although it can easily be demonstrated that Islām has many archaic survivals in its developed ritual and thought forms and that many Muslims are profoundly affected by archaic influence in their own personal and folk religious orientation, yet there remains a vast segment of the Islamic experience that does not fall within the realm of the archaic. This segment is, furthermore, historically the most important portion of the Islamic tradition, for it is here that one finds the elements that went into the formation of the brilliant Islamic civilization of classical and medieval times. Though it may have sprung originally from a "primitive" context and carried some signs of its origin with it (as what religion has not?), Islām is not a "primitive" religion, nor is it the connection with its "primitive" roots that constitutes its historical significance.

The point may be put in a more formal and academic fashion through Max Weber's famous distinction between two great groups of religions, the "traditional" religions and the "rationalized" religions—those that express themselves primarily, if not exclusively, in non-rational ways and those that have attained a rational and self-conscious mode of expression. Roughly, the distinction corresponds to what have sometimes been called the "lower" and the "higher" religions. On the whole, historians of religions in the past forty years have found the first group to be more interesting and more instructive. The conceptual tools they have evolved were created in response to the problems of dealing with and understanding primarily traditional and non-rationalized forms of religious expression, which are characteristic of "primitive" religions and the earlier phases of the "higher" religions. Is it not possible that the cause for the failure in communication between Islamicists and historians of religions to which I have alluded lies precisely here? For though it shares some characteristics with the first group, Islām clearly belongs to the second great division, and the methods proper to the study of the first type of religious response and expression are but ill adapted to the study of the second. It would appear necessary that attention be given to the peculiar problems of systematic understanding of the higher religions before we shall have the benefit of truly *religionswissenschaftliche* study that embraces Islam, Judaism, and Christianity in their full historical sweep. I realize well that the task of analyzing the "higher" religious traditions is enormously difficult, even more difficult in my opinion than bridging the gap between our own and the archaic world. Among the reasons for the direction scholarship in the History of Religions has taken, the sheer magnitude and formidability of giving a systematic *religionswissenschaftliche* account of the "higher" religions may, perhaps, rank with the most important. Nevertheless, until development along these lines occurs, students of Islam are likely to cling to their present historical and philological approach to their studies and to be relatively indifferent to the possibilities opened up by comparative and systematic methods.

As a final point in this essay, I should like to call attention to what many sensitive students of Islām consider to be the most important new problem on their scholarly horizon. It is a problem that historians of religions generally have yet to acknowledge. In fact, to acknowledge it and to allow oneself to be consciously concerned with it would seem for many scholars to be a betrayal of scholarship itself, a departure from the proper function of the scholar and a renunciation of the objectives of scientific inquiry.

The problem may be put simply thus: in our day Muslims hear and respond to what Islamicists say. In former times the Western scholar interested in Islam could afford to be indifferent to the reception his writing might have among those people whose heritage was his subject matter. In all likelihood there would have been no response anyway since such writing was intended for a small closed audience of like-minded scholars and would scarcely be known beyond such circles. The character of the modern world with its easy communications has changed all of that. What is said in Chicago and what is written in Montreal are heard and read in Cairo and Karachi. The response is immediate and strong, and, moreover, it is important. This new situation, which has forced itself increasingly upon the attention of students of Islām in recent years, has given a novel dimension to Islamic Studies and has a number of implications that have been the cause of much pondering and of some departures in thought.

One of the implications is that the Islamicist now finds himself drawn into personal relations with the modern representatives of the tradition he is endeavoring to study. But the responses that his work inevitably evokes, if he is at all sensitive, he is made vividly aware that he is speaking of historical events, developments, documents, personalities, and so on, that have a profound and immediate religious meaning in the lives of some millions of his contemporaries. Such a realization is sobering, for it lays a moral responsibility upon anyone who ventures into discussion of matters so charged with emotion and value. If he is alive to human feelings, he does not deal lightly and indifferently with things that represent the most precious insights and values of others. The scholar's new situation of writing and speaking in the glare of public scrutiny poses some extraordinarily intractable dilemmas. Although he is now compelled to be sensitive to the tone of his words and the responses they will create, as a scholar he is also under obligation to be true to his own best insights. It will never do to distort or to forego stating what one sincerely believes to be the truth because of the possible discomfort it may give to another. A Western Islamics scholar does not speak from the perspective of Islamic faith and can scarcely be expected to; but whether he will or not, he enters into communication with persons who receive his words and respond to them in the light of such faith. There is here an important and complex issue requiring the attention of everyone who labors in the Islamics field. The dilemma will be clear if one reflects upon a concrete problem, for example, the attitude appropriate to a scholar working with the Qur'an. If he treats that famous book as he would any other piece of literature, considering it as the product of the personality of the prophet and of historical and environmental factors in his life, he cannot avoid coming afoul of Muslim convictions and giving grave offense to Muslim sensibilities. What to a Western-trained scholar appears as a straightforward critical stance toward the Qur'an may be seen by Muslim eyes as an attack on the Holy Book and, indeed, upon the entire structure of Muslim religiosity. To ignore what critical historical scholarship has taught, however, would be unthinkable for the Western scholar. The tension between these seemingly irreconcilable demands is part of the problem that the new situation poses for Islamics scholars.

A second implication of the new situation is that Islamicists are confronted by a new criterion for the adequacy of their understanding and formulations. In our day whatever may be put forward as an interpretation of any aspect of Islamic experience will be quickly and searchingly examined by those who themselves share Islamic faith and who are formed by its outlook. When the Islamicist declares that the meaning of a given institution, doctrine, practice, or development is thus and so, he must be prepared to face the judgment of the very people he is talking about. If from the depths of their own involvement they find his grasp of the matter to be inadequate, there is no higher court of appeal to which he may turn. His purpose, after all, is to describe the religion of Muslims in its reality and its depth. If Muslims cannot recognize his descriptions as applying to themselves and saying something true about themselves and the tradition which has formed them, the conclusion is almost unavoidable that his scholarship has missed the mark. It is not a mere consideration of sentiment or desire to avoid hurting or displeasing Muslims that figures here; there is a substantive problem of considerable weight. The Islamicist is being challenged by his novel circumstances in the modern world to learn to speak in two realms of discourse at the same time. To be adequate to his task, he must be able to satisfy all the conditions demanded by rigorous critical study, that is, to communicate with his colleagues in the academic tradition of historical and philological scholarship and in the same moment to speak in words that reflect faithfully and truly what is happening in Muslims' hearts and minds. Satisfaction with anything less seems to me admission of a duality of truth that I find unacceptable.

The point just stated is susceptible of easy distortion and caricature. Obviously, one cannot allow the unlettered peasant or the narrow-minded ʿĀlim to sit in judgment over the learned scholar with serious intentions. For many Muslims it would undoubtedly be most desirable if Western scholars and other non-Muslims kept their opinions about Islām to themselves. It is not such persons or the necessity of securing their agreement to scholarly understanding that I have in mind when I suggest that Muslim reaction constitutes a serious criterion for the earnest scholar. What must be taken seriously are the responses of learned and sober Muslims of good will. Similarly, it is possible to object that the criterion suggested has no relevance to the study of the Muslim past. The men of long ago are no longer with us, and at best we can only speculate about what their responses to the work of present-day scholars might be. Furthermore, on the face of it, there is no obvious reason why a Muslim should necessarily have a better grasp of the Islamic past and its mood than anyone else. There are numerous instances in the history of scholarship to suggest that an outsider enjoys some advantage in the attempt to win a critical grasp of a religious tradition and its development. These arguments are weighty and must be taken seriously. But so far as studies of the recent past and of contemporary developments are concerned, they do not weaken the point. The point also has relevance for every effort to state the enduring religious meaning of aspects of Islām, which is the peculiar concern of the historian of religions. Even with respect to the distant past, it must be remembered that the Muslim scholar is the inheritor of that tradition which still lives in him; he enjoys, therefore, an initial advantage over most of those others who seek to recreate and interpret that tradition through their scholarship. In any event, the point that Islamics scholarship should be conscious of its judgment by Muslim opinion is not a suggestion for some kind of arrangements for submitting proposed publications to a Muslim jury. It is rather the attempt to indicate a standard and an ideal for scholarship, toward which we in the Islamics field should strive regardless of the practical difficulties, disappointments, and even rebuffs that we may face. The argument is also a recognition of the new situation we face in the contemporary world, as individual men and as scholars.

The third implication of the new situation for students of Islām is this: they have, even as disinterested scholars and as outsiders, become participants in the process of Islamic becoming. We have already made the point that Muslims read and know what is written and thought in distant places. The results of scholarship are taken up by Muslims as part of the equipment with which they approach and appropriate their own heritage. That is to say, not only do Muslims respond externally to the views of scholars; they take up into themselves new advances in understanding so that their own view of themselves and of the past of their community is changed and reformed by these new elements. One may in all soberness claim that a major causal factor in the present-day upsurge or renaissance of Muslim self-consciousness has been Western Islamics scholarship. The devoted and laborious efforts of Western students of Islām, particularly during the nineteenth century but continuing into this one, rediscovered for the uses of Muslim piety, as well as for the uses of scholarship, many treasures of the Islamic past to which Muslims themselves had long since grown oblivious. One large reason why Muslims have a new interest in being Muslims and a new confidence in the richness of their heritage lies in the work of Western and non-Muslim editors of texts who have made it possible to know what the heritage really was. The scholar may not intend or want to affect the modern development of Islām, or even be in the slightest interested in that development, but to the extent that his scholarship has merit and depth he will become a factor in the new outreach of Muslims in spite of himself. This is true even of the scholar who studies very early periods of Islamic history and development. As an example consider Ignaz Goldziher's monumental study of the *aḥādīth* of the Prophet.[7] Though Goldziher was the very ideal exemplification of the philollogist-historian with purely scientific objectives before his eyes, he has, nonetheless, been a powerful element in shaping the directions that Muslim thought is now taking. His contribution has been not only to the understanding of the Islamic past but also to the newly unfolding and still emerging self-understanding of the Muslims of the present. Goldziher's work is a part of the fabric of scholarship, but it is also a constituent of the fabric of Islam itself in the twentieth

[7] The reference is to Ignaz Goldziher, "Über die Entwicklung des Hadiths," *Muhammadanische Studien* (Hildesheim: Georg Olms, 1961), Vol. II.

century. And all of this has occurred without Goldziher willing it or, perhaps, even being aware of the possible consequences of his researches. We Islamicists, whether we wish it or not and whether we like it or not, have been precipitated by the conditions of modern life into a new relationship with those whom we study. Since we cannot avoid affecting our Muslim contemporaries in quite vital ways through our work, is it not better that we should become self-conscious about what we are doing? And is it not also an aspect of our very scholarship that we should seek this self-consciousness? Surely, it is neither shameful nor unscholarly to attempt to see clearly the implications of what one does. The experience of the contemporary Islamicist in his new situation has forced him to recognize, as others apparently have not yet done, that his scholarship bears a contemporary and religious relevance of the most profound kind.

Allāhu a'lam.

9

Toward a Unified Interpretation of Japanese Religion

H. BYRON EARHART

In spite of some pioneering studies on Japanese religion in general and on specific individual religions of Japan, it must be admitted that, in the West, there is no unified interpretation of Japanese religious history. It is unfortunate that Western studies of Japanese religions have tended to splinter apart into isolated treatments rather than to contribute toward a general understanding of Japanese religious history as forming one major religious tradition.[1] Even the best Western studies of Japanese religion represent just so many fragmented, separate glimpses of the Japanese scene. Indeed, it is sometimes difficult to see how these studies could have been conducted within the context of the same historical tradition. A major premise of this essay is that Japanese religious history forms a logical area of research which deserves a more comprehensive understanding than can be supplied by unconnected studies. This essay will advance some important reasons why such a unified interpretation has not been achieved and then suggest how it might be achieved: first, a hypothesis will be posed outlining briefly four reasons why this unified interpretation has not appeared; second, to support this hypothesis, some Western literature and Western scholarship on Japanese religion will be treated;[2] and

[1] Joseph M. Kitagawa has given a general picture of the earliest Japanese religion in his "Prehistoric Background of Japanese Religion," *History of Religions*, II (Winter, 1963), 292–328. His recent book, *Religion in Japanese History* (New York: Columbia University Press, 1966), was not available at the time of writing.

[2] Only a minimum of Western literature can be cited. To document this essay exhaustively would require a bibliographical monograph, but this is not our task. For the same reason, no attempt has been made to treat the Japanese literature on these questions.

third, illustrations from the writer's limited research will be presented to suggest how a unified interpretation might be achieved.

In this essay I would like to maintain a critical attitude toward previous Western literature in presenting my proposal for a rather new approach to the study of Japanese religious history. Accordingly, it may even be of some value to overemphasize the criticism of previous literature in order to contrast it more effectively with the proposed method of study. The writer's purpose is to argue for the validity of a new approach; once this new approach is recognized, any overstatement will be corrected in extending this approach to concrete material.

At the outset it is best to list some basic reasons why a unified interpretation of Japanese religions has not been achieved.

(1) The first and primary reason has to do with the way in which the study of Japanese religion in the West began. It began with the study of mythology, and subsequently there has remained the mistaken tendency to confuse an official mythology with the religious life of the people.

(2) The second reason for failure is the limited aspects of Japanese religions that have been taken up for study. The overwhelming tendency has been to investigate the formal organization of the various religions, not only the official mythology but also the formal shrine organization of *Shintō*; in Buddhism, attention has been focused especially upon scriptures and doctrine; even in the study of the so-called new religions there has been a one-sided emphasis on the ethical and theological aspects. All this has resulted in the neglect of folk religion and popular aspects.

(3) The third reason is the high degree of compartmentalization, separating not only *Shintō* and Buddhism, but also folk religion, on the one hand, and *Shintō* and Buddhism, on the other hand. This compartmentalization does not correspond to the historical realities of mutual influence among

these three religious currents; furthermore, it artificially excludes such important religious movements as *Shugendō* and *Onmyō-dō.*

(4) The fourth reason, more general in nature, is that there simply has been no method for interpreting the religions of Japan. For example, *Shintō* has been seen in terms of *Shintō*, and Buddhism in terms of Buddhism, and other religious factors have sometimes been forced into these categories. The general methodological suggestion of this essay is that we must analyze such topics as religious phenomena within Japanese history, acknowledging all the relevant elements and influences and arriving at a general interpretation. It is not sufficient to label elements Buddhist or *Shintō* or to use such general terms as Taoistic and shamanistic influences. On the contrary, it is always necessary to demonstrate concretely the religious function of a symbol or ritual and to verify the actual significance of Taoistic or shamanistic influence.[3] That is, we must define religious phenomena within the history of Japanese religion, without compartmentalizing them artificially. In this process, of course, the problem of hermeneutics or interpretation, which is crucial to all religious studies, will arise. However, if my approach is followed, we should reap a twofold reward: on the one hand, we should acquire a deeper understanding of the individual religious phenomena, and, on the other hand, we should develop a more coherent picture of how these individual religious phenomena constitute the fabric of Japanese religious history.

In the second part of this essay we will examine in greater detail the four important reasons for the failure to achieve a unified interpretation of Japanese religions. We will take them up individually, showing how each of them constituted an obstacle to a more comprehensive understanding of Japanese religious history in Western scholarship.

[3] See Mircea Eliade, "Methodological Remarks on the Study of Religious Symbolism," in *The History of Religions: Essays in Methodology*, ed. Mircea Eliade and Joseph M. Kitagawa (Chicago: University of Chicago Press, 1959), pp. 86–107.

(1) Let us examine the proposition that from the beginning of Western studies on Japanese religion an undue emphasis has been placed on mythology. This proposition is clarified by comparing early Western studies of Japanese religion with the contemporary Science of Religion, which was just emerging as a scholarly discipline. It is widely recognized that *Religionswissenschaft* – known in English as Science of Religions or Comparative Religion and, more appropriately, as History of Religions – began as a modern discipline with F. Max Müller. This "father" of History of Religions, like his collaborators and first successors, was able to establish the new discipline mainly because of the accumulation of philological work already completed on Indian scriptures and Indian religion. Of course, Müller himself was instrumental in increasing such scholarly materials, through his own personal scholarship as well as through the publication of the *Sacred Books of the East*. And, to be sure, even in Müller's day there was some literature on topics such as anthropology, Islam, and Chinese religion. But it is difficult to overestimate the influence of Western research in Indian philology, mythology, and religion on the founding of the History of Religions. Indian studies began early, and, more important, there was the very natural connection between matters "Indian" and "European." The familiar adjective "Indo-European" has been applied to philology, mythology, and even religion. Thus, the various disciplines dealing with India, such as Indology, philology, and Buddhology, came to be grafted onto the earlier European studies of languages, classics, and religion. Because of this long-standing interest and because of the voluminous scholarly research available, the study of the History of Religions in the West – even to this day – has been associated first and foremost with the religions of India.

However, the development of Western studies of Japanese religion contrasts sharply with that of Western studies of Indian religion. For research on Japan, especially research on Japanese religion, has been played two nasty tricks by historical fate. In the first place, Japan was a relatively isolated country until the Meiji Restoration of 1867, when the policy of isolation was replaced by a policy of openness to the West.[4] In the second place, even after study of Japan had begun, it was neither stimulated nor maintained actively by the kind of natural linguistic and historical links which existed between India and Europe. In short, the study of Japanese religions began much later than the study of Indian religions and has progressed rather slowly with fewer scholars.[5] Therefore, there is not yet a large corpus of translations and research concerning Japanese religion.

If we continue the comparison with the study of Indian religions, there are at least two points of similarity in the emerging study of Japanese religion. The first point of similarity is that the earliest studies of Japanese religion, as one might expect, were philological, or at least "literary," in their emphasis upon the ancient records. The second point of similarity is equally predictable: especially in the analysis of ancient records, *Shintō* was taken to be the indigenous religion of Japan and interpreted by means of the current scholarly theories of "nature worship" and "ancestor worship."[6] We shall see that the study of Japanese religion has never escaped this early mode of interpretation.

[4] In 1867 Müller had already used the term "Science of Religion" in the sense of an independent discipline for the study of religion. See F. Max Müller, *Chips from a German Workshop*, Vol. I (sub-titled "Essays on the Science of Religion") (New York: Charles Scribner and Co., 1869), pp. xi, xix–xxi. In 1872 this was followed by *Lectures on the Science of Religion* . . . (New York: Charles Scribner & Co., 1872). The lectures were delivered in 1870.

[5] Even in the study of Indian religions there was the tendency to neglect popular religion or at least to separate it from the literary and more philosophical traditions. "This preoccupation with philosophical forms excluded the possibility of taking ritual, cultic and liturgical expressions, acts and objects very seriously. It implied the study of the traditional writings of an elite; hence, hardly any attention was given to popular religious forms in the villages and among the tribal peoples." (See Kees W. Bolle, "Devotion and Tantra," *Studies of Esoteric Buddhism and Tantrism* [Koyasan, Japan: Koyasan University, 1965], p. 217). This kind of problem is with us in every area of the history of religions but has been especially acute in the study of Japanese religions.

[6] An interesting statement of the conflict between these two rival theories for explaining Japanese religion was given by Michel Revon at a time (1908) when scholarly argument was still hotly joined. See his "Ancestor-Worship and Cult of the Dead (Japanese)," *Encyclo-*

Now let us look at two translations of ancient records which were crucial for the early study of Japanese religion. In 1882 Basil Hall Chamberlain published his translation of "*Ko-ji-ki*, or Records of Ancient Matters."[7] In 1896 W. G. Aston brought out his translation of *Nihongi: Chronicles of Japan from the Earliest Times to A.D. 697*.[8] These two works may be described briefly as including the cosmogony, mythology, religious practices, and "history" of early Japan recorded by court order. Although these two translations are obviously important for the study of Japanese religion, in Western literature – especially secondary literature – they have assumed an importance completely out of proportion to their actual significance. Along with Aston's *Shinto, the Way of the Gods*;[9] they have probably exerted a more widespread influence upon the Western interpretation of Japanese religion than any other scholarly works. Handbooks of Comparative Religion and most secondary treatments of Japanese religion in particular persist in treating Japanese religion largely in terms of these two translations. That is, they have tried to see in this mythology of court and priests the watershed of the religious life and faith of the Japanese people. However, even though these ancient works are valuable sources, they have their own limitations. Contemporary scholars of Japanese religion are well aware of this fact, but it is worth repeating. In the words of one Japanese scholar,

> When we go through other parts of the above-mentioned two books [*Kojiki* and *Nihongi*], *Shoku-nihon-gi* (Chronicles of Japan, Continued) and the entire *Manyoshu* (Ancient Japanese Anthology), we know

paedia of Religion and Ethics, I (1908), 455–57. For a more recent treatment, see Franz Kiichi Numazawa, *Die Weltanfänge in der Japanische Mythologie* (Freiburg in der Schweiz: Paulusdruckerei, 1946), pp. 207–35, esp. p. 217.

[7] Published in *Transactions of the Asiatic Society of Japan*, Vol. X (1882), Suppl.

[8] Originally published in *Transactions of the Japan Society* (London, 1896), Suppl. I (2 vols.); reprinted, two volumes in one with original pagination, by Allen and Unwin in 1956.

[9] Published by Longmans, Green in 1905. Nor should we overlook the pioneering work of E. M. Satow and Karl Florenz.

> that the deities in the myths have, with very few exceptions, nothing to do with those actually believed in and enshrined.[10]

But in spite of the relatively unimportant role of formal mythology in Japanese religion, handbooks have persistently over-valued its significance by their use of these readily available translations. As I have indicated, this prevalent misunderstanding of the older Japanese mythology originated, at least in part, in the dominant emphasis on mythology in the early stages of the development of the Science of Religion.[11] To discuss this problem further would detract us from our major concern, but we must not forget the historical and methodological lessons to be drawn from this discussion. Historically, the study of Japanese religion began with the study of mythology. This starting point has meant, methodologically, that mythology has too often been mistaken for religion.

(2) Next we shall examine the second reason — over emphasis on the formal organization of the various religions — why a unified interpretation of Japanese religion has not been realized. We have just seen that early Japanese mythology is often mistaken as the source and mainstay of Japanese religion. Stated in the extreme, another mistaken conception, which builds upon the former, holds that *Shintō* includes all indigenous and folk religion in Japanese history. However, the highly organized present-day form of *Shintō*,

[10] Toshiaki Harada, "The Origin of Community Worship," in *Religious Studies in Japan* (Tōkyō: Maruzen, 1959), pp. 213–18, esp. p. 216.

[11] The day is long past when Greek religion, for example, could be viewed solely in terms of myth and mythology. As W. K. C. Guthrie has remarked, "Yet although the science of religious history was born, it remained in essence mythology. . . . Before the study of Greek religion could be set on a wider and firmer basis, two other sciences had to be developed which as yet could hardly be said to exist, namely archaeology and anthropology." Guthrie has given a finely balanced treatment of the study of Greek religion by a judicious use of these approaches, side-stepping the rationalistic interpretations of the last century. See his *The Greeks and Their Gods* (Boston: Beacon Press, 1950, 1954), Intro. and Chap. I, esp. p. 6. A similar reinterpretation of Japanese religion on broader lines is long overdue.

which should properly be called "shrine *Shintō*" (*jinja Shintō*), not only is a relatively late product but in fact includes within it both Chinese and Buddhist influence.[12] And to put the problem quite honestly, there are dominant themes within Japanese folk religion which must be recognized in order to understand both *Shintō* and Japanese Buddhism.[13] As far as Western scholarship is concerned, a new interpretation of *Shintō* is required, one that incorporates integrally the festivals and beliefs of the people as well as the various historical influences.

It is ironic that, even in the study of Japanese folk religion, popular traditions and practices have been greatly neglected. No Western scholar has made such careful and extensive studies of Japanese folklore as the late M. W. de Visser, but even his work, according to a contemporary Dutch scholar of Japanese folk religion (who borrows Robert Redfield's terminology), relies almost completely on the "great tradition" and leaves the "little tradition" almost untouched.[14]

[12] In part, this confusion is a matter of terminology and definition. For example, *Shintō* can be broken down into "Popular Shinto," "Domestic Shinto," "Sectarian Shinto," "Imperial Household Shinto," "Shrine Shinto," "The Grand Shrine of Ise," and "State Shinto." For a *Shintō* scholar's interpretation see Sokyō Ono, *Shintō. The Kami Way* (Tokyo: Bridgeway Press, 1962), pp. 12–15. However, it is not simply a matter of terminology, for the multiplication of so many "Shinto" cattegories is quite ambiguous and forced. One could even argue that greater clarity would be lent to the discussion if use of the word "Shinto" were temporarily suspended.

[13] The writer was firmly persuaded of this fact in an analysis of religious phenomena associated with Japanese mountains. Documentation cannot be given here, but there is sufficient evidence to conclude that both *Shintō* and Buddhism were absorbed into a common current of folk belief and folk practices. See my "A Religious Study of the Mount Haguro Sect of *Shugendō*: An Example of Japanese Mountain Religion" (unpublished Ph.D. dissertation, University of Chicago, 1965), esp. Vol. I, Part II, pp. 79–234. (This dissertation is cited hereinafter as "Haguro *Shugendō*.")

[14] C. Ouwehand, *Namazu-e and Their Themes. An Interpretative Approach to Some Aspects of Japanese Folk Religion* (Leiden: E. J. Brill, 1964). On page x Ouwehand says, "It may seem that I am now picking up, fifty years later, the thread spun by my predecessor at the National Museum of Ethnology, the late Professor M. W. de Visser, in his pioneering monographs, but there are in fact great differences between then and now." He cites the fact that "Yanagita Kunio inaugu-

We shall not elaborate here upon the problem of Japanese folk religion but only say that in general the state of Western scholarship on Japanese folk religion is similar to that of *Shintō* scholarship in the West: genuinely popular elements have been almost completely overlooked, and even when they have been recognized, they have not been related to the religious expressions of the priestly and literary classes. This matter will be discussed later.

The study of Japanese Buddism is marked by the publication of several outstanding works. One thinks immediately of De Visser's two-volume work *Ancient Buddhism in Japan*[15] and Sir Charles Eliot's *Japanese Buddhism.*[16] The former is concentrated on the use of scriptures, and the latter emphasizes doctrine. Even if one were to concentrate on such formal aspects of Buddhism as these, one would find very few studies of Buddhist rites.[17] A much more serious deficiency is the great neglect of Buddhism as a truly Japanese development. Like Sir Charles Eliot, most Western scholars approach Japanese Buddhism in terms of Indian Buddhism. If we wished to caricature this approach, we might say that Eliot climbed the highest Japanese mountain and faced India in order to trace Japanese Buddhism back to India. At any rate, Eliot's approach is more concerned with "Buddhism in Japan" than with *Japanese* Buddhism. Merely to mention

rated modern Japanese folklore study," and although De Visser became aware of Yanagita's work, he left such research for his students. Ouwehand concludes that "since de Visser had no more opportunity to draw on the unceasing stream of publications produced by the study of Japanese folklore for which Yanagita provided so firm a foundation, his work in this field, carried out with such meticulousness and assiduity, remained limited to a systematic compilation of data taken primarily from the sources of the 'great tradition.'"

[15] De Visser, *Ancient Buddhism in Japan. Sūtras and Ceremonies in Use in the Seventh and Eighth Centuries A.D. and Their History in Later Times* (Leiden: E. J. Brill, 1935).

[16] Eliot, *Japanese Buddhism* (London: Edward Arnold, 1935; reprinted, London: Routledge & Kegan Paul, 1959).

[17] For example, see Shōjun Bandō *et al., A Bibliography on Japanese Buddhism* (Tokyo: The Cultural Interchange Institute for Buddhists Press, 1958). In almost all the sects there are proportionately many more studies on "Texts and Commentaries" and "Doctrine" than on "Rites and Ceremonies."

the topic of "*Japanese* Buddhism" immediately involves us in the question of the unity of Japanese religion in general and the plurality of Japanese religions in particular. This question of unity and plurality will be postponed briefly, but we must preview here its implications for the study of Japanese Buddhism. Some scholars will surely question the propriety of calling Buddhism "a Japanese religion." In English there is frequent reference to "Japanese Buddhism" and even "Buddhist Japan," but it is time to establish a newer and more radical approach to the problem. Not only must we recognize that Buddhism in Japan does constitute a "Japanese religion," but we must also acknowledge the more significant fact that "Japanese religion" itself is heavily Buddhist in influence and orientation. If we choose but one point of intimate contact between Buddhist influence and Japanese religious life, we may cite the example of *Jizō* (*Kshitigarbha*, in Sanskirt) and the distinctive Japanese concern for souls of the dead in after-life. *Jizō* as the savior of the dead (among his many functions) is technically a Buddhist contribution, but he has been believed in by all groups of Japanese people without awareness of its Buddhist origin.[18] Indeed, once we stop limiting our attention to the formal aspects of Japanese religion, we realize more acutely the mutual influence among the several religions. This leads us to our third proposition or reason for the deficiencies in Western scholarship on Japanese religion.

(3) The third reason why a unified interpretation of Japanese religion has not been realized is compartmentalization of the several religious traditions in Japan, which has led to a failure to recognize adequately their complex characters and mutual influence. Most Western scholarship has attempted to deal with either *Shintō* or Buddhism or folk religion almost as separate entities, in the process neglecting or minimizing the mutual influence among them. The best

[18] See M. W. de Visser, *The Bodhisattva Ti-tsang (Jizō) in China and Japan* (Berlin: Oesterheld, 1914), esp. pp. 65–177. As Ouwehand has already remarked, De Visser draws predominantly on the "great tradition."

way to document this tendency is to summarize the historical model for Japanese religion that is followed faithfully by most handbooks and secondary treatments of Japanese religion. This historical model is quite simple in outline. The first stage is indigenous Japanese religion, which is treated as animism, nature worship, or ancestor worship or according to some other theory drawn from "primitive religion." This early stage is thought to have developed into *Shintō*, and folk religion is either included in *Shintō* implicitly or covered explicitly under the category of "folk *Shintō*." Buddhism is treated as a foreign religion that entered Japan in the middle of the sixth century and had become "amalgamated" with *Shintō* by the ninth century in the form of *Ryōbu Shintō*. Actually this "amalgamation" is treated primarily as an intellectual affair in terms of the system of *honji-suijaku*. (This system organized the *kami*[19] of *Shintō* and the Buddhist objects of worship by means of corresponding pairs.) The period of amalgamation is interpreted as continuing down to the Meiji Restoration in 1867, when Buddhism and *Shintō* were officially separated by government order and once more assume their independent status. Those influences or elements which did not constitute a separate religious system are somehow sandwiched into this historical model. Noteworthy in this connection are the Chinese influences of religious Taoism (*yin-yang* or *Onmyō-dō*) and Confucianism (or Neo-Confucianism). Unfortunately, this scheme overlooks important religious movements such as *Shugendō*, and popular Buddhism is slighted as the vulgarization of orthodox Buddhism.

It is high time that this historical model be abandoned, because it distorts practically every aspect of Japanese religion which it touches on. Above all it overlooks the complex character of Japanese religion and religions. A few examples of this distortion will suffice. To begin with, even the "indigenous" religion of Japan is a compound of different ele-

[19] *Kami* is the Japanese word for "god" or "divinity," especially in *Shintō*.

ments from diverse geographical sources.[20] The mythological accounts themselves were specific, limited traditions within early Japan whose composition was influenced by Chinese and other sources. The very word *Shintō* is of Chinese origin and was adopted, as is well known, to distinguish the native tradition from the new tradition of Buddhism. However, this *Shintō* was capable neither of including the totality of indigenous religion nor of excluding "foreign" influence. Furthermore, there was never a monolithic organization of *Shintō*; rather there were various schools of *Shintō*, which gradually developed in different ways. These *Shintō* schools are patently influenced by Buddhist theories. The *Shintō* which centered around the emperor (sometimes known as "Imperial Household *Shintō*"), although often considered the most uniquely *Shintō* or Japanese in character, is itself pervaded by Chinese influence. In addition, the festivals which *Shintō* observes, and the calendar by which they are observed, both exhibit considerable Chinese influence.

Turning to Buddhism, we see that Buddhism was received initially in terms of foreign *kami*, whose presence was interpreted alternatively as now beneficial, now harmful. Throughout the Nara period (710–94) scholarly-monastic Buddhism existed predominantly as an aristocratic, courtly affair. Buddhism gained followers and achieved geographical expansion through non-intellectual media such as the popular preachers who recited charms (*darani*, or *dharani* in Sanskrit). The development of devotion to Buddhist "gods" such as *Jizō*, *Amida*, and *Kannon* was another important factor. Chronologically, the Heian period (794–1185) with the "new

[20] See Kitagawa, *loc. cit.* It is unfortunate that brilliant methodological insights are not always applied to concrete research in religion. Joachim Wach long ago noted that the growth of every religion must be studied according to its own principles. He also wrote, "Every religion has its prehistory, and when it seems to be absent, then one does not understand it, and has not yet investigated it adequately. In this aspect every religion is a 'syncretism.'" (*Religionswissenschaft: Prolegomena zu ihrer wissenschafts-theoretischen Grundlegung* [Leipzig: J. C. Hinrichs'sche Buchhandlung, 1924], pp. 85–86.) Here I have extended Wach's remarks concerning an individual religion to the general religious history of Japan.

Buddhism" of the *Shingon* and *Tendai* sects was responsible for this new impetus.[21] However, we must not overlook the influence of religious Taoism on two levels. From the beginning of the Japanese governmental system, which was patterned directly on Chinese models, there was a bureau of *yin-yang* (the *Onmyō-ryō*).[22] This bureau gradually lost its official character and gave way to a movement of unofficial practitioners (*onmyō-ji*) of divination and magic. These practitioners used material from religious Taoism and gradually adopted Buddhist charms, too. In turn, popular Buddhist practitioners (*gyōja*), unordained vendors of Buddhist formulas, adopted the forms of religious Taoism.[23] In addition to this early influence, religious Taoism was later reintroduced in the Heian period as an integral part of the *Shingon* sect of Buddhism. Religious Taoism contributed to the pantheon, ceremonies, and charms of *Shingon*; generally these contributions were accepted within *Shintō* without change.[24] An extremely interesting form of religious Taoism which penetrated Buddhism, *Shintō*, and folk belief is the phenomenon of *Kōshin* or "the belief in three worms."[25]

We need not carry this historical sketch farther. It will be

[21] This development is treated comprehensively by Ichirō Hori, "On the Concept of *Hijiri* (Holy-Man)," *Numen*, V (1958), Fasc. 2, 128–60; Fasc. 3, 199–232.

[22] See George B. Sansom, "Early Japanese Law and Administration," Pt. I, *Transactions of the Asiatic Society of Japan*, 2d ser., IX (1932), 67–109, esp. 81. *Yin-yang*, the Chinese term for the two polar aspects of reality, such as female-male, gradually pervaded both religious Taoism and Confucianism (and later Neo-Confucianism). In Japan these characters are pronounced *onmyō* or *inyō*. The bureau (*ryō*) called *onmyō-ryō*, which the Japanese borrowed from the Chinese, dealt with divination, astrology, and the calendar. An excellent study of just one aspect of *Onmyō-dō* (the "way" of *yin-yang*) has been made by Bernard Frank, "Kata-imi et Kata-tagae. Étude sur les Interdits de direction à l'époque Heian," *Bulletin de la Maison Franco-Japonaise*, Nouvelle Série, V (1958), Nos. 2–4, pp. 1–246.

[23] See Hori, *op. cit.*

[24] For further references and material, see the writer's dissertation, "Haguro *Shugendō*," I, 287–317.

[25] See Noritada Kubo, "Introduction of Taoism to Japan," in *Religious Studies in Japan* (Tōkyō: Maruzen, 1959), pp. 457–65; and "Haguro *Shugendō*," I, 287–317.

sufficient to say that *Shintō* and Buddhism, to mention only the two most conspicuous religious traditions, became so thoroughly mixed in actual practice and popular belief that even the official policy of the Meiji Restoration could not separate them. To this day there remains much evidence to deny that a separation ever took place in popular piety. Furthermore, throughout this long historical development, folk religion continued both within and outside of the official traditions. The religious movement of *Shugendō*, with which the writer is most familiar, is the best example of a unified religious tradition based on "indigenous" beliefs and incorporating in a unique fashion elements of *Shintō*, Buddhism, and also religious Taoism. The example of *Shugendō* will be treated at greater length in Part III of this essay.

The rejection of these older "compartmentalized" notions clears the way so that Japanese religion may be studied more as a unity. On the other hand, there will always be a tension in this study between the general unity of Japanese religion and the plurality of Japanese religions. That is, this essay aims to avoid either extreme. On the one hand, we do not favor a positivistic (or nihilistic) approach which simply negates the existence of any separate religious traditions. On the other hand, we must not advance a hypothetical "Japanese Religion" which by its overarching unity swallows up individual traditions into one super-religion. If we are to avoid these two extremes, we must pay attention to the historical situation and analyze the units of religious tradition by way of their historical formation and phenomenological unity.[26] These guiding rules may sound rather abstract, but

[26] The term "phenomenological" or "phenomenology of religion" has been used in so many different ways that its meaning here must be specified. For example, in his work entitled *Religionswissenschaft* (as well as in later works), Wach insisted on the historical and systematic character of the discipline *Religionswissenschaft*. (See his *Religionswissenschaft: Prolegomena . . .*, p. 72.) In pointing out the aspects of Japanese religion that we must study, I might have written "historical formation and *systematic* unity" and still have been within the bounds of Wach's notion of *Religionswissenschaft*. Indeed, in a later work he defines phenomenology as follows: "We use the term not in the sense of Husserl and Scheler but to indicate the systematic, not the historical, study of phenomena like prayer, priesthood, sect, etc." (*Sociology of*

several concrete pointers may be added. For one thing, we must never lose sight of the fact that all forms of religion in Japan were forced to rub elbows with one another in a narrow island country that was relatively isolated. There was a significant connection among these religious forms that went beyond mere physical proximity. Therefore, Japanese religion constitutes a logical area of religious investigation. Unity and diversity, or unity and plurality, may be discussed meaningfully within this geographical and historical context. These considerations lay the foundation for the more strictly methodological discussion to follow.

(4) Finally, we must investigate the fourth reason why a unified interpretation of Japanese religion has not been achieved: lack of a sound method for interpreting the religions of Japan. To this point, three specific reasons have already been suggested as direct causes for the general confusion in Western studies of Japanese religion. At bottom, however, these three reasons indicate a basic lack of method. Generally speaking, in Western scholarship on Japanese religion, there has been no fundamental methodology capable of recognizing, analyzing, and interpreting religious phe-

Religion [Chicago: University of Chicago Press, 1944], p. 1.) Therefore, I have used the term "phenomenological" to mean, at least in part, the systematic treatment of religious phenomena. In recent years there has been an increasing tendency to emphasize the need for co-operation between "historical" and "phenomenological" research. Here phenomenology is defined as a study of the structures of religious phenomena. (See Raffaele Pettazzoni, "History and Phenomenology in the Science of Religion," in his *Essays on the History of Religions*, trans. H. J. Rose [Leiden: E. J. Brill, 1954], pp. 215–19; this article first appeared as the introductory essay for the periodical *Numen*, as "Aperçu introductif," *Numen*, I [1954], Fasc. 1, 1–7. See also Pettazzoni's "The Supreme Being: Phenomenological Structure and Historical Development," in *The History of Religions: Essays in Methodology*, ed. Mircea Eliade and Joseph M. Kitagawa [Chicago: University of Chicago Press, 1959], pp. 59–66. For two other articles treating this problem see Mircea Eliade, "History of Religions and a New Humanism," *History of Religions*, I [Summer, 1961], 1–11; and C. J. Bleeker, "The Phenomenological Method," *Numen*, VI [1959], Fasc. 2, 96–111.) This is not the proper place to discuss the relationship between historical and phenomenological (systematic) research, but I would like to insist upon the complementary and inseparable character of the two tasks.

nomena as such. Instead, isolated phenomena have been treated in terms of the ambiguous contexts of *Shintō*, Buddhism, and folk religion. In this essay we are not directly concerned with Japanese scholarship, but we cannot fail to mention that the compartmentalization of religious studies within Japanese scholarship is partly responsible for the compartmentalization within Western scholarship. Japanese scholarship has turned out an amazing amount of research concerning Japanese religion, but – to the Westerner – this research seems rigidly specialized. For example, not only is Buddhism the almost undisputed field of Buddhists, but Buddhist scholars usually restrict themselves to a study of their own sects. The same is true of *Shintō* and folk religion and even of such limited fields of study as Taoism. Of course this high degree of specialization reflects a high level of scholarship and a vast amount of scholarly publications. It would be a serious mistake to criticize Japanese scholarship simply because it is specialized; however, it is unfortunate that scholars have tended to confine themselves to the materials and approaches of their own area of specialization. For example, the study of Japanese folklore founded by the late Kunio Yanagita was pursued only by his "school," and for the most part, *Shintō* and Buddhist scholars have not concerned themselves with such scholarship.[27] We must not forget that *Religionswissenschaft* in Japan (*shūkyōgaku*, in Japanese) has a rather long and distinguished history, but until recently, it has been concerned primarily with non-Japanese materials. Scholars such as the late Hideo Kishimoto

[27] This problem has too many facets to be described in a simple statement. One difficulty is that the Yanagita school of folklore has persisted in interpreting all data in terms of a Japanese origin and the Japanese spirit. This interpretation has erected insurmountable obstacles for interaction with other areas of study. For scholars of Buddhism and Taoism (religious Taoism in Japan), it practically denied in principle the possibility of cultural borrowing. For scholars of *Shintō*, it posed a dichotomy between an original and pure religious belief or practice, on the one hand, and a later, distorted organization of that belief or practice in (shrine) *Shintō*, on the other hand. This is but one example of how scholarly disciplines in Japan have inherently discouraged interaction among themselves. For references and discussion concerning Yanagita, see "Haguro *Shugendō*," I, 140.

and also Ichirō Hori have led the way in insisting upon a more co-operative and comprehensive study of Japanese religion.[28] We look forward to the scholarship of the coming generation of scholars trained by these men.

Returning to our central topic of Western scholarship, we note at present an increasing number of Western scholars who can utilize the vast resources of Japanese publications. These Western scholars are not limited to Japanologists per se but include members of all the traditional disciplines. Although some are specialists in anthropology, history, political science, and sociology, others are concentrating on the study of *Shintō*, Buddhism, folklore, or the so-called new religions. For the future of the study of Japanese religion, the systematic method with which these scholars approach the Japanese material, especially Japanese secondary scholarship, is crucial. I think it would be a tragedy if Western scholars limited their research to the material of only one Japanese discipline—say, folklore. In effect, this would duplicate the compartmentalization of Japanese scholarship and would certainly not serve the best interests of Western scholarship. It would serve to confuse rather than to clarify the Western interpretation of Japan and Japanese religion. It is imperative that Western scholars adopt a systematic method for interpreting Japanese religion and utilize relevant materials from all areas of Japanese scholarship. It is to be expected that Western scholars will not all agree on the method to be adopted; nevertheless I will venture a preliminary discussion of method based on my own limited research.

In proposing a method for interpreting Japanese religion, several general considerations must be kept in mind. In the first place, we should admit that there is no special methodology for interpreting Japanese religion: a methodology by definition should be capable of analyzing the relevant materials regardless of their date or geographical

[28] Even Masaharu Anesaki, first holder of the chair of *shūkyōgaku* at Tōkyō University (from 1905), encouraged wider studies. See the obituary of Hideo Kishimoto by Joseph M. Kitagawa, in *History of Religions*, IV (Summer, 1964), 172–73.

location. Thus, we are primarily concerned with a methodology for interpreting religious materials. In the second place, we cannot hope for widespread agreement on such a methodology: at present we confront a rather sharp compartmentalization in Western scholarship. Nevertheless, it should be clear that I am proposing a methodology in the context of *Religionswissenschaft*, or History of Religions. With these two general considerations in mind, we will suggest a methodology for interpreting religious phenomena and demonstrate its relevance for the religious scene in Japan.

A methodology presupposes a discipline with a body of material. Herein we are concerned with the discipline of History of Religions, which takes as its object of study the innumerable expressions of man's religious history. A methodology also presupposes the existence of certain limited problems. That is, it is impossible to survey the complete history and geography of man's religious expressions. Therefore, we must focus upon the various related problems within this larger context. A problem may be recognized in terms of a certain historical period or geographical division, but inevitably we are forced to deal with it in terms of the religious documents that expose it. It is absolutely indispensable for scholars to analyze the relevant myths, legends, rituals, religious careers, folk beliefs, symbols, doctrines, and philosophical concepts. This type of analysis is historical in the sense that it traces the emergence, development, and transformation of the religious phenomenon in order to grasp its basic form. It is structural in that it must demonstrate — much as in a work of art — the form that defines the dramatic significance of the religious phenomenon.[29] One of the aims of such an analysis is to search out all the related religious materials. Another aim is to per-

[29] It is at this point, I think, that the phenomenological task must be seen as both "systematic" and "structural" and, in turn, as complementing the historical task. For example, in the case of *Shugendō*, we can see both a historical and a phenomenological unity of religious material connected with mountains.

ceive the actual unities of religious phenomena that constitute meaningfully related religious structures.

These observations are somewhat pedestrian, but they rest on the working experience of every historian of religions: namely, that we have an endless number of discrete facts among which we must recognize the significant relationships. These few remarks on methodology are only preliminary considerations — the initial mechanics of approaching material. There remains the more difficult task of hermeneutics — the interpretation of the religious phenomena. The present task, however, is to direct a methodological concern to Japanese religion. Therefore, we will forego the problem of hermeneutics itself in order to indicate the implications of our methodology for the study of Japanese religion.

In one respect, this methodology forces us to recognize more sharply the long history of Japanese religion. In another respect, it forces us to acknowledge more profoundly the extent of mutual influence among religious forms in Japan. Now it is well known that Japanese people may be affiliated simultaneously to two religions (*Shintō* and Buddhism) or even three religions (if we include Confucianism). This observation is not altogether incorrect — if anything it is an understatement rather than an overstatement of the case. But to perceive the real meaning of this observation, we must go to the concrete religious forms. In analyzing these concrete religious forms, we shall realize the significance of the above-mentioned methodological considerations.

The significance of such a methodology and its relevance for treating Japanese religion may be demonstrated by means of C. Ouwehand's study.[30] He has taken as his task the understanding of some "catfish pictures" (*namazu-e*) that were sold as protective charms against earthquakes, particularly after the serious earthquake of 1855. At first glance these pictures seem to be the spontaneous and meaningless reaction stimulated by an extraordinary social experience. Ouwehand has shown — by painstaking research in Japanese folk religion, *Shintō*, anthropology, and comparative

[30] Ouwehand, *op. cit.*, pp. ix–xii, 51 ff., 182 ff.

study—that this was no mere spontaneous, meaningless emergence. Rather it is an important religious theme in Japanese history, which is, in turn related to many other aspects of Japanese religion. A general view of Ouwehand's work bears this out. He has discovered old Japanese beliefs in the catfish as a kind of monster which lives under the world and causes earthquakes when it moves about. The catfish or monster is subdued or pacified by means of a special stone placed over it. Ouwehand gives interesting comparative material of the same nature as well as convincing evidence from the Japanese scene. Indeed, the catfish pictures are explicated not only in terms of folk beliefs but also in terms of the structure of *Shintō* shrines. For usually there is one figure in the *Shintō* pantheon who is responsible for placing the stone on the catfish; in the precincts of the *Shintō* shrines dedicated to this figure are found the stones which were used for this purpose and which are therefore sacred. Ouwehand even finds a form of the "catfish" theme in a *Zen* (Buddhist) proverb (or *kōan*). Readers may refer to the book for Ouwehand's own analysis, but for our purpose it is his analytical approach that is quite significant. He has shown that a recent charm of seeming insignificance can be interpreted meaningfully in the context of ancient folk beliefs and other Japanese religious expressions.[31] In the next section, the writer will propose a somewhat similar example from his own research.

All the considerations in this paper presuppose a much wider familiarity with Japanese religion than the writer possesses. Nevertheless, a certain degree of boldness is required in any methodological statement, because there is never a time when all the evidence is in. It is my responsibility, however, to show concretely what a unified interpretation of Japanese religions has meant in my own limited research. Remarks on methodology and interpretation stand

[31] Study of the so-called new religions could profit well from the example of Ouwehand's persistence in searching out all the relevant religio-historical materials.

or fall in their application to the relevant material. The aspect of Japanese religious history with which I am most familiar is the movement known as *Shugendō*. First, I shall give a brief sketch of *Shugendō*; and second, I shall discuss what a "unified interpretation" of *Shugendō* means.[32]

The religious movement known as *Shugendō* is an especially appropriate subject for our investigation of a unified interpretation of Japanese religious history since it includes elements and influences from most of the religious traditions in Japan. *Shugendō* emerged from indigenous beliefs and practices associated with the Japanese mountains. From ancient times in Japan, there were notions that mountains were sacred in a number of ways: as the place where the mythological figures descended to earth, as the abode of mythological figures or objects of worship, as the source of water and fertility, as the regional center of religious faith and worship. *Shugendō* accepted these notions (*sangaku shinkō*, or religious phenomena in the mountains) and first emerged in the context of the sacred mountains. As it took shape around the mountains, *Shugendō* absorbed the influences of religious Taoism, *Shintō*, and Buddhism. With the introduction of Chinese influence along with Buddhism, there appeared various "Taoistic" ideals such as the notion of the "wizard" (*hsien*, in Chinese; usually *sennin*, in Japanese), who retreated into the mountains for religio-ascetic and magical purposes. The Buddhist influence, with its notion of asceticism, also seems to be the major motivation for the religio-ascetic practice of climbing the mountain. Before Buddhism, the religious rites connected with mountains appear to have been performed only at the foot of the mountains and to have been agricultural in character.[33]

[32] Some of these remarks were first made in a transcribed discussion with Hitoshi Miyake, "Taidan: Nihon Shūkyō no Kenkyū Hōhō" ("Methodological Discussion of the Study of Japanese Religions"), *Kokusai Shukyo News* (*International Religious News*), V (May-June, 1946), 26–37.

[33] There are still a number of unsolved problems in the early period of "*sangaku shinkō*," or "mountain cult," one of which is the exact nature of the Japanese hunters known in recent times as *matagi*. See "Haguro *Shugendō*," I, 95–104.

The legendary founder of *Shugendō* was depicted in the light of the traditions of *Shintō*, Taoism, and Buddhism in the setting of the ancient sacred mountains. The many ascetics (*gyōja*), who made a religious career of living in the mountains and guiding lay believers to the holy mountains, were living synthesizers of these several traditions. They performed purifications borrowed from the *onmyō-ji*, or popular practitioners of *Onmyō-dō* (religious Taoism); they often wore the white costume of *Shintō* priests and visited *Shintō* sanctuaries; increasingly, they memorized Buddhist scriptures and formulas as charms, adopted Buddhist tools such as the *shakujō* (in Sanskrit, *khakkhara*), and assumed Buddhist dress.

Especially within the context of esoteric (*Mikkyō*) Buddhism of the Heian period (that is, the *Tendai* and *Shingon* sects), they developed local headquarters on many mountains throughout Japan.[34] Although the earliest centers of *Shugendō* were in the mountains of Yoshino, Kumano, and Ōmine, these gradually came to be established throughout the main Japanese island of Honshū and also on Kyūshū and Shikoku. Each one of these local headquarters constituted a rather unique blending of the oldest beliefs and practices of the area, affiliation with the *Shintō* shrines, and alignment with a particular *Shugendō* branch of either the *Shingon* or *Tendai* sect. From the time they emerged, down to the abolishment of *Shugendō* in 1872, the local forms of *Shugendō* were distinct unities which included these historical influences as constitutive elements; in other words, these elements were parts of the whole phenomenon of *Shugendō*. As these local *Shugendō* groups became more highly organized, they developed elaborate ritual periods for asceticism, worship, and pilgrimage within the mountains.[35] They developed not only complex, peculiar systems

[34] I have sketched the influence of esoteric Buddhism on one aspect of *Shugendō*, the tradition of the founder En no Gyōja, in my article, "Shugendō, the Traditions of En no Gyōja, and Mikkyō Influence," *Studies of Esoteric Buddhism and Tantrism* (Koyasan, Japan: Koyasan University, 1965), pp. 297–317.

[35] See "Haguro *Shugendō*," II, 501–92; and a short article by the

of doctrine, but also elaborate hierarchical priesthoods usually centered around the mountain and spreading a network of priestly control over the surrounding area.[36] The organizational forms were predominantly Buddhist, and for this very reason, the members of *Shugendō* were instrumental in spreading Buddhism to the populace.[37] The national influence of this movement can be judged by an estimate that just before its abolition in 1872 there were approximately 191,000 *Shugendō* leaders of the highest rank; this of course does not count the untold numbers of lower-ranking leaders or the lay believers. *Shugendō* influence was important for the founding of several of the so-called new religions, and in the freedom of the postwar period, a number of *Shugendō* sects per se have reappeared. This brief sketch will serve to introduce the historical development and constitution of the movement of *Shugendō*.

Next, as we move to the question of a "unified interpretation of *Shugendō*, we face the problem of what to do with all the discrete phenomena of *Shugendō* — that have been gathered by scholars of several academic fields. Information bearing on *Shugendō* is reported from such widely separated fields as archeology, ancient mythology, Japanese history, Buddhist studies, *Shintō* studies, folklore studies, and even art history. This diversity of sources is not unusual for historical research; however, in the case of our subject, either no definition of *Shugendō* is given or a different definition is given by each scholar in a different field of study. Scholars see *Shugendō* as a form of either *Shintō* or Buddhism or folk religion, depending upon their scholarly point of departure. The student of *Shugendō* is faced with the initial dilemma of whether it is indeed possible to see *Shugendō* as a religious movement possessing its own unity. Before we attempt to demonstrate positively this religious unity, it will be worthwhile to review the ways in which we cannot arrive

---

writer, "Four Ritual Periods of Haguro Shugendō in Northeastern Japan," *History of Religions*, V (Summer, 1965), 93–113.

[36] See "Haguro *Shugendō*," II, 411–54.

[37] *Shugendō* was also quite influential in spreading belief in *Kōshin* and several art forms.

at a unified interpretation. That is, until we surmount the obstacles to a unified interpretation, as listed in the first part of this essay, we will not be able to work our way through the material to a sense of religious unity.

(1) The first obstacle pointed out was the persistent attempt to interpret Japanese religion by means of classical mythology. In the case of *Shugendō*, we can say definitely that the mythological approach will not work. *Shugendō* can be defined as the Japanese mountain religion par excellence; but it is very significant that the large number of *kami*, or mythological figures, directly associated with mountains in classical mythology have almost nothing to do with the founding of *Shugendō*. It is En no Ozunu, a minor personage in the ancient records, who is revered as the founder of *Shugendō* – and then only after he assumed the combined form of a Taoistic-Buddhistic worker of incantations.[38] Of course, we must take into account the mythological literature to understand the ancient religious importance of sacred mountains. But *Shugendō* developed within the context of sacred mountains in its own way, without adopting the worship of any member of the formal mythological pantheon.

(2) The second obstacle pointed out was overemphasis of the formal organization of Japanese religion. This obstacle has in fact actually blocked a unified understanding of *Shugendō*. One of the few Western references to *Shugendō* defines it as "Buddhist associations formed by the *Shingon* and *Tendai* sects."[39] Indeed, this is a prominent interpreta-

[38] The mythological figure *Hito-koto-nushi* does enter into the problem of the role of En no Ozunu in the ancient literature; however, the conclusive fact is that none of the mountain *kami* (or "divinities") of the formal *Shintō* pantheon became objects of worship in *Shugendō*. See "Haguro *Shugendō*," I, 157–81, 235–49.

[39] E. Papinot, "Shugendō," *Historical and Geographical Dictionary of Japan* (Ann Arbor, Mich: Overbeck Co., 1948), p. 593. The first Western publication devoted solely to *Shugendō* has just appeared in French: G. Renondeau, "Le Shugendō: histoire, doctrine et rites des anachorètes dits *yamabushi*," *Cahiers de la Société Asiatique*, XVIII (1965), 1–150. This is an excellent, concise statement of *Shugendō*, based on Japanese materials and recognizing the mixed background of the movement. Nevertheless, it does not recognize *Shugendō* as a re-

tion even in Japanese scholarly circles. This mistaken conclusion is reached by focusing one's attention on the outer forms of the fully developed *Shugendō* of the Tokugawa period. But even if we limit our attention to the heavily Buddhist-oriented *Shugendō* of Tokugawa times, we cannot explain it in terms of "Buddist associations." For the ethos of *Shugendō* is closely akin to religious practices in the mountains, and Buddhism possesses no inner rationale for practices in the mountains. *Shugendō* organizations were formed by ascetics for temporary or lifetime confinement *in the mountains* and by believers for devotion toward or actual pilgrimage to the mountains. Even the most formal and abstract aspect of *Shugendō* — its doctrine — is oriented toward the mountain. One of the most common doctrines of *Shugendō* groups is that one may become a Buddha by practice in the mountains. We cannot understand *Shugendō* merely in terms of its later and formal organization, which admittedly presents a dominantly Buddhist appearance.

(3) The third obstacle pointed out was the high degree of compartmentalization between different religious traditions in Japan. In the case of *Shugendō* this makes no sense at all, even though we can find examples treating it this way in Western literature. The German physician Engelbert Kaempfer wrote his account of *Shugendō* just before the turn of the eighteenth century in terms of "Sintos Hermits," that is, *Shintō* hermits.[40] A more recent Western scholar has corrected Kaempfer's interpretation, but in a Buddhist direction. "The 'Jamabuxis' (Yamabushi or Shugenja) are treated by the 'Sumario' of 1557 as well as by Kaempfer (II 43 ff.), as representatives of Shintoism. They really belong however to the Buddhist Tendai and Shingon sects

ligious phenomenon in its own right but attaches it either to *Shingon* or to *Tendai:* "Le *shugendō* n'a jamais constituté une secte (*shū*) indépendante. Ses adeptes relèvant soit de la secte Shingon, soit de la secte Tendai" (p. ix).

40 Engelbert Kaempfer, *The History of Japan. Together with a Description of the Kingdom of Siam 1690–92*, trans. J. G. Scheuzer, F.R.S. (Glasgow: James MacLehose, 1906). The section on *Shugendō*, or "Jammabos," is in Vol. II, pp. 43–56, of the 1906 edition.

who were of course strongly influenced by *Shintō* teaching and practice."[41] In Japanese literature this sharp separation is not explicit, but in actual practice scholars have tended to comment only on that aspect of *Shugendō* which fell within their scholarly province. Buddhist scholars have emphasized the conspicuousness of Buddhist symbols and doctrine, neglecting the popular aspects; folklorists have recorded popular beliefs, practices, and festivals connected with *Shugendō*, discounting Buddhist doctrine as an intellectual superimposition that is not of the essence of *Shugendō*. From the viewpoint of the compartmentalists, there are only two ways of studying *Shugendō*: either *Shugendō* must be forced into one or another of the categories of *Shintō*, Buddhism, or folk religion, or it must be dissected into three or more distinct components. It should be obvious by now that neither alternative is capable of grasping *Shugendō* without greatly distorting it.

(4) The fourth obstacle pointed out — and the most basic — was the lack of a fundamental method for interpreting Japanese religion. We may condense much of what has gone before in the statement that until this time there has been no method which is capable of approaching and interpreting *Shugendō*. The standard procedure of separation into *Shintō* and Buddhism will not work, even if a third category of folk religion or a fourth category of religious Taoism is added. In actual fact, these elements constitute a religious movement of its own kind. Nor does the standard historical model of Japanese religion — as previously mentioned — correspond to the realities of *Shugendō*. We have already proposed in Part II the need for a methodology that would be capable of taking at face value the pertinent religious phenomena, analyzing them historically and structurally, and interpreting them on the basis of this analysis. Such a methodology would not be thwarted by the presence

[41] Georg Schurhammer, *Shin-to. The Way of the Gods in Japan According to the Printed and Unprinted Reports of the Japanese Jesuit Missionaries in the 16th and 17th Centuries* (Bonn: Kurt Schroeder, 1923; German and English texts in double columns), p. 135. For other references and discussion, see "Haguro *Shugendō*," I, 39–60.

of influences from several religious traditions. My remaining task is to give a few examples of how this method might be useful to approach and interpret *Shugendō* in a unified manner.

Since *Shugendō* is quite complex as the result of assimilating diverse influences, it can be seen from a number of perspectives. Nevertheless, in my dissertation I have documented the basic ethos of this religious movement as a physical and devotional orientation toward sacred mountains. Although it should be admitted that not all *Shugendō* phenomena are directly related to mountains, they are the orienting force that holds the other elements together into a unity. Furthermore, the orientation toward sacred mountains is the basic clue to discovering a "unified interpretation" of *Shugendō*, both in terms of its long-range development and transformation and in terms of a cross section of its elements at any one period.

The idea that the historical unity of *Shugendō* can be traced in terms of religious beliefs and practices connected with the Japanese mountains has already been suggested in the brief sketch of *Shugendō*. Rather than advance further documentation for this idea, we shall point out the significance of this kind of historical unity for understanding Japanese religion. Of the greatest significance is the fact that we can now recognize a continuing relationship between religious phenomena in the mountains from ancient or even prehistoric times up through the ages to the present. In this long historical span *Shugendō* molded into one religious movement a number of different forms of religiosity associated with mountains. In the most ancient times there were beliefs that the mountains were sacred as the abode of the *kami* ("gods") and as the revered source of irrigation water. Archeological evidence indicates that rituals were performed at the foot of mountains. Also in ancient times there were some vague ideas of a priesthood in the mountains, increasingly influenced by Taoist ideas of a career of retreat into the mountains and eventually overwhelmed by the Buddhist ideal of asceticism in the depths of the mountains.

These early aspects of developmental *Shugendō* carry over into certain themes of folk religion in later times. One dominant theme of folklore is that the souls of the dead go to the mountains; another theme is the seasonal alternation of an agricultural *kami* between the mountains and the rice fields. These themes, too, became related to *Shugendō*, even though they also continued in other contexts. These few examples point up the historical unity of *Shugendō* and, in turn, lend greater unity and meaning to Japanese religious history. Seen in this context, the aforementioned religious phenomena cease to be isolated practices and beliefs — they now fall into place as integral segments of a long, continuous history of religiosity associated with the Japanese mountains. This type of approach illustrates how we should read ancient documents or classical mythology, not simply out of antiquarian curiosity, but in order to gain a better understanding of subsequent religious history.

If we jump to more recent history, we can see that some of the ancient religious themes were present as influences in the founding of the so-called new religions. For example, it is no accident that several of the founders of "new religions" gained their inspiration from wandering in the mountains or at the direct hands of *Shugendō* practitioners.[42] Once we recognize the historical unity of *Shugendō*, we begin to realize the implications of this unity for other religious phenomena in Japanese history, such as the "new religions." It is worth noting that these unities are discovered through a patient searching of all the related religious phenomena, correlated with careful historical and structural analysis.

As we have seen, religious orientation to mountains is the basic clue to the historical unity of *Shugendō*; and at the same time, this orientation is the unifying factor in a cross

42 Illustrative material on such founders has been collected by Hori in "Penetration of Shamanic Elements into the History of Japanese Folk Religion," in *Festschrift für Ad. E. Jensen*, ed. Eike *et al.* (München: Klaus Renner Verlag, 1964), I, 245–65.

section of the religious life of *Shugendō*. To rephrase this point, religious orientation to mountains constitutes the phenomenological unity of *Shugendō*. One of the most striking illustrations of the phenomenological unity of *Shugendō* is the division of the ritual year into four seasonal periods of religious activity in the mountains. Even the ritual periods are called by the names of the four seasonal "mountains" or "peaks." We have already mentioned historical influences present in these ritual periods, but here we are more interested in the kinds of religious activity. In short, *Shugendō* has accepted all kinds of religious activity, blending them distinctively into a religious life lived within the mountains or conceived in terms of mountains. In the four ritual periods, we find such elements as New Year's rites and regeneration of time, agricultural celebrations connected with the coming of spring, a long summer period of pilgrimage to the mountains by believers, and a fall period of ascetic confinement in the mountain temples for *Shugendō* professionals. This theme has been documented elsewhere,[43] and so we shall characterize only the total picture of these four ritual periods—together they portray a religio-dramatic unity acted out in the setting of the mountains. In this light we see not a number of separate "superstitions" and activities accidentally linked with mountains but a unified, though complex religious world that is lived out in the setting of sacred mountains.

It may be added that in actuality the "historical unity" and "phenomenological unity" of *Shugendō* are inseparable. Just one striking example can be given. In the fall ritual period of Haguro *Shugendō*, the professional leaders spent a period of ascetic confinement in and around the sacred area of Mount Haguro. Procession into the mountains involved symbolic acts and rites depicting death, conception, growth of the foetus in the womb (confinement in the mountain), and finally rebirth (exit from the mountains) as the fulfillment of the ascetic practices. The concrete material, which is extremely

[43] See "Haguro *Shugendō*," II, 501–92; and "Four Ritual Periods of Haguro Shugendō in Northeastern Japan."

complex, is oversimplified in this summary. On the one hand, there are ancient Japanese beliefs that souls of the dead go to the mountains and are reborn from the mountain, especially in the fertilizing form of mountain streams. These ancient elements are obviously present in the fall ritual period of Mount Haguro. On the other hand, within the same rituals, we find the complex symbolism of Buddhist fulfilment in reaching the stage of *bodhisattva* or even becoming Buddha. These rituals also have some connection with Buddhist conceptions of rebirth.

Thus through historical investigation we have discovered the historical or over-all unity of both popular and Buddhist contributions to the theme of rebirth in the mountains, but we have stopped short of interpreting the various meanings of confinement within the mountain. To solve this problem, we must analyze the structure of the four ritual periods. I have attempted to show in an analysis of these ritual periods that they constitute one religio-dramatic segment of the larger unity of the religious year, all of which is acted out in relation to the sacred mountains.[44] In spite of the seemingly contradictory elements, there is a religio-dramatic unity which utilizes both sets of elements (Buddhist and popular) to express its purpose. The orientation to mountains — the focus of religiosity — is an abstract way of expressing *Shugendō's* phenomenological unity. Any other aspect of *Shugendō* — be it the priestly hierarchy or the system of doctrine — when analyzed carefully, can be interpreted within this over-all religious unity. The significance of such an analytical method is that it enables us to surmount the previously described "obstacles" and to arrive at a unified interpretation.

In conclusion, we admit that the case of *Shugendō* is not to be construed as applicable to all Japanese religion or the separate religions in Japan. At the same time, it must be argued that *Shugendō*, as an extreme example of the interrelationship and mutual borrowing within Japanese religion, is quite appropriate for testing a new methodology. A methodol-

[44] See "Haguro *Shugendō*," II, 540–92; and "Four Ritual Periods of Haguro Shugendō in Northeastern Japan," pp. 109–12.

ogy capable of interpreting *Shugendō* as a unity should be capable of interpreting any religious phenomenon within Japanese history. Although there will always be room for argument about the unity and diversity or unity and plurality of religion within Japanese history, it is crucial that the argument be based on and integrally related to the expressions of religion. Ouwehand has made a remarkable integration of Japanese fork religion, beginning with some apparently insignificant pictures and paying attention to all the relevant material; the writer would like to suggest that his own study of *Shugendō* represents another integration of Japanese religion, based on the phenomena of *Shugendō*. A similar impression emerges from both of these works, I think: that Japanese religion is like a vast interrelated nervous system. To study this nervous system at any one point involves one, inevitably, in tracing the relationship of this point to the whole system. (The analogy cannot be carried too far, of course, since the nervous system includes a control center for the whole system, and there is no clearly defined center in Japanese religion.) To study Japanese religion with this interrelatedness in mind should help us achieve more perceptive studies of limited problems and also contribute a wider understanding of Japanese religious history. On the one hand, we will be better able to understand such limited problems as the "new religions" when we view them in terms of their wider religious setting, and on the other hand, as we begin to accumulate a corpus of monographs of this kind, we will be led naturally into a general and total understanding of Japanese religious history.[45]

[45] I am now revising for publication a short introduction to Japanese religion based on the methodological approach elaborated in the present article.

10

Symbol and Reality among the Trobriand Islanders

JEROME H. LONG

The Trobriand group of islands lies roughly 130 miles to the east of Papua, about 151° east longitude and 9° south latitude. It is comprised of the large islands of Kiriwina, Kaileuna, and Vakuta as well as many small islands of lesser importance. The natives who inhabit these islands are of Papuo-Melanesian stock and speak a Melanesian language.

The Trobrianders engage in a variety of activities and pursuits. They make canoes, pottery, and baskets, raise pigs, and fish. They are daring sailors and once a year take a long and often dangerous voyage known as the *kula*. But they are horticulturalists first and last. As Bronislaw Malinowski writes:

> The Trobriander is above all a cultivator, not only by opportunity and need, but also by passion and his traditional system of values. . . . Half of the native's working life is spent in the garden and around it centres perhaps more than half his interests and ambitions. In gardening the natives produce much more than they actually require, and in any average year they harvest perhaps twice as much as they can eat.[1]

Social organization proceeds along matrilineal lines; however, the male in some cases actually exercises the power which he has derived from his mother's or aunt's side of the family.

[1] Bronislaw Malinowski, *Coral Gardens and Their Magic: A Study of the Methods of Tilling the Soil and of Agricultural Rites in the Trobriand Islands*, Vol. 1: *The Description of Gardening* (New York: American Book Co., 1935), p. 8.

Primary research in the Trobriand Islands was done by Bronislaw Malinowski, and it is to his works that primary reference will be made.

The purpose of this paper is to examine a number of living symbols which function in the life of the Trobrianders. In so doing I hope to disclose the structure of reality which these symbols express.

G. van der Leeuw defines "structure" as "reality significantly organized."[2] The important ideas in this definition are "organization" and "significance." Both are constituent of reality itself. Organization brings out and preserves the specificity and concreteness of reality. Significance refers to the dimension of meaning inherent in reality as well as to its tendency toward comprehensiveness. The forms or modalities in which this significant organization of reality is expressed we call symbols. Therefore it follows that what we call "reality" is never just "there" in its nakedness but appears to us in the form of symbols, and the only means whereby one is able to experience, appropriate, and understand reality are certain symbols which disclose the structure of the real. The Trobrianders classification of their oral literature can perhaps illustrate and clarify this relation between symbol, structure of reality, and significance.

The Trobrianders possess a great store of oral literature. They have themselves divided this literature into certain classes according to content and also in terms of when certain stories are to be told and by whom. The three classes are called *kukwanebu, libwogwo*, and *liliu*. Malinowski translates *kukwanebu* as "folk tale" or "fairy tale." This type of story is told only during late November when wet weather is setting in. Certain *kukwanebu* are owned by certain members of the tribe and are usually narrated only by the owner. The fairy tale is usually an account of how a man, animal, or plant is punished for some impropriety. The purpose of the story is entertainment, and its success depends upon the ability of the

[2] G. van der Leeuw, *Religion in Essence and Manifestation*, trans. J. E. Turner (New York: Harper & Row, 1963), II, 672.

storyteller to change his voice as he takes the part of various characters and to gesture entertainingly.

Libwogwo, the second type of story, are historical accounts, legends, and hearsay tales. These tales often concern some great feat by an individual or family in the tribe. They are regarded as historically true, and they arouse interest not as a performance or entertainment like the *kukwanebu* but because they concern success in activities considered important by the Trobrianders.

The term for the third class of stories, *liliu,* Malinowski translates as "myths." Myths by their content and intention constitute for the Trobriander a different kind of class of narrative altogether. *Liliu* tell how death came into the world, thereby robbing man of his power of eternal rejuvenation; they relate how the Trobrianders emerge from the underworld; they tell how the first *kula* was undertaken and then established by cultural heroes. *Liliu* are sacred stories. In the words of Malinowski, "These stories . . . are to the natives a statement of a primeval, greater and more relevant reality, by which the present life, fates, and activities of mankind are determined. . . ."[3]

In terms of our previous definition of the relation of symbol and structure, the following can be said. All three classes of stories — fairy tales, historical accounts and legends, and myths — are symbolic. However, a distinction among them can be made in terms of their significance and their organization. The organization of myths discloses the many different levels on which significant realities are expressed. For example, only a myth can aptly express how the Trobrianders appropriate the earth mother in their social system or why the Trobrianders derive so much joy from gardening; only a myth can reveal how death first entered the world, thus robbing mankind of his capacity for eternal rejuvenation. Myths are significant because their particular content probes the depths of human existence and reflects how man experiences, appropriates, and understands his world.

[3] Bronislaw Malinowski, *Magic, Science and Religion and Other Essays* (Garden City, N.Y.: Doubleday & Co., 1948), p. 108.

Because myths deal with significant realities, they contain the primary symbols that must be investigated by those who wish to understand that specific mode of reality which we call human. This mode of reality cannot be understood without some reference to transcendence, that is, to that power which stands outside and over against man. Symbols convey the specific modes in which transcendence is made available. For example, in mythical times Tudava, the cultural hero, showed the Trobrianders how to build canoes. He also organized the first *kula*. Now building canoes and going on the *kula* are significant human activities for the Trobrianders because of their transcendent origin in mythical times and because both acts were done first by transcendent beings, that is, gods. In contrast to building canoes, pearl diving is not a significant human activity because it has no transcendent reference point. We call those modes of reality that imply some notion of transcendence "religious symbols." It follows that the study of religious symbols is the study of significant realities which inform the life of a particular people.

The primary religious symbol of the Trobrianders is the earth. By "primary" here I mean that all other events, things, and places are "real" only insofar as they are related to the earth or one of its several homologues. The earth is the origin and source of all reality for the Trobrianders. The remaining part of this paper will attempt to show the different manifestations of the earth as a religious symbol and how each manifestation informs different aspects of the life of the Trobrianders.

Among the Trobrianders the earth is experienced on a variety of levels and planes. According to myth, all the clans, subclans and families of the Trobrianders emerged out of the ground at a particular place. These clans emerged from the ground in a definite order. The pattern of emergence established for all time the rules of social intercourse among the different clans. The social organization of the Trobrianders is real for them only in terms of this emergence.

The fact that the Trobrianders have a matriarchal social system and trace their line of descent through the female side of the family is another reflection of the pervasive influence of the symbol earth. The earth is represented as female and her most immediate homologue is woman. The woman is directly or indirectly the center of political and social power for the Trobrianders. Even though the chief of the clan is often male, he derives his authority from the female side of his family. The woman is the source of authority because she more than anything else resembles the earth; her menstrual cycle is homologous to the cycles of the moon, which, according to the Trobrianders, also emerged from the earth. Certain Trobriand myths establish woman as the source of power because she was first to appear on earth. The Trobrianders say: "You see we are so many on the earth because women came first. Had there been many men, we would be few."[4]

The symbol of the earth is interiorized and given expression by the Trobrianders in their social structure. By such interiorization, the pattern of social relationships is made real and significant for them.

The same kind of interiorization and expression of the earth mother can also be seen in the gardening of Trobrianders. Each stage of the gardening process is inaugurated by certain formulas, rites, or gestures which clearly express this process of interiorization:

> The belly of my garden leavens,
> The belly of my garden rises,
> The belly of my garden reclines,
> The belly of my garden grows to the size of a bush-hen's nest,
> The belly of my garden grows like an ant-hill,
> The belly of my garden rises and is bowed down,
> The belly of my garden rises like the iron-wood palm,
> The belly of my garden lies down,
> The belly of my garden swells,
> The belly of my garden swells as with a child.[5]

[4] Bronislaw Malinowski, *The Sexual Life of Savages in North-Western Melanesia* (New York: Harcourt, Brace & World, Inc., 1929), p. 182.

[5] Malinowski, *Coral Gardens and Their Magic*, I, 169.

Gardening for the Trobriander derives its significance from the fact that it was instituted in mythical time by Tudava, the cultural hero and the son of the earth mother. At a certain moment in the gardening process, a rite known as the "anchoring of the garden" occurs. During the rite reference is made to Tudava:

> Anchoring, anchoring of my garden,
> Taking deep root, taking deep root in my garden,
> Anchoring in the name of Tudava,
> Taking deep root in the name of Malita,
> Tudava will climb up, he will seat himself on the
> high platform.
> What shall I strike?
> I shall strike the firmly moored bottom of my *taytu*.
> It shall be anchored.[6]

By such formulas economic activity is transformed into a symbol and thereby becomes available and possible for the Trobrianders. These formulas are not just accretions to the gardening process. Rather they are constitutive of the process itself. They serve to humanize the process and thereby transform it into a mode of significant reality.

It is very difficult for us to comprehend the intimacy between the Trobriander and the earth mother. Perhaps a linguistic example will clarify the depths of this relationship. The Trobriander calls the hairs on his body *unu'unu*. The stringy hairs on yams are called by the same name. The Trobrianders are literally "people of the land." They seek to live as closely as possible to the reality of the earth mother.

The cosmic dimension of the earth mother can also be seen in the following myth, reported by Malinowski:

> . . . a woman called Mitigis or Bolutukwa, mother of the legendary hero Tudava, lives quite alone in a grotto on the seashore. One day she falls asleep in her rocky dwelling, reclining under a dripping stalactite. The drops of water pierce her vagina, and thus deprive her of virginity.

[6] *Ibid.*, p. 129.

> Hence her second name, Bolutukwa: *bo*, female, prefix *litukwa*, dripping water.[7]

Tudava, the sun, the moon, and fire emerged from Mitigis after her vagina was opened.

What is important here is that the birth process occurred without any form of male participation. The creative power of the female is unlimited and comprehensive. Although the Trobrianders contend that the opening of the vagina is necessary before conception can occur, they stoutly maintain that it does not have to be opened by the male and that artificial means can be just as effective.

This myth, which establishes the priority of the female in the process of conception, provides the basis for the Trobrianders' understanding of the biological causes of conception and birth. According to the Trobrianders, all children come from the island of Tuma, where the spirits of the dead (*baloma*) reside. When a spirit of the dead becomes tired of his life on Tuma, he simply sheds his skin by bathing in salt water and becomes an infant once more. Then he goes to the sea and drifts on logs, scum, or leaves until he reaches the main island. A native continues the story:

> A child floats on a drift log. A spirit sees it is good-looking. She takes it. She is the spirit of the mother or of the father of the pregnant woman. Then she puts it on the head, in the hair of the pregnant woman, who suffers headache, vomits, and has an ache in the belly. Then the child comes down into the belly, and she is really pregnant. She says: "Already it [the child] has found me; already they [the spirits] have brought me the child." [8]

This account of the biological origin of a Trobriander child is another illustration of the primary role of the female as a homologue of the earth and also discloses something about the significant reality of biological life. Life on the biological plane becomes significant because each birth is always a rebirth. In

[7] Malinowski, *The Sexual Life of Savages*, pp. 182–83.
[8] *Ibid.*, p. 173.

the economy of the sacred, nothing is ever lost. Death is only a change in the mode of being — it is never final.

We have mentioned the importance of the earth mother in establishing social, economic, and biological realities. Now we shall see how the symbol of the earth mother determines the understanding of time for the Trobrianders.

For the Trobrianders the word *milamala* has three meanings: "(a) the marine annelid known as the palolo worm, (b) a name for a particular month, (c) a long dancing season associated with this month." [9] The appearance of the palolo worm (*Eunice viridis*) signals the beginning of the preparations for the *milamala* festival.

According to Malinowski, the palolo worm "makes its appearance on the surface of the sea for spawning only once a year, at the full moon falling within the period from October 15 to November 15." [10] The palolo worm is a fascinating creature. Marine biologists recognize in it an extreme case of sexual dimorphism. W. McM. Woodworth writes:

> We have then in the palolo, combined in the same individual, an atokal and an epitokal part corresponding to the anterior and posterior ends of the animal, and it is the posterior epitokal part, the "Palolo," that is periodically cast off and leads such an ephemeral existence, while the anterior atokal part remains in the galleries of the reef-rock to regenerate, by a process of strobilization, a new posterior atokal sperm or egg sac, which at the appointed time is again set free.[11]

The Trobrianders may or may not be aware of the exact morphology and the intricate processes of regeneration of the

[9] E. R. Leach, "Primitive Calendars," *Oceania*, XX (June, 1950), 245.

[10] Bronislaw Malinowski, "Lunar and Seasonal Calendar in the Trobriands," *Journal of the Royal Anthropological Institute of Great Britain and Ireland*, LVII, 212. The palolo worm also figures in the religious ceremonies of the Samoans, the Fiji Islanders, and the natives of Malekula.

[11] W. McM. Woodworth, "The Palolo Worm, Eunice viridis (Gray)," *Bulletin of the Museum of Comparative Zoology, Harvard*, LI (1907), 6–7.

palolo worm. But for our purposes, it is only important that the palolo worm is able to evoke certain images and symbols for the Trobrianders which extend far beyond its biological existence. This is not a question of worshipping the palolo as a natural structure. Rather it discloses among the Trobrianders a profound experience of and refined sensitivity to this natural form. This experience allows the Trobrianders to see in the periodical occurrence and disappearance of this worm the reality of the regenerative powers of the cosmos which in the last analysis overcome time and death.

The palolo worm is caught in the same cycle of periodic return as the moon and other "moon creatures" such as the lizard, snake, crab, and iguana. Like the moon, which "dies" or disappears only to return, these creatures disappear (go underground), slough off their skins, and reappear in a new form. Unlike man, who also possessed the power of rejuvenation in mythical times, these creatures did not lose this power.

The symbolic significance of the palolo worm is also evident in the name given it – *milamala* – by the natives. Now *milamala* is the name of the first moon of the new year. The Trobrianders use a lunar calendar and usually number ten moons in a year.[12] The *milamala* festival occurs after the harvest, which marks the end of the old year, and before the planting, which signals the start of the new year.

During the *milamala* time the usual pattern and routine of village life ceases. The people do not work in the gardens or do any kind of work which is not related to the *milamala*; instead they build special huts in which the harvested yams are ceremoniously piled. The entire period is marked by a super-abundance of everything.

The high point of the *milamala* festival is the mass return of the *baloma* (spirits of the dead) from the island of Tuma. It is this return that marks the *milamala* as a religious festival and indicates the Trobrianders' experience and understanding of time.

[12] This is the number of moons recorded by Malinowski on his first visit to the Trobriand Islands. Later he changed the number to thirteen. The thirteen-moon year was later disputed by E. R. Leach. (See E. R. Leach, "Primitive Calendars," *Oceania*, XX [June, 1950].)

Like all significant realities, the *milamala* festival was first established in mythical times. The myth states that in primeval times even after people died they remained (if they wished) in the villages with the survivors. Malinowski's account of the myth continues,

> But one day an old woman spirit who was living with her people in the house crouched on the floor under one of the bedstead platforms. Her daughter, who was distributing food to the members of the family, spilled some broth out of the coconut cup and burnt the spirit, who expostulated and reprimanded her daughter. The latter replied: "I thought you had gone away; I thought you were only coming back at one time in the year during the *milamala*." The spirit's feelings were hurt. She replied: "I shall go to Tuma and live underneath." She then took up a coconut, cut it in half, kept the half with the three eyes and gave her daughter the other. "I am giving you the half which is blind, and therefore you will not see me. I am taking the half with the eyes, and I shall see you when I come back with other spirits." This is the reason why the spirits are invisible, though they themselves can see human beings.[13]

Another version of the origin of the *milamala*, which is perhaps older, is also recorded by Malinowski:

> A woman of Kitava died leaving a pregnant daughter behind her. A son was born, but his mother had not enough milk to feed him. As a man of a neighboring island was dying, she asked him to take a message to her own mother in the land of spirits, to the effect that the departed one should bring food to her grandson. The spirit woman filled her basket with spirit food and came back wailing as follows: "Whose food am I carrying? That of my grandson to whom I am going to give it; I am going to give him his food." She arrived on Bomagema beach in the island of Kitava and put down the food. She spoke to her daughter: "I bring the food; the man told me I should

[13] Malinowski, *Magic, Science and Religion*, p. 133.

bring it. But I am weak; I fear that people may take me for a witch." She then roasted one of the yams and gave it to her grandson. She went into the bush and made a garden for her daughter. When she came back, however, her daughter received a fright for the spirit looked like a sorceress. She ordered her to go away saying: "Return to Tuma, to the spiritland; people will say that you are a witch." The spirit mother complained: "Why do you chase me away? I thought I would stay with you and make gardens for my grandchild." The daughter only replied: "Go away, return to Tuma." The old woman then took up a coconut, split it in half, gave the blind half to her daughter, and kept the half with the eyes. She told her that once a year, she and other spirits would come back during the *milamala* and look at the people in the villages, but remain invisible to them. And this is how the annual feast came to be what it is.[14]

During the *milamala* the spirits of the dead return to the island to observe the festivities. By this return, mythological time is re-created; it is present. The commingling of the living and the dead as if there were no distinction and the superabundance of food and heightened social activities suggest a return to mythical time when all forms of life were full, overflowing, and pregnant with possibilities. The *milamala* is not a re-enactment of what occurred in mythical time; that is, there is no drama which portrays the emergence of the clans from the earth or the mighty acts of Tudava, the cultural hero. Rather it is a celebration of the power that brought all of these acts into being. During the *milamala*, mythical time is made present and the power of the cosmos is experienced. It is significant that the *milamala* occurs at the start of the new year. The first meal of the *milamala* is dedicated to the *baloma*: "Let us give up last year's food, O old men; let us eat the new food instead."[15] The *milamala* provides a proper orientation and basis for all significant events which will occur during that year. The

[14] *Ibid.*, pp. 133–34.
[15] Malinowski, *Coral Gardens and Their Magic*, I, 167.

milamala is a configuration of significant time. The significance and reality of time for the Trobriander are acquired by its relation to situations which occurred in mythical time.

The *milamala* also indicates the creativity, freshness, and power of mythical times. It is a cosmic regeneration, a rejuvenation of all forms. One can see the parallel imagery here between the moon (which is also called *milamala*), certain moon creatures (the palolo worm, snakes, crabs, and so on), and the earth. All slough off their skin – the old form which time has worn out – and appear new and fresh.

In this paper I have attempted to show the primary importance of religious symbolism for an understanding of the religious life of the Trobrianders. I have tried to illustrate the structural relationship between symbol and reality, that is, that all significant organizations of reality are couched in a particular complex pattern of symbols, and therefore, that symbols are generic to reality itself. Two other points concerning symbolism were also made: (1) Symbols are expressed on a variety of levels – hence their polyvalent character – and (2) symbols are expressed in a concrete and particular manner. For example, there is only *one* specific way in which the Trobrianders may garden; a *particular* species of marine life – the palolo worm – heralds the *milamala* festival; and *specific* rules govern the pattern of social relationships. All of these particular patterns of behavior and events suggest particular choices on the part of the Trobrianders; and these particular choices suggest the concreteness of the structure of reality which is conveyed in the symbol.

Moreover, I have attempted to show what kinds of realities are implied in the symbol of the earth mother for the Trobrianders – how the symbol of the earth mother, by establishing its own rhythm, influences certain modes of reality for the Trobrianders. The realities I have chosen to present are the economic order, the social order, the processes of procreation and birth, and death and time.

In writing papers of this sort one lays himself open to

the charge of dealing with antiquities which, although they may provide interesting reading, are quite irrelevant to man's present mode of being in the world. One can plead innocent to such a charge only if he has a view of history which holds that certain historical meanings, though realized in the past, can be made available to and appropriated by persons not living in the same historical period. An understanding of the history of mankind as the history of religious symbols is one of the ways in which such a view can be projected. This is so because religious symbolism is never exhausted by the historical or cultural period in which it appears. In fact, the cultural epoch does not give meaning to the symbol; it is the symbol which nurtures and gives life and meaning to a particular cultural epoch. The meanings which are implied in the symbol are generic to man's way of being in the world. As A. Portmann, a biologist, writes,

> . . . our openness to the world—our unique way of being in the world—is not just an airy realm of the spirit all by itself created as an epiphenomenon by organic living matter, but that this way of being is deeply rooted in our organic nature.[16]

It is this openness to the world which is embodied in religious symbols. These symbols are never lost, although they may be buried under layers of historical and human atrophy. It is at this point that historians of religions by an examination of symbols can strip off the layers of historical and human atrophy and allow the symbols to speak to contemporary man. A reappropriation of the symbols of archaic man can be seen in the works of the sculptor Henry Moore. His sculpture shows that the archetype of the feminine depicted in the form of an earth goddess can still excite the passions of modern man and call forth meanings which were thought to have been lost or forgotten.

Just as this view of religious symbols can lead to a new understanding of history it can also lead to what Portmann

[16] Adolphe Portmann, "Preface to a Science of Man," *Diogenes*, No. 40 (Winter, 1962), p. 14.

calls a "basic anthropology." The whole of human history and not just the history of the West would be the resource for the formation of such an anthropology. Portmann writes,

> Such a basic anthropology seeks to go beyond the many warring conceptions of our place in the world to bring out our essentially human traits; it can be neither Christian nor Marxist nor Buddhist, and it is no new attempt at syncretism. All these attitudes claim to be final and conclusive, even when they pretend to be "scientific" in their respective spheres. Every one of these efforts must be labeled a "terminal" anthropology, as opposed to a "basic" one. . . .
>
> . . . But the science we are here envisaging will not try to establish any one end or solve the problem of the meaning of life in any final way. Such modesty is not to be construed as indecisiveness or as scepticism about the possibility of an answer. It arises from a single source—the recognition of the fundamentally enigmatic nature of human life which makes the quest for the meaning of life a task which no generation can dispense with and of which it cannot be relieved.[17]

A study of the history of religious symbolism can show in what ways man has expressed his humanness in a variety of historical and cultural situations. Such a history will also be able to throw light on the religious potentialities of man. To end with one more quotation from Adolphe Portmann:

> [A basic anthropology] will be able to show that it is a function of human life to give meaning to it, that this is a powerful urge, and that the lack of meaning in our lives leads to various kinds of breakdown. But it will also be able to show that the loss of faith in all interpretations of the meaning of life offered at a given time belongs as much to the essential tools of social life, for this doubt is one of those openings in the social structure by which our species prepares for change.[18]

[17] *Ibid.*, p. 24.
[18] *Ibid.*, p. 25.

11

The Significance of the History of Religions for the Systematic Theologian

PAUL TILLICH

In this lecture, I wish to deal with three basic considerations. I call the first one "two basic decisions." A theologian who accepts the subject, "The Significance of the History of Religions for the Systematic Theologian," and takes this subject seriously, has already made, explicitly or implicitly, two basic decisions. On the one hand, he has separated himself from a theology which rejects all religions other than that of which he is a theologian. On the other hand, if he accepts the subject affirmatively and seriously, he has rejected the paradox of a religion of non-religion, or a theology without theos (also called a theology of the secular).

Both of these attitudes have a long history. The former has been renewed in our century by Karl Barth. The latter is now most sharply expressed in the so-called theology-without-God language. For the former attitude, either the one religion is *vera religio*, true religion, against all others, which are *religiones falsâe*, false religions, or as it is expressed in modern terms, one's own religion is revelation, but any other religion is only a futile human attempt to reach God. This becomes the definition of all religion – a futile human attempt to reach God.

Therefore, from this point of view it is not worthwhile to go into the concrete differences of the religions. I remember the half-hearted way in which, for instance, Emil Brunner did it. I recall the theological isolation of historians of religion like my very highly esteemed friend, the late Rudolf Otto, and even today the similar situation of a man like

Friedrich Heiler. One also recalls the bitter attacks on Schleiermacher for his use of the concept of religion for Christianity. I remember the attacks on my views when for the first time (forty years ago) I gave a seminar on Schleiermacher at Marburg. Such an approach was considered a crime at that time.

In order to reject both this old and new orthodox attitude, one must accept the following systematic presuppositions. First, one must say that revelatory experiences are universally human. Religions are based on something that is given to a man wherever he lives. He is given a revelation, a particular kind of experience which always implies saving powers. One can never separate revelation and salvation. There are revealing and saving powers in all religions. God has not left himself unwitnessed. This is the first presupposition.

The second presupposition is that revelation is received by man in terms of his finite human situation. Man is biologically, psychologically, and sociologically limited. Revelation is received under the conditions of man's estranged character. It is always received in a distorted form, especially if religion is used as a means to an end and not as an end in itself.

There is a third presupposition that one must accept. When systematic theologians assume the significance of the history of religions, they must also believe not only that there are particular revelatory experiences throughout human history but that there is a revelatory process in which the limits of adaptation and the failures of distortion are subjected to criticism. Such criticism takes three forms: the mystical, the prophetic, and the secular.

A fourth presupposition is that there may be — and I stress this, there *may* be — a central event in the history of religions which unites the positive results of those critical developments in the history of religion in and under which revelatory experiences are going on — an event which, therefore, makes possible a concrete theology that has universalistic significance.

There is also a fifth presupposition. The history of religions in its essential nature does not exist alongside the history of culture. The sacred does not lie beside the secular, but it is its depths. The sacred is the creative ground and at the same time a critical judgment of the secular. But the religious can be this only if it is at the same time a judgment on itself, a judgment which must use the secular as a tool of its own religious self-criticism.

Only if the thelogian is willing to accept these five presuppositions can he seriously and fully affirm the significance of the history of religions for theology against those who reject such significance in the name of a new or an old absolutism.

On the other hand, he who accepts the significance of the history of religions must stand against the no-God-language theology. He must also reject the exclusive emphasis on the secular or the idea that the sacred has, so to speak, been fully absorbed by the secular.

The last of the five points, the point about the relation of the sacred and the secular, has already reduced the threat of the "God is dead" oracle. Religion must use the secular as a critical tool against itself, but the decisive question is: *Why any religions at all?* Here one means religions in the sense of a realm of symbols, rites, and institutions. Can they not be neglected by a secular theologian in the same way he probably neglects the history of magic or astrology? If he has no use for the idea of God, what can bring him to attribute high significance to the history of religions?

In order to affirm religion against the attack from this side, the theologian must have one basic presupposition. He must assume that religion as a structure of symbols of intuition and action — that is, myths and rites within a social group — has lasting necessity for even the most secularized culture and the most demythologized theology. I derive this necessity, the lasting necessity of religion, from the fact that spirit requires embodiment in order to become real and effective. It is quite well to say that the Holy, or the Ultimate, or the Word is within the secular realm, and I myself have done so innumerable times. But in order to say that something is *in* something, it must have at least a possibility of being *outside* of it. In other words, that which is *in* and that *in* which it is, must be distinguishable. In some way their manifestations must differ. And this is the question: *In what does the merely secular differ from that secular which would be the object of a secular theology?*

Let me say the same thing in a well-known, popular form. The reformers were right when they said that every day is the Lord's Day and, therefore, devaluated the sacredness of the seventh day. But in order to say this, there must have been a Lord's Day, and that not only once upon a time but continuously in counterbalance against the overwhelming weight of the secular. This is what makes God-language necessary, however untraditional that language may be. This makes a serious affirmation of the history of religion possible.

Therefore, as theologians, we have to break through two barriers against a free approach to the history of religions: the orthodox-exclusive one and the secular-rejective one. The mere term "religion" still produces a flood of problems for the systematic theologian, and this is increased by the fact that the two fronts of resistance, though coming from opposite sides, involve an alliance. This has happened and *still* happens.

Both sides are reductionistic, and both are inclined to eliminate everything from Christianity except the figure of Jesus of Nazareth. The neo-orthodox group does this by making him the exclusive place where the word of revelation can be heard. The secular group does the same thing by making him the representative of a theologically relevant secularity. But this can be done only if the picture and message of Jesus is itself drastically reduced. He must be limited to an embodiment of the ethical call, especially in the social direction, and the ethical call is then the only thing which is left of the whole message of the Christ. In *this* case, of course, history of religion is not needed any longer, not even the Jewish and Christian. Therefore, in order to have a valued, evaluated, and significant understanding of the history of religions, one has to break through the Jesus-centered alliance of the opposite poles, the orthodox as well as the secular.

Now I come to my second consideration: a theology of the history of religions. The traditional view of the history of religions is limited to the history that is told in the Old and New Testament, enlarged to include church history as the continuity of that history. Other religions are not qualitatively distinguished from each other. They all are perversions of a kind of original revelation but without particular revelatory experiences of any value for Christian theology. They are pagan religions, religions of the nations, but they are not bearers of revelation and salvation. Actually, this principle was never fully carried through. Jews and Christians were both influenced religiously by the religions of conquered and conquering nations, and frequently these religions almost suffocated Judaism and Christianity and led to explosive reactions in both of them.

Therefore, what we need, if we want to accept the title of this lecture, "The Significance of the History of Religions for the Systematic Theologian," is a theology of the history of religions in which the positive valuation of universal revelation balances the critical valuation. Both are necessary. This theology of the history of religions can help systematic theologians to understand the present moment and the nature of our own historical place, both in the particular character of Christianity and in its universal claim.

I am still grateful, looking back on my own formative period of study and the time after it, to what in German is called the *religionsgeschichtliche Schule*, the School of History of Religions in biblical and church historical studies. These studies opened our eyes and demonstrated the degree to which the biblical tradition participates in the Asia Minor and Mediterranean traditions. I remember the liberating effect of the understanding of universal, human motives in the stories of Genesis or in Hellenistic existentialism and

Persian eschatology, as they appeared in the late periods of the Old and New Testament.

From this point of view, all of the history of religions produced symbols for savior figures, which then supplied the framework for the New Testament understanding of Jesus and his work. This was liberating. These things did not fall from heaven like stones, but there was a long preparatory revelatory history, which finally, in the *kairos*, in the right time, in the fulfilled time, made possible the appearance of Jesus as the Christ. All this was done without hurting the uniqueness of the prophetic attack on religion in the Old Testament and the unique power of Jesus in the New Testament. Later on, in my own development, as in that of many other theologians, the significance was made clear of both the religions that surrounded the Old and New Testament situation and the religions farther removed from Biblical history.

The first question confronting a theology of the history of Israel and of the Christian Church is the history of salvation; but the history of salvation is something within the history. It is expressed in great symbolic movements, in *kairoi* such as the various efforts at reform in the history of the Church. In the same vein, nobody would identify history of religions and history of salvation, or revelation, but one searches for symbolic moments. If the history of religions is taken seriously, are there *kairoi* in the general history of religions? Attempts have been made to find such *kairoi.* There was the Enlightenment of the eighteenth century. Everything for these theologians was a preparation for the great *kairos*, the great moment, in which mature reason is reached in mankind. There are still religious elements in this reason: God, freedom, immortality. Kant developed it in his famous book, *Religion within the Limits of Pure Reason.*

Another attempt was the romanticist understanding of history, which led to Hegel's famous effort. From his point of view, there is a progressive history of religion. It progresses according to the basic philosophical categories which give structure to all reality. Christianity is the highest and last point, and it is called "revealed religion," but this Christianity is philosophically demythologized. Such a view is a combination of Kantian philosophy and the message of the New Testament.

All earlier religions in Hegel's construction of the history of religions are *aufgehoben*, which can only be translated by two English verb forms, namely, "taken in" and "removed." In this construction, therefore, that which is past in the history of religion has lost its meaning. It is only an element in the later development. This means, for instance, that for Hegel the Indian religions are long, long past, long ago finished, and have no contemporary meaning. They belong to an early stage of history. Hegel's attempt to develop a theology of the history of religion resulted in the experiential theology which was very strong in America about thirty years ago. It was based on the idea of remaining open to new experiences of a religious character in the future. Today men like Toynbee point in this direction—or perhaps look for that in religious experience which leads to a union of the great religions. In any case, it is a post-Christian era that is looking for such a construction.

It is also necessary to mention Teilhard de Chardin, who stresses the development of a universal, divine-centered consciousness which is basically Christian. For him, Christianity takes in all spiritual elements of the future. I am dissatisfied with such an attempt. I am also dissatisfied with my own, but I will give it in order to induce you to try yourself, because that is what one should do if he takes the history of religions seriously.

My approach is dynamic-typological. There is no progressive development which goes on and on, but there are elements in the experience of the Holy which are always there, if the Holy is experienced. These elements, if they are predominant in one religion, create a particular religious type. It is necessary to go into greater depth, but I will only mention a tentative scheme, which would appear as follows. The universal religious basis is the experience of the Holy within the finite. Universally in everything finite and particular, or in this and that finite, the Holy appears in a special way. I could call this the sacramental basis of all religions — the Holy here and now which can be seen, heard, dealth with, in spite of its mysterious character. We still have remnants of this in the highest religions, in their sacraments, and I believe that without it a religious group becomes an association of moral clubs, as much of Protestantism has, because it has lost the sacramental basis.

Then, there is a second element, namely, a critical movement against the demonization of the sacramental, that is, making it into an object that can be handled. This element is embodied in various critical ways. The first of these critical movements is mystical. The mystical movement indicates a dissatisfaction with any of the concrete expressions of the Ultimate, of the Holy. Man goes beyond them. He goes to the one beyond any manifoldness. The Holy as the Ultimate lies beyond any of its embodiments. The embodiments are justified. They are accepted, but they are secondary. Man must go beyond them in order to reach the highest, the Ultimate itself. The particular is denied for the Ultimate One. The concrete is devaluated.

Another element, or the third element in the religious experience, is the element of "ought to be." This is the ethical or prophetic element. Here the sacramental is criticized because of demonic consequences like the denial of justice in the name of holiness. This is the whole fight of the Jewish prophets against sacramental religion. In some of the words of Amos and Hosea the fight is carried so far that the whole cult is abrogated. This criticism of the sacramental basis is decisive for Judaism and is one element in Christianity. But again I would say, if religious experience is without the sacramental and the mystical element, it becomes moralistic and finally secular.

I would like to describe the unity of these three elements in a religion which one could call — I hesitate to do so, but I don't know a better word — "the religion of the concrete spirit." And it might well be that one can say the inner *telos*, which means the inner aim of a thing, such as the *telos* of the acorn is to become a tree — the inner aim of the history of religions is to become a religion of the concrete spirit. But we cannot identify this religion of the concrete spirit with any actual religion, not even Christianity as a religion. But I would dare to say — of course, dare as a Protestant theologian — that I believe that there is no higher expression of what I call the synthesis of these three elements than in Paul's doctrine of the Spirit. There we have the two fundamental elements, the ecstatic and the rational elements, united. There is ecstasy, but the highest creation of the ecstasy is love in the sense of *agape*. There is ecstasy, but the other creation of ecstasy is *gnosis*, the knowledge of God. It is knowledge, and it is not disorder and chaos.

The postive and negative relation of these elements or motives now gives the history of religions its dynamic character. The inner *telos* of which I spoke, the religion of the concrete spirit, is, so to speak, that toward which everything drives. But we cannot say that this is a merely futuristic expectation. It appears everywhere in the struggle against the demonic resistance of the sacramental basis and the demonic and secularistic distortion of the critics of the sacramental basis. It appears in a fragmentary way in many moments in the history of religions. Therefore, we have to absorb the past history of religions and annihilate it in this way; but we have a genuine living tradition that consists in the moments in which this great synthesis became, in a fragmentary way, reality. We can see the whole history of religions in this sense as a fight for the religion of the concrete spirit, a fight of God against religion within religion. And this phrase, a fight of God against religion within religion, could become the key for understanding the otherwise extremely chaotic, or at least seemingly chaotic, history of religions.

Now, as Christians we see in the appearance of Jesus as the Christ the decisive victory in this struggle. There is an old symbol for the Christ, Christus Victor, and this can be used again in this view of the history of religions. And thus it is already connected in the New Testament with the victory over the demonic powers and the astrological forces. It points to the victory on the cross as a negation of any demonic claim. And I believe we see here immediately that this symbol can give us a Christological approach which could liberate us from many of the dead ends into which the discussion of the Christological dogma has led the Christian churches from the very beginning. In this way, the continuation of critical moments in history, of moments of *kairoi* in which the religion of the concrete spirit is actualized fragmentarily, can happen here and there.

The criterion for us as Christians is the event of the cross. That which happened there in a symbolic way, which supplies the criterion, also happens fragmentarily in other places, in other moments, has happened and will happen even though they are not historically or empirically connected with the cross.

Now I come to a question which was very much in the center of this whole conference, namely, How are these dynamics of the history of religions related to the relationship of the religious and of the secular? The holy is not only open to demonization and to the fight of God against religion as a fight against the demonic implications of religion. But the holy is also open to secularization. And these two, demonization and secularization, are related to each other insofar as secularization is the third and most radical form of de-demonization. Now, this is a very important systematic idea.

You know the meaning of the term *profane*, "to be before the doors of the sanctuary," and the meaning of *secular*, "belonging to the world." In both cases, somebody leaves the ecstatic, mysterious fear of the Holy for the world of ordinary rational structures. It would be easy to fight against this, to keep the people in the sanctuary, if the secular had not been given a critical religious function by itself. And this makes the problem so serious. The secular is the rational, and the rational must judge the irrationality of the Holy. It must judge its demonization.

The rational structure of which I am speaking implies the moral, the legal, the cognitive, and the aesthetic. The consecration of life which the Holy gives is at the same time the domination of life by the ecstatic forms of the Holy and the repression of the intrinsic demands of goodness, of justice, of truth and of beauty. Secularization occurring in such a context is liberation.

In this sense, both the prophets and the mystics were predecessors of the secular. The Holy became slowly the morally good, or the philosophically true, and later the scientifically true, or the aesthetically expressive. But then, a profound dialectic appears. The secular shows its inability to live by itself. The secular that is right in fighting against domination by the Holy becomes empty and becomes victim of what I call "quasi-religions." And these "quasi-religions" imply an oppressiveness like that of the demonic elements of the religions. But they are worse, as we have seen in our century, because they are without the depths and the richness of the genuine religious traditions.

And here, another *telos*, the inner aim of the history of religions, appears. I call it *theonomy*, from *theos* – God – and *nomos* – law. If the autonomous forces of knowledge, of aesthetics, of law and morals, point to the ultimate meaning of life, then we have theonomy. Then they are not dominated, but in their inner being they point beyond themselves to the Ultimate. In reality, there takes place another dynamic struggle, namely, between a consecration of life, which becomes heteronomous, and a self-actualization of all the cultural functions, which becomes autonomous and empty.

Theonomy appears in what I called the religion of the concrete spirit in fragments, never fully. Its fulfilment is eschatological; its end is expectation which goes beyond time to eternity. This theonomous element in the relation of the sacred and the secular is an element in the structure of the religion of the concrete spirit. It is certainly progressive, as every action is. Even to give a lecture has in itself the tendency to make progress in some direction, but it is not progressivistic — it doesn't imagine a temporal fulfilment. And here I differ from Teilhard de Chardin, to whom I feel very near in so many respects.

And now my third and last consideration: the interpretation of the theological tradition in the light of religious phenomena. Let me tell you about a great colleague, a much older colleague at the University of Berlin, Adolph Harnack. He once said that Christianity in its history embraces all elements of the history of religions. This was a partially true insight, but he did not follow it through. He did not see that, if this is so, then there must be a much more positive relationship between the whole history of religion and the history of the Christian Church. And so, he narrowed down his own constructive theology to a kind of high bourgeois, individualistic, moralistic theology.

I now want to return my thanks on this point to my friend Professor Eliade for the two years of seminars and the cooperation we had in them. In these seminars I experienced that every individual doctrinal statement or ritual expression of Christianity receives a new intensity of meaning. And in terms of a kind of apologia, yet also a self-accusation, I must say that my own *Systematic Theology* was written before these seminars and had another intention, namely, the apologetic discussion against and with the secular. Its purpose was the discussion or the answering of questions coming from the scientific and philosophical criticism of Christianity. But perhaps we need a longer, more intensive period of interpenetration of systematic theological study and religious historical studies. Under such circumstances, the structure of religious thought might develop in connection with another or different fragmentary manifestation of theonomy or of the religion of the concrete spirit. This is my hope for the future of theology.

To see this possibility, one should look to the example of the emphasis on the particular which the method of the history of religions gives to the systematic theologian. It is to be seen in two negations: against a supranatural theology and against a natural theology. First, there is the method of supranatural theology, which was the way classical Protestant orthodoxy formulated the idea of God in systematic theology. This concept of God appears in revelatory documents which are inspired but were not prepared for in history. For orthodoxy, these views are found in the biblical books, or for Islam, in the Koran. From there, dogmatic statements are prepared out of the material of the holy books by the Church, usually in connection with doctrinal struggles, formulated in creeds or official collections of doctrines, and theologically explained with the help of philosophy. All this is done without looking beyond the revelatory circle which one calls one's own religion or faith. This is the predominant method in all Christian churches.

Then there is the method of natural theology, the philosophical derivation of religious concepts from an analysis of reality encountered as a whole and especially from an analysis of the structure of the human mind. Often these concepts, God and others, are then related to traditional doctrines; sometimes they are not related.

These are the two main methods traditionally used. The method of the history of religions takes the following steps: first, it uses the material of the tradition as existentially experienced by those who work theologically. But since the historian of religions works theologically, he must also have the detachment which is necessary to observe any reality. This is the first step.

In the second step, the historian of religions takes over from the naturalistic methodology the analysis of mind and reality to show where the religious question is situated in human experiences both within ourselves and within our world; for instance, the experience of finitude, the experience of concern about the meaning of our being, the experience of the Holy as Holy, and so on.

Then the third step is to present a phenomenology of religion, showing the phenomena, especially that which shows itself in the history of religion—the symbols, the rites, the ideas, and the various activities. And the fourth step consists in the attempt to point out the relation of these phenomena — their relatedness, their difference, their contradictions — to the traditional concepts and to the problems that emerge from this. Finally, the historian of religions tries to place the reinterpreted concepts into the framework of the dynamics of religious and secular history and especially into the framework of our present religious and cultural situation. Now these five steps include parts of the earlier methods, but they apply them in the context of the history of the human race and into the experiences of mankind as expressed in the great symbols of religious history.

The last point, namely, putting everything into the present situation, leads to another advantage or, if you wish to call it so, to a new element of truth. It provides the possibility of understanding religious symbols in relation to the social matrix within which they have grown and into which we have to reintroduce them today. This is an exceedingly important step. Religious symbols are not stones falling from heaven. They have their roots in the totality of human experience, including local surroundings in all their ramifications, both political and economic. And these symbols can then be understood partly as in revolt against these surroundings. And in both cases, this is very important for our way of using symbols and reintroducing them.

A second positive consequence of this method is that we can use religious symbolism as a language of the doctrine of man, as the language of anthropology, not in the empirical sense of this word, but in the sense of doctrine of man — man in his true nature. The religious symbols say something to us about the way in which men have understood themselves in their very nature. The discussion about the emphasis on sin in Christianity and the lack of such emphasis in Islam is a good example. This shows a fundamental difference in the self-interpretation of two great religions and cultures, of men as men. We enlarge our understanding of the nature of man in a way which is more embracing than any particular technical psychology.

But now my last word. What does this mean for the

theologian's relationship to his own? His theology remains rooted in its experiential basis. Without this, no theology at all is possible. But he tries to formulate the basic experiences which are universally valid in universally valid statements. The universality of a religious statement does not lie in an all-embracing abstraction which would destroy religion as such but in the depths of every concrete religion. Above all, it lies in the openness to spiritual freedom both from one's own foundation and for one's own foundation.

Biographical Notes

JERALD C. BRAUER is professor of church history and the dean of the Divinity School of the University of Chicago.

JOACHIM WACH (1898–1955) taught at Leipzig, 1927–35, and Brown University, Providence, R.I., 1935–46, and served as professor and chairman, History of Religions field, in the Divinity School of the University of Chicago, 1946–55. He was also a member of the Committee on History of Culture.

PAUL TILLICH (1886–1965) started his teaching career in 1919 at Berlin. Subsequently he taught at Marburg, Dresden, and Frankfurt, in Germany, as well as at Union Theological Seminary, New York, and Harvard University. At the time of his death, he was the John Nuveen Professor of Theology at the Divinity School of the University of Chicago.

MIRCEA ELIADE taught at the University of Bucharest and at the Ecole des Hautes Études (Sorbonne) before coming to the University of Chicago, where he holds the Sewell L. Avery Distinguished Service Professorship. He is the chairman and professor, History of Religions field, in the Divinity School, and is also a member of the Committee on Social Thought.

JOSEPH M. KITAGAWA is professor of History of Religions both in the Divinity School and in the Department of Far Eastern Civilizations at the University of Chicago. He is also a member of the Committee on South Asian Studies.

CHARLES H. LONG is associate professor of History of Religions in the Divinity School and teaches in the College of the University of Chicago. He is also a member of the Committee on African Studies.

CHARLES J. ADAMS is director of the Institute of Islamic Studies, McGill University. He was instructor in the Department of Religion, Princeton University, 1953–54, and a Ford Foundation Overseas Training Fellow, 1955–57, before going to McGill in 1957. He is editor of *A Reader's Guide to the Great Religions* (1965) and of *McGill Islamic Studies*.

THOMAS J. J. ALTIZER is associate professor of religion in the College of Arts and Sciences of Emory University. He is the author of *Oriental Mysticism and Biblical Eschatology* (1961), *Mircea Eliade and the Dialectic of the Sacred* (1963), *The Gospel of Christian Atheism* (1966); and the forthcoming *The New Apocalypse; The Radical Christian Vision of William Blake*; and co-author with William Hamilton of *Radical Theology and the Death of God* (1966).

PHILIP H. ASHBY is professor of the History of Religion, Princeton University. He studied under Joachim Wach, 1946–50. He is the author of *The Conflict of Religions*, (1955), *The History and Future of Religious Thought*, (1963), and "The History of Religion," in *Religion*, edited by P. Ramsey (1965).

KEES W. BOLLE is associate professor in the Department of History at UCLA. He is a pupil of Mircea Eliade and studied in Madras under V. Raghavan for two years as a Rockefeller scholar. He is the author of *The Persistence of Religion* (1965) and has contributed to the *New Catholic Encyclopedia* and to *Studies of Esoteric Buddhism and Tantrism* (1965). He translated and wrote the introduction to Jan de Vries' *The Pageant of the History of Religions*.

H. BYRON EARHART is a member of the faculty of the Department of Religion at Western Michigan University. He taught at Vanderbilt University in 1965–66. He has written articles for *History of Religions*, *Numen*, and Japanese publications. His first book, to be published soon, is a historical introduction to Japanese religion utilizing the approach outlined in his present article. He is revising his dissertation on Shugendo for publication.

JEROME H. LONG is a member of the faculty of the Department of Religion at Western Michigan University. He is a student of Mircea Eliade and is currently engaged in writing his dissertation.

CHARLES S. J. WHITE is assistant professor of religious thought and teacher in the South Asia Regional Studies program in the University of Pennsylvania. He has published articles in *History of Religions* and *The Encyclopaedia Britannica* and is currently engaged in preparing a book on medieval Indian devotional religion.

Acknowledgments

Most of the articles included in the present volume were presented at the Alumni Conference of the Field of History of Religions, October 11–13, 1965, celebrating the seventy-fifth anniversary of the University of Chicago as well as the one hundredth anniversary of the Divinity School of the University of Chicago. The papers by Professors Tillich and Eliade were given as public lectures. (Tillich's article, which became his last one before his death, has been published as a part of his posthumous book, *The Future of Religions* [New York: Harper & Row, 1966].) Instead of writing the usual introduction, we decided to include an article by the late Joachim Wach, who spent the last ten years of his life teaching at Chicago. The following faculty members of the University of Chicago served as discussants for the papers presented by the alumni: Robert M. Grant (for Philip H. Ashby), Marshall G. S. Hodgson (for Charles J. Adams), Charles H. Long (for Thomas J. J. Altizer), Mircea Eliade (for Kees W. Bolle), Norman H. Zide (for Charles S. J. White), and Joseph M. Kitagawa (for H. Byron Earhart). Unfortunately, limitations of space in this volume have made it impossible to include a summary of discussions by the participants. The papers have been revised, however, in the light of the helpful comments made by the discussants and other participants. We are very grateful to Mr. Alan L. Miller, who not only assisted Miss Kathryn West in the planning of the Conference but also served as editorial assistant and prepared the manuscript for publication. Some of the chapters have been read by Dr. Charles

S. J. White, who made many helpful stylistic suggestions. Thanks are also due to the staff of the University of Chicago Press for their careful and thoughtful assistance and to Mrs. Helen Bailey whose meticulous typing made the editorial task a pleasant one.

Passages from the following books are quoted by permission of the respective publishers: Mircea Eliade, *The Myth of the Eternal Return* (trans. from the French by Willard R. Trask [Bollingen Series, No. XLVI; Pantheon Books, 1954] pp. 10–11 and 22); E. E. Evans-Pritchard, *Social Anthropology* (New York: Macmillan Co., 1952); Bronislaw Malinowski, *Magic, Science, and Religion and Other Essays* (New York: Macmillan Co., 1948); Adolphe Portmann, "Preface to the Science of Man," *Diogenes*, No. 40 (Winter, 1960; International Council for Philosophy and Humanistic Studies, Unesco House, Paris); Bronislaw Malinowski, *Coral Gardens and Their Magic*, Vol. I (London: George Allen & Unwin, Ltd., 1935); W. Mcm. Woodworth, "The Palolo Worm, Eunice viridis (Gray)," *Bulletin of the Museum of Comparative Zoology*, LI (1907).

Index